"Mahri Leonard-Fleckman sets an incredibly rich table for us to ponder the Sunday Scriptures, giving us a potent mix of biblical scholarship, prayer, and practical advice. She invites individuals and groups to sink deeply into the readings, to go beyond a surface study of the Scriptures in order to let them take flesh in their own lives and the lives of their communities. Her thoughtful instructions for group *lectio divina* challenge us to hear the many ways the texts open up to our sisters and brothers, inviting us into a world of bracing conversations."

> —Michelle Francl-Donnay
> Author of *Prayer: Biblical Wisdom for Seeking God*

"A biblical scholar accepts an invitation to lead a weekly study of the Sunday Scriptures in an active and gritty downtown parish. Mahri Leonard-Fleckman is the 'expert' but, as it turns out, so are the diverse participants from the neighborhood who share the Word of God and their lives with one another. *Ponder: Contemplative Bible Study* is the fruit of these encounters. This is a terrific resource for preachers and catechists, as well as for personally reflecting on and praying with the Sunday Scriptures."

> —Jude Siciliano, OP
> Preacher and editor, PreacherExchange.com

"Catholic laity have not always felt they had permission to interpret biblical texts. In *Ponder*, Mahri Leonard-Fleckman does better than grant permission: she empowers. Joining traditional Catholic spiritual practices of *lectio divina* and Ignatian contemplation with the fruits of modern critical biblical scholarship, Leonard-Fleckman equips readers with background knowledge and practical tools for their own deep engagement with the readings proclaimed at Mass each Sunday. Through contemplative practice grounded in dialogue and community, she invites readers to engage the Scriptures with mind *and* heart, curiosity and compassion."

> —Anathea Portier-Young
> Associate Professor of Old Testament, Duke Divinity School

"I strongly recommend *Ponder* not only for preachers but for all Christians regularly engaging the appointed scriptural texts in their Lord's Day worship. Just as the author gracefully bridges serious scholarship with personal prayer in the context of a community of faith, so readers may learn to integrate heart and head in the encounter with God's Word through attention to the process and insights of *Ponder*."

—Jan Michael Joncas
Artist in Residence and Research Fellow in Catholic Studies,
University of St. Thomas

"*Lectio divina* as a form of individual and communal prayer with the Scriptures has grown in popularity. This book will help those who wish to combine prayer based on the Sunday Scriptures with some study of the texts. Both prayer groups and individuals will welcome this book as they center their prayer on the Scriptures."

—*The Bible Today*

"Here is an outstanding resource for studying the Sunday lectionary and, more importantly, for learning how *to pray* with the lectionary."

—Frank J. Matera
Professor Emeritus, The Catholic University of America

Ponder

CONTEMPLATIVE BIBLE STUDY
FOR YEAR C

MAHRI LEONARD-FLECKMAN

LITURGICAL PRESS
Collegeville, Minnesota

www.littlerockscripture.org

Cover design by Amy Marc. Cover art courtesy of Getty Images.

Scripture readings in this work are from the *Lectionary for Mass for Use in the Dioceses of the United States of America, second typical edition* © 2001, 1998, 1997, 1986, 1970 Confraternity of Christian Doctrine, Inc., Washington, DC. Used with permission. All rights reserved. No portion of this text may be reproduced by any means without permission in writing from the copyright owner.

Other Scripture texts in this work are taken from the *New American Bible, revised edition* © 2010, 1991, 1986, 1970 Confraternity of Christian Doctrine, Washington, D.C., and are used by permission of the copyright owner. All Rights Reserved. No part of the New American Bible may be reproduced in any form without permission in writing from the copyright owner.

Where noted, Scripture quotations are from New Revised Standard Version Bible © 1989 National Council of the Churches of Christ in the United States of America. Used by permission. All rights reserved worldwide.

Excerpts from the English translation of *The Roman Missal* © 2010, International Commission on English in the Liturgy Corporation. All rights reserved.

© 2021 by Mahri Leonard-Fleckman
Published by Liturgical Press, Collegeville, Minnesota. All rights reserved. No part of this book may be used or reproduced in any manner whatsoever, except brief quotations in reviews, without written permission of Liturgical Press, Saint John's Abbey, PO Box 7500, Collegeville, MN 56321-7500. Printed in the United States of America.

1	2	3	4	5	6	7	8	9

Library of Congress Cataloging-in-Publication Data

Names: Leonard-Fleckman, Mahri, author.
Title: Ponder : contemplative Bible study / Mahri Leonard-Fleckman.
Description: Collegeville, Minnesota : Liturgical Press, 2020- | Contents: Year C | Summary:
    "Ponder: Contemplative Bible Study for Year C is the second book in a three-volume
    series designed to accompany hearers and preachers of the Word as they pray with and
    ponder the Sunday readings throughout the liturgical year. The Sunday readings are
    provided, along with brief commentary, reflections, and guidance on how to use this
    resource alone or with a group"— Provided by publisher.
Identifiers: LCCN 2020015109 (print) | LCCN 2020015110 (ebook) | ISBN 9780814665824
    (Year A : epub) | ISBN 9780814665008 (Year B : paperback) | ISBN 9780814665572
    (Year A : paperback) | ISBN 9780814665824 (Year A : mobi) | ISBN 9780814665824
    (Year A : pdf) | ISBN 9780814665251 (Year B : epub) | ISBN 9780814665251 (Year B :
    mobi) | ISBN 9780814665251 (Year B : pdf) | ISBN 9780814665589 (Year C : paperback)
    | ISBN 9780814665831 (Year C : epub) | ISBN 9780814665831 (Year C : mobi) | ISBN
    9780814665831 (Year C : pdf)
Subjects: LCSH: Church year meditations. | Bible—Meditations. | Catholic Church—Prayers
    and devotions. | Catholic Church. Lectionary for Mass (U.S.)
Classification: LCC BX2170.C55 L46 2020 (print) | LCC BX2170.C55 (ebook) | DDC
    242/.3—dc23
LC record available at https://lccn.loc.gov/2020015109
LC ebook record available at https://lccn.loc.gov/2020015110

To the members of St. John's Bible Study,
who prayed *Ponder* into being,
and to all those who thirst for God's word.

O God, you are my God—
it is you I seek!
For you my body yearns;
for you my soul thirsts.

Psalm 63:2

Contents

Season of Easter

Ordinary Time

Acknowledgments

In the summer of 2012, I attended my first international meeting of the Catholic Biblical Association of America. I was overwhelmed. The conference was held at Notre Dame—which seemed a formidable place at the time—and I was an introverted graduate student. I remember escaping down to the book exhibit one afternoon for a moment of quiet. As chance (or providence) would have it, I met Mary Stommes, the editor of *Give Us This Day*. She was kind and gracious, and after talking for a while, she invited me to write for the publication. That moment marked the beginning of my relationship with Liturgical Press, for which I am deeply grateful.

I wish to thank the wonderful staff at Lit Press who have made this project possible. I am indebted to my editor Amy Ekeh, whom I have come to trust completely, and whom I suspect should be called my coauthor rather than my editor for all the "ponders" she has helped to shape lovingly and prayerfully. Peter Dwyer believed in the idea of *Ponder* at an early stage and worked hard with me to craft the proposal. I must also express my thanks to Hans Christoffersen, whose presence through the years has been important in many other ways, especially in his dedication to the Wisdom Commentary series. And to Mary Stommes, who first brought me into the fold: thank you. Liturgical Press feels like a family to me; I am honored to be part of it.

Outside of Liturgical Press, I also wish to thank the Rev. William Campbell, SJ, who read the Introduction to the manuscript when it was still in the beginning stages and whose insights and suggestions have been invaluable.

Above all, my thanks to the members of the Bible study at St. John's parish in Worcester, Massachusetts, for praying this project into being with me. We began our Bible study in the fall of 2014, and it continues to live on in these pages. This second volume of *Ponder* is dedicated not only to the members of St. John's Bible Study, but to all those who hunger and thirst for God's word. May this book help you on your journey.

Introduction

Our Roots: St. John's Bible Study or "Neighborhood"

To explain the goals and format of this Bible study, let me first describe its roots, the community from which it emerged. It began at St. John's Catholic Church, a mid-nineteenth-century parish that is known historically as the "mother church" of Worcester in central Massachusetts. It is a flourishing, gritty, downtown parish that draws a rich and diverse mix of people. Its mission is to serve the poor, and it hosts the largest daily soup kitchen in the city. St. John's also hosts thriving devotions, including its yearly Novena of Grace in Honor of Saint Francis Xavier, also called "The Lenten Retreat of the City of Worcester."

The rectory next door is a sprawling building that once housed priests in the diocese and now provides transitional sober housing for men. The setting for our weekly Bible study is the rectory dining room, a tired but dignified space. We gather at a well-worn table with old, wide, high-backed armchairs. The dining room sits just behind the Worcester train station, close enough that in summer evenings with the windows open, we have to shout to hear ourselves above the sound of trains pulling in and out. In the winter, the old furnace pumps out enough heat directly into the dining room to give us heat stroke, while the rest of the house remains drafty.

We gather after Mass on Tuesday evenings for one hour. Ours is a simple, drop-in, lectionary-based study that regularly gathers five to fifteen people. I provide a handout with the readings for the upcoming Sunday and some corresponding notes. Together, we pray with and then discuss one of the readings, sometimes two, then offer up communal prayers and go on our way.

The group that has been meeting for the past five years, in shifting forms and combinations, is a ragtag community, a mismatch of members. What unites us is our faith. Generally, we are Roman Catholic. Many of us would not rub shoulders outside the Bible study,

1

excepting perhaps sporadic handshakes in the pews. One member (Matthew) called our Bible study a "neighborhood" of bracing experiences and ideals, as distinguished from the "mutual admiration and unchallenged agreement" that so often marks the sameness of the people we choose to socialize with. "As it is with the neighborhood," said Matthew, "so it is with the Bible study."[1]

And so it is. When gathering each week, one never knows who will show up or what the discussion dynamics will be. Lord knows, sometimes the results aren't pretty! Yet we come back and try again. We are conservative, liberal, and moderate. We range in age from our twenties to our eighties. We are blue collar and white collar, jobless, retired, and working. Over the years, some of our participants have had homes to live in and others have not. Some of us come with mental or physical illnesses or histories of addiction. Our pastor attends regularly to prepare for Sunday's homily. And I, the Bible scholar, "lead" the group, but the term is loose. When I am unable to make it (which once lasted a full year while I was teaching out of state), other members step in and guide the group with only the aid of the weekly handout.

Over the years, some members of the St. John's Bible Study have carefully collected these handouts in order to have a full, three-year set. Returning to earlier handouts years later, I find myself surprised by how much I gain from these notes and reflections, as if they were written by someone else. They have become a rich, ongoing treasure in my own personal prayer life. Now that these handouts have been gathered together into this series of books, I hope they may become a valuable resource in your prayer life too.

The Format

To truly understand this study and the flexibility it offers to individuals or groups, I invite you to use your liturgical imagination. The format on the following pages is simple. Some would perhaps even

---

1. Matthew was reflecting on and quoting from Christopher Lasch's *Revolt of the Elites and the Betrayal of Democracy* (New York; London: W.W. Norton & Company, 1996), in particular Lasch's discussion of "communities" of like-minded people versus "neighborhoods" in which people meet as equals, without regard to race, class, or national origins (Lasch, 117, 119–21).

consider it simplistic, though this perception would be misguided. Most importantly, the simplicity of the format allows for freedom and independence of prayer and study. First, I provide the entirety of Sunday's readings so that participants have easy access to the texts without having to consult additional Bibles or missalettes. Only the psalm is missing, not because it is less important, but for issues of space. Having the readings easily accessible has proven invaluable in our own slightly chaotic parish, where the notion of ordering extra Bibles and somehow keeping them together in one space is daunting.

Under each reading are my commentary notes. These notes provide some basic background and information about the readings. The goal is not to lead readers into viewing the texts a certain way (in other words, my way), but to invite readers into their own deep knowledge of the texts, a kind of full-bodied understanding that I like to call "bone knowledge." Therefore, these notes are streamlined to create minimal mental clutter. They include historical and literary context, discussions of translation choices from the Hebrew or Greek (sometimes Aramaic), the broader contexts from the surrounding passages and books, and references to other Sunday readings. In these short summaries, I have distilled my own ideas, in consultation with commentaries and study Bibles, into what I consider to be the most pertinent information for a wide-ranging audience.

Finally, I include a section called "Ponder" that provides possible connections, essential ideas, or ongoing questions to consider from the texts. I have placed these last so as not to overly influence participants at the outset of the study; the goal is to refrain from reading them as long as necessary. This section, connected with the commentary notes below each reading, may be particularly helpful for those who lead the Bible study or are preparing to preach.

Together, the readings, notes, and "ponderings" provide a valuable yet simple tool for ongoing prayer and study. They also create a sort of Sunday missalette that some of our Bible study members take into the pews on Sunday for continued prayer and thoughtful preparation.

Union of Heart and Mind

As for the core principle of this Bible study, it is simple: union of heart and mind. The study takes the words of Vatican II's *Dei Verbum* seriously: Scripture, "the force and power of the word of God," is so great that it stands as "the church's support and strength, imparting robustness to the faith of its daughters and sons and providing food for their souls. It is a pure and unfailing fount of spiritual life."[2] This Bible study is, first and foremost, a practice in gaining intimacy with God through intimacy with our sacred texts. It is to learn to trust our ability to hear God speak to us with great love through Scripture, and to become increasingly comfortable opening our hearts and minds to hear God's word. We gain this intimacy by full-bodied attention to the text, just as love of God calls for the full-bodied union of heart, spirit, mind, and strength (Mark 12:30).[3] Through prayer and study of Scripture, then, the goal of this study is that each of us knows, deeply and profoundly, that the Scriptures are "nourishment" which "enlightens" our minds, "strengthens" our wills, and "fires [our] hearts . . . with the love of God."[4]

As a Hebrew Bible scholar,[5] I must admit that I find this distinction between "mind" and "heart" woolly. There is no word for "mind" in the Hebrew Bible, and in the ancient world there was little use for that messy jumble inside our heads. Rather, the ancient Israelites were an embodied people. Everything was rooted in felt experience, including thinking. When we read the term "mind" in our translated Hebrew Bibles, the literal term in Hebrew is most often "heart" or "spirit." Sometimes it is even liver, intestines or "kidneys," as in Psalm 26:2, which translates literally, "Examine me, LORD, and test me, search my kidneys and my heart." According to this ancient people, the heart was the seat of all knowledge. Our intentionality and thinking, our

---

2. Dogmatic Constitution on Divine Revelation, *Dei Verbum* (November 18, 1965) 21, in Austin Flannery, ed., *Vatican Council II: Constitutions, Decrees, Declarations; The Basic Sixteen Documents* (Collegeville, MN: Liturgical Press, 2014).

3. The word for "mind" in Mark 12:30, *dianoia*, also translates as "intention" or "purpose." Mark's Gospel draws from Deut 6:5, which translates literally from the Hebrew as: "You shall love YHWH your God with all your heart, with all your life force, and with all your muchness." The Gospel adds "mind" to the list of faculties.

4. *Dei Verbum* 23.

5. I use the phrase "Hebrew Bible" rather than "Old Testament" intentionally. Though an imperfect expression, for me it reflects the reality that this inspired corpus of texts is considered holy for both Jews and Christians. As Christians, we use the expression "Old Testament" to reflect our commitment to both the Old and New Testaments. For Jews, we simply refer to "the Bible" or, more specifically, the Tanakh (the Torah or "teaching," the Prophets, and the Writings).

ability to follow God's teachings comes from within our "inmost being," as knowledge "inscribed upon the heart" (cf. Jer 31:33).

In our contemporary world, saturated as it is with studies of the mind, mindfulness, and mental training, I find myself leaning back into this ancient worldview of the heart as the seat of knowledge (don't tell my neuroscientist husband!). Particularly in a Bible study focused on genuine connection to and understanding of the text, personal experience and prayer are crucial starting points. This heart-centered practice then leads to more careful, authentic reading and attention. In this Bible study, the movement from heart to mind often happens organically, the most thoughtful ideas and challenging questions emerging from a strong grounding in prayer. And this is not a practice that I subscribe to only with Bible study. I have found that even in my own more cerebral, scholarly work, some of the best intellectual questions and insights bubble up organically while marinating in heart-centered reflection.

The Heart

That said, we begin our Bible study by praying with a Scripture text. This period sometimes takes twenty minutes; sometimes it leads to reflections that take up the majority of the hour. We choose one of the Sunday readings and, without introduction, read and pray with it together. Further below, you'll find the specific instructions that we use to guide our Bible study sessions. Here, I'll describe the two key forms of prayer that our group uses: *Lectio Divina* and Ignatian Contemplation.

Lectio Divina

This ancient form of Christian prayer translates imperfectly as "Divine Reading." It is a tool for recollection, contemplation, and, ultimately, resting in God. In group *Lectio Divina*, we begin by having a participant read one of the Sunday texts aloud, slowly and prayer-fully. (If done as personal prayer outside of a group, the person reads the text on their own in the same way, though with greater freedom to stop, linger, and contemplate or "chew" on any words, phrases, or images that come to mind.) As we listen for the first time in the group, we open our hearts to the text, listening as if we have never heard it before, entering into it with curiosity and imagination. Trusting that the Holy Spirit guides us, we allow it to break open and speak to us. After the first read-through of the text and a moment of silence, we go around the room and share a word or phrase that especially struck us (we say *only* the word or phrase, without further explanation). Participants can always simply say "pass" when their turn comes. One of the gems that comes from this group practice is the creation of a prayer or litany in the repetition of certain words or phrases as we move around the room (again, without any additional commentary).

After this first read-through and response, we repeat, this time with a different voice. (It's important to have distinct and diverse voices throughout the process.) This second person reads the same passage again, slowly and meditatively. As they do so, we continue to sink into the text, digesting it. Perhaps we linger on the word or phrase we heard in the first read-through of the text. Perhaps another insight presents itself to us. After another moment of silence following the reading, we may go around the room again and take turns offering heart-based reflections on how the text spoke to us, or we may simply open up the space for these reflections in a less-structured way, as participants feel pulled to speak.

Another way of describing "heart-based" here is "experience-based." In other words, people speak from their *personal experience* of the text, saving the intellectual questions and ideas for later. Examples of experience-based reflections include what thoughts or feelings arose in the person while praying with the text, how the text spoke to them personally, how a particular phrase struck them, etc.

This process is a shortened form of group *Lectio Divina*, the full practice of which often includes three repetitions of the same passage: the first for hearing a word or a phrase, the second for listening for how God speaks to us, and the third for hearing an invitation, or how God calls or invites us to live and act. Sometimes, our group chooses to do a third reading of the same passage, but I have found that in a one-hour period, reading the selected passage twice is enough to ground us firmly enough in our hearts and personal experiences before moving on.

Further Resources

Casey, Michael. *Sacred Reading: The Ancient Art of Lectio Divina*. Liguori: Liguori/Triumph, 1995.

Hall, Thelma, r.c. *Too Deep for Words: Rediscovering Lectio Divina.* New York: Paulist Press, 1998.

Pennington, M. Basil. *Lectio Divina: Renewing the Ancient Practice of Praying the Scriptures.* New York: Crossroads, 1998.

Ignatian Contemplation

Some of the passages that we read, especially Gospel passages as well as some stories in the Hebrew Bible, are conducive to Ignatian Contemplation. According to Ignatian spirituality, one of many ways that God speaks to us is through the imagination. The imagination becomes a tool to tap into our natural curiosity, to enter into a text and experience it in a fresh way, and to pay attention to the sometimes subtle ways that God meets us and invites us through this practice. Ignatian spirituality is not disconnected from *Lectio Divina*, which similarly invites us to curiosity, imagination, and contemplation. Both assume cooperation with and guidance by the Holy Spirit, whom we invite into the practice. Yet the tools in Ignatian spirituality are more precise and particular in terms of active engagement in and through a passage.

In our Bible study, then, when a text is particularly promising for engaging the imagination, I offer this tool to participants in our second reading of a text. I invite the group to enter into a scene and to notice every detail. I tell them to notice the sights, the smells, the sounds, the feel of the scene. I invite them to linger on the people, those described in the text as well as those who go unseen, unnoticed. I invite them to lose themselves in the scene and perhaps to become part of it. Perhaps they become an observer, an anonymous member of a crowd, a disciple, or a prophet. As they use their imaginations, I invite them to consider how God is speaking to them and calling to them through the text. My friend and spiritual director uses the expression "daydream as prayer" to describe how the imagination can become prayer when we are open to and trust the Spirit's guidance.[6]

After the second read-through, we open up the space as usual for sharing around the table. Reflections on this Ignatian practice will often arise naturally. At times, after the reflection period is over, I will ask further questions of the group, such as where they found

---

6. My thanks to Rev. William Campbell, SJ, for this insight.

themselves in the scene, and what insights or questions this vantage point gave to them.

Further Resources

Barry, William, SJ. *Letting God Come Close: An Approach to the Ignatian Spiritual Exercises.* Chicago: Loyola, 2011.

Martin, James, SJ. *The Jesuit Guide to (Almost) Everything: A Spirituality for Real Life.* New York: HarperCollins, 2012.

O'Brien, Kevin, SJ. *The Ignatian Adventure: Experiencing the Spiritual Exercises of St. Ignatius in Daily Life.* Chicago: Loyola, 2011.

The Mind

At some natural transition point, our group moves from sharing our reflections after the second reading (a time when we allow one another to speak, but without responding or entering into discussion) to open, more intellectual discussion about the text. At this point, the commentary notes can be helpful as an aid for context and meaning. I would suggest waiting until the very end of your time together to explore the notes in the "Ponder" section as a group, or even refraining from reading them altogether. These final "ponderings" can be useful for ongoing personal reflection and exploration during the week. Yet each Bible study group should feel the freedom to follow its own format as needed.

As for leaders or group facilitators, you may consider reading over the commentary notes and even the final "Ponder" section in preparation for the Bible study. Some of the Bible study leaders at St. John's have told me that they like to go into the Bible study unprepared and learn alongside the group (and these are leaders without any formal training in Scripture). The most important task for the leader in this second half of the Bible study is to keep people focused on the text; I have found that when we shift from prayer to "study," a common tendency is to move away from the text altogether and begin to speak in theological generalities or platitudes rather than remaining grounded in the passage. As a Bible study leader, I often find that my role is less "leader" and more "nagger," whose main task is to remind people to allow the text to guide their thinking, rather than to place their thinking on the text. My most common comments at this stage are: "Let's remember to stay focused on the text"; "Where do you see that in the text?"; or, "That's an interesting theological statement, but what does the text say?" For example, we may like to talk about God as "all-knowing," but in the creation stories of Genesis 1–11, God seems to be constantly surprised by the outcome of creation (particularly the messiness of humans) and slowly figuring out what to do as a result. Remember that theology cleans up what the Bible often leaves untidy. Our goal is to give the text its space to speak, even to the "untidiness" of God's word and our lives.

In closing, I hope that you will find this Bible study life-giving. Personally, as a scholar, I don't often have the opportunity to bridge serious scholarship with personal prayer and a community of faith. In writing this Bible study, I have been grateful for the opportunity to do just this sort of bridging between scholarship, prayer, and practice. I have done my very best to sink into the weekly readings, to pray with the texts and present them as authentically as I possibly can. I pray that you enjoy this pondering, and that our great God draws you closer through the words on the following pages.

Mahri Leonard-Fleckman, PhD
College of the Holy Cross
Worcester, MA

How to Use this Study—Groups

A basic "how-to guide" can be found on the inside front cover of this book, but the following description will provide more detailed guidance. Of course, you should feel free to adapt the following approach as needed to suit the needs, time constraints, and temperament of your group.

Silence. The group leader may invite everyone to settle into silence and come home to God if they've been "away" for a while. Remind the group that God is always present. Allow silence to take root for several long moments.

Opening Prayer. You will find an Opening Prayer on the inside front cover of this book.[1] You may wish to say this together, or your group may choose an alternative Opening Prayer.

Lectio Divina **(20–30 min.).** Choose one of the Sunday readings (the first reading, the second reading, or the Gospel) and two people from your group to read. At this point, the group leader may wish to offer an invitation such as the following: "In this reading of our text, I invite us to open our hearts to this passage, to be curious, and to listen as if we've never heard this passage before. I invite us to listen, in particular, for a word or phrase that speaks to us today. At the end of the reading, we'll go around the room and simply speak our words or phrases out loud, without any explanation. As always, when your turn comes, you can simply pass."

Read the text slowly. One of the readers reads the selected text slowly and meditatively. The group listens for a word or phrase that especially speaks to them.

Share a word or phrase. After a moment of silence, group members speak their words or phrases out loud with no elaboration or discussion (or they may "pass"). Savor this litany of shared words.

---

1. The opening prayer is my translation of Psalm 19:15 (v. 14 in some English translations).

Read the text a second time. The second reader now reads the same text slowly and meditatively. The group continues to sink into the text and ponder the word or phrase they have heard, listening for how God might be speaking to or calling them.

Engage in Ignatian Contemplation if desired. At this point, if the text is conducive to an imaginative exercise, your group may engage in Ignatian Contemplation. Using the method for Ignatian Contemplation described above, the group leader may invite participants into the scene.

Share experience-based reflections. After a moment of silence, participants can share their thoughts and reflections on the text. Allow everyone to speak as prompted by the Spirit. At times, it may be helpful for the group leader to remind participants to stay in their hearts and leave any intellectual questions aside for the moment. The leader may also need to steer the sharing away from discussion and debate, keeping everyone focused on the text. Allow this sharing to continue until a natural stopping point.

Bible Study (20–30 min.). At this point, your group can move into the Bible "study" portion of your time together. Invite participants to move from "heart" to "mind." Begin with discussing the reading you selected for *Lectio Divina,* but feel free to explore other readings if you exhaust your discussion of the originally selected text. Your group may wish to read the commentary notes together and discuss any lingering questions or insights. Along the way, you may need to remind the group to stay rooted in the text (see notes above on "The Mind").

Ponder. Hold off on this section for as long as possible—or even avoid it altogether—so that participants can use this material for further pondering of the Sunday readings throughout the week.

Closing Prayer. At the end of the hour, draw the discussion to a natural close. Invite the group to join in prayer with an invitation such as: "For what shall we pray tonight?" After prayers are offered, you may offer a conclusion such as: "For these prayers that we speak out loud, and for those that we hold in the silence of our hearts, we pray together in the words that Jesus taught us." Join together in praying the "Our Father."

How to Use this Study—Individuals

For those using this study as individuals, you may find the group guide helpful, but the flow will be much freer and up to the movement of the Spirit. You will essentially follow the steps for individual practice of *Lectio Divina*. There are four parts to this practice: *lectio* (reading), *meditatio* (meditation), *oratio* (prayer), and *contemplatio* (contemplation). For further resources and explanation, see the above descriptions for *Lectio Divina* and Ignatian Contemplation.

Begin by finding a quiet and comfortable space. Often, people find that committing to a specific place for daily prayer, whether a particular chair or room, or perhaps even a specific church pew, can be conducive to regular practice. You may want to set a timer for your prayer period. I used to pray in the pews for twenty minutes before Mass, so the beginning of the Mass became my natural "timer."

I would suggest picking one text (or a part of a text) for your prayer period. Don't attempt to go beyond that reading, unless you are strongly pulled to do so. Before beginning, open with a prayer or an intention for your prayer period. Then begin by reading the text slowly and meditatively. Do not try to get through the entire reading! Allow yourself to stop on any word, phrase, or image that strikes you. Rather than trying to move on quickly, stop and "sit" with this word or phrase. Marinate in it. Ingest it as a cow might chew its cud, chewing and swallowing, regurgitating and re-chewing to swallow again. This is the practice of *meditatio* or meditating on Scripture. If the imagery is particularly vivid, you might also find yourself drawn to Ignatian Contemplation, allowing your imagination to draw you into the scene and play with the word or image.

As you see fit, allow this practice of *meditatio* to open you to pray with God (*oratio*). You might reflect on why you were drawn to a particular word, phrase, or imagery. You might reflect on how God is speaking to you through the text. You may find yourself praying aloud or silently to God. You may experience God calling you to a particular form of action or "being" through the word. You may simply feel God's presence.

The ultimate aim of this practice is to lead you to *contemplatio,* the practice of stillness or resting in God. Prayer is a winding ladder that we ascend and descend regularly, and this last stage is up to God's grace that helps draw you further and further into the quiet and stillness. This sense of interior stillness is what we call "recollection," when the mind and the senses become quiet and focused on listening to God. *Contemplatio* does not always happen. Yet praying with Scripture is ultimately about intimacy with God, and this stillness before God, this practice of *listening* rather than speaking to God, is the deepest form of intimacy.

During this period of prayer, you may end up praying through the entire passage. Or, you may never make it through the first verse. Just remember that there are no set "rules," and there is nothing to accomplish! You may spend the entire time meditating on a particular word. You may end up speaking to God about something on your heart and mind. You may never make it to *contemplatio.* You may even end up feeling like the whole time was a waste. Don't worry; this is all part of the practice! Even if the prayer period felt difficult or dry, like nothing was happening, trust that God was present. The fact that you made time for prayer reveals your desire and God's desire working through you. That is enough.

As you finish your period of prayer, take a few moments to reorient yourself slowly. You might take a few moments simply to sit silently, and to express gratitude for the time. Whatever you do, be sure to close with a prayer. In group *Lectio Divina,* we pray the "Our Father" together. On your own, you may be drawn toward another prayer that feels more authentically yours.

As you shift from this heart-centered practice, you may be drawn to integrate the heart with the mind by reading the commentary notes under your passage. I would suggest waiting on these notes until you are finished with your period of prayer, though some may find that beginning with the commentary notes are helpful for sinking into prayer. You may also be drawn to peruse the other readings and consider how the readings are meant to fit together. Or perhaps you wish to remain in the heart and ponder further, in which case I would suggest reading the "Ponder" sections, which are created for deeper reflection on the readings.

Above all, remember that the format of this Bible study is open and flexible. How you use it is entirely up to you and the movement of the Spirit.

About the Sunday Readings

As you engage in this lectionary-based study, it may be useful to review the types of readings we hear proclaimed each Sunday and to have a sense of how these readings are selected.

As you probably know, the Sunday readings are on a three-year cycle: Years A, B, and C. You can easily orient yourself to the current liturgical year with some simple math. Year C is always divisible by three. So, for example, the year 2022 is divisible by three and is therefore Year C. (You can quickly determine this by adding the digits of the year together and dividing by three. No need to do long division!) Once you locate Year C, you can determine that the previous year is Year B, and the following year is Year A. Note that the liturgical year begins with the First Sunday of Advent of the prior year. So, in our example above, Year C (2022) actually begins with Advent of 2021.

You will find a volume of *Ponder: Contemplative Bible Study* published for each liturgical year: A, B, and C.

Now let's turn to the structure of each Sunday. During the Liturgy of the Word at each Sunday Mass, we hear a series of four readings:

1. **The first reading** is taken from the Hebrew Bible (the Christian Old Testament). This reading is selected to correspond with the Gospel reading for the day, so it may come from anywhere in the Hebrew Bible. We have no "semi-continuous" readings of a single book in the Hebrew Bible on Sundays (semi-continuous means that a reading continues from what was read the previous Sunday, though often skipping over verses or even chapters to do so). This lack of continuity is one reason why Christians lack familiarity with the Hebrew Bible. (Note that during the Easter season, the first reading comes from a New Testament book: The Acts of the Apostles.)

2. **The responsorial psalm.** The psalm, which is often sung, is intended to be a *response* to the first reading. Its theme may tie directly into a theme of the first reading. For space purposes (not for lack of importance!), we have not included the full text of the Sunday psalm, but you will find the reference if you wish to look it up.

3. **The second reading** is taken from the New Testament, usually from one of Paul's letters. Unlike the first reading, this reading is semi-continuous. While we do not typically read an entire New Testament letter, we may read large sections of one letter over the course of multiple weeks. This also means that, unlike the first reading, the second reading may or may not clearly correspond with the Gospel reading.

4. **The Gospel.** The Sunday Gospel readings in Year A feature the Gospel of Matthew; Year B features Mark; and Year C features Luke. The Gospel of John is sprinkled throughout the three years, mostly during the Lent and Easter seasons (except in the case of Year B, in which we have more readings from John's Gospel because Mark's Gospel is relatively short and doesn't fill the entire year). The Gospel readings are fairly continuous, but we do not read the entire Gospel from beginning to end.

Navigating the Church Year

It may be helpful to have a basic understanding of the church's liturgical calendar as you navigate this book from Sunday to Sunday.

We begin the liturgical year with Advent and Christmas, followed by a period of Ordinary Time (I). Next come Lent and Easter, followed by another period of Ordinary Time (II). Because the number of Sundays in Ordinary Time I and II differs from year to year (due to variation in the dating of Easter), Ordinary Time is organized in a single section in this book.

The following guide will help you navigate your way through the year.

Season of Advent	Four Sundays of Advent
Season of Christmas	From Christmas Day through The Baptism of the Lord
Ordinary Time I	**4-8 WEEKS** From the Second Sunday in Ordinary Time through the Sunday in Ordinary Time that falls before Ash Wednesday
Season of Lent	Five Sundays of Lent and Palm Sunday
Season of Easter	From Easter Day through Pentecost Sunday
Ordinary Time II	**APPROXIMATELY 6 MONTHS** Begins with Most Holy Trinity and Most Holy Body and Blood of Christ (Corpus Christi).

Ordinary Time II picks up
where Ordinary Time I leaves off
(though often skipping a few Sundays
in Ordinary Time
due to variation in the calendar).
The season concludes with Our Lord Jesus
Christ, King of the Universe.

Here's another useful tip: if you aren't sure how to locate the current Sunday in the liturgical year, you can consult the daily readings calendar at usccb.org. Each day of the church year is clearly identified, and the lectionary readings are provided.

First Sunday of Advent

The days are coming, says the LORD,
   when I will fulfill the promise
   I made to the house of Israel and Judah.
In those days, in that time,
   I will raise up for David a just shoot;
   he shall do what is right and just in the land.
In those days Judah shall be safe
   and Jerusalem shall dwell secure;
   this is what they shall call her:
   "The LORD our justice."

Jeremiah lived from Judah's golden age (late 600s BCE) through the Babylonian conquest and destruction of Judah (ca. 597–586 BCE). During this time, many Judeans were dispersed and exiled to Babylon or Egypt. Jeremiah himself died in Egypt. Jeremiah began prophesying while the people were in imminent danger of exile and continued after they had experienced the trauma of exile from Judah. Our text likely comes from the very end of the reign of the final Judean king, Zedekiah, and Jerusalem's final destruction (ca. 588–586 BCE). Jeremiah promises the people's return and the restoration of the Davidic line, the "just shoot" who will rebuild Jerusalem and the temple. This restoration will take place through the power of Israel's God, whose primary attribute is "justice" or "righteousness" (NRSV). The "just shoot" is another expression for "messiah" or "anointed one" (from *māšaḥ* in Hebrew, meaning "to anoint"), and was a political term for kings. The word "messiah" slowly developed into a purely religious term. For the early Jewish followers of Jesus in the first century CE, and then for Gentile believers, Jesus was this Messiah.

RESPONSORIAL PSALM   PSALM 25:4-5, 8-9, 10, 14

To you, O Lord, I lift my soul.

SECOND READING   1 THESSALONIANS 3:12–4:2

Brothers and sisters:
May the Lord make you increase and abound in love
    for one another and for all,
    just as we have for you,
    so as to strengthen your hearts,
    to be blameless in holiness before our God and Father
    at the coming of our Lord Jesus with all his holy ones. Amen.

Finally, brothers and sisters,
    we earnestly ask and exhort you in the Lord Jesus that,
    as you received from us
    how you should conduct yourselves to please God
    —and as you are conducting yourselves—
    you do so even more.
For you know what instructions we gave you through the
        Lord Jesus.

First Thessalonians is Paul's first letter and our earliest New Testament text (ca. late 40s CE). It is a letter of encouragement to the early Christian community in Thessalonica (northern Greece). The early Christians expected Christ to return during their lifetimes. Paul urges them to remain vigilant and alert in awaiting this return, even in the face of social pressure and persecution. The reading begins as a community prayer for love and the strengthening of hearts to be perfect, or "blameless in holiness," as the people await the "coming" (Greek *parousia* or "presence") of Christ. Paul then issues ethical instructions. He reminds the community to conduct themselves (literally "walk") in a way that is pleasing to God with the goal of obedience to God. The final reference to "instructions" refers back to earlier instructions in the letter.

GOSPEL   LUKE 21:25-28, 34-36

Jesus said to his disciples:
"There will be signs in the sun, the moon, and the stars,
    and on earth nations will be in dismay,
    perplexed by the roaring of the sea and the waves.
People will die of fright
    in anticipation of what is coming upon the world,
    for the powers of the heavens will be shaken.
And then they will see the Son of Man
    coming in a cloud with power and great glory.
But when these signs begin to happen,
    stand erect and raise your heads
    because your redemption is at hand.

"Beware that your hearts do not become drowsy
    from carousing and drunkenness
    and the anxieties of daily life,
    and that day catch you by surprise like a trap.
For that day will assault everyone
    who lives on the face of the earth.
Be vigilant at all times
    and pray that you have the strength
    to escape the tribulations that are imminent
    and to stand before the Son of Man."

Today we begin a new liturgical year with the Gospel according
to Luke. His is a unique story of Jesus that includes Zechariah and
Elizabeth, Simeon and Anna, and the particular traditions of the
Canticles of Mary (*Magnificat*) and Zechariah (*Benedictus*) that are
so precious to the church. According to tradition, Luke was a physician and a Gentile who shared a body of sources about Jesus with
Mark and Matthew. Luke was also a gifted writer. Although he tells
the same basic story as Mark and Matthew, Luke emphasizes God's
compassion for the most marginalized members of society, including key stories about women, tax collectors, the poor, the sick, the
oppressed, and even the Pharisees, who all interact with Jesus more
prominently in this Gospel than in any other. For Luke, Jesus's story
is a natural continuation of the story of the people of Israel. Because

the beginning and end of every liturgical year focus on the end times and the importance of vigilance, we begin the year deep into the Gospel with remarkable imagery of powerful signs in the natural world that point toward the end times. These signs are not cause for fear but for celebration: the disciples' redemption is near. They are to be ready and awake.

Ponder

The name of Israel's God is mystical, unknowable. Throughout the Hebrew Bible, God responds enigmatically when humans ask for God's personal name. (See, for example, Exodus 3:13-14, where Moses asks for God's name, and God responds, "I am who I am.") Yet in our first reading, the prophet Jeremiah names God "our justice [righteousness]." Jeremiah names this God "Justice" to give hope to a people who are living through traumatic experiences. This God, Justice, will ultimately have the last word over the pain of current historical situations. What does it mean to us as Christians to know that our ultimate hope, in the midst of our own pain and historical crises, is rooted in God's name as Justice?

The early Christian community lived in a state of urgency and hope, believing the "end times," or eschaton, would come in their lifetimes. This did not happen. Yet God's time is not linear. Our readings and the beginning of this liturgical season invite us to wake up yet again, like the early Christians, and reflect on what the "end times" mean for us. Each of us will have our own personal eschaton or death. Ongoing catastrophes, immense tragedies, and painful conflicts in this world remind us—as they did for the early Christians—that this life is fleeting and delicate. The Gospel calls us to be watchful and alert, while Paul exhorts us to strengthen our hearts. How do we practice being present now, while remaining alert to what has not yet fully come?

Second Sunday of Advent

Jerusalem, take off your robe of mourning and misery;
   put on the splendor of glory from God forever:
wrapped in the cloak of justice from God,
     bear on your head the mitre
     that displays the glory of the eternal name.
For God will show all the earth your splendor:
   you will be named by God forever
   the peace of justice, the glory of God's worship.

Up, Jerusalem! stand upon the heights;
   look to the east and see your children
gathered from the east and the west
     at the word of the Holy One,
     rejoicing that they are remembered by God.
Led away on foot by their enemies they left you:
     but God will bring them back to you
     borne aloft in glory as on royal thrones.
For God has commanded
     that every lofty mountain be made low,
and that the age-old depths and gorges
     be filled to level ground,
     that Israel may advance secure in the glory of God.
The forests and every fragrant kind of tree
     have overshadowed Israel at God's command;
for God is leading Israel in joy
     by the light of his glory,
     with his mercy and justice for company.

The book of Baruch was written in Greek in the second or first century BCE, though it is set during the events that led up to and followed the exile to Babylon in 586 BCE. Our reading draws from a long "Poem of Consolation" (4:5–5:9) that begins by calling the people to take courage. Throughout the poem, the author interweaves quotes from the book of Isaiah to describe the events after the exile when Jerusalem, the Holy City, will be renamed and become a physical manifestation of God's glory and throne (see Isa 40:3-4, 9-11; 62:1-12). Judeans will return to the Holy City from where they have been dispersed across the known world while God leads them in mercy and justice. The imagery from this text, and especially the citations from Isaiah, link directly into our Gospel reading.

RESPONSORIAL PSALM   PSALM 126:1-2, 2-3, 4-5, 6

The Lord has done great things for us; we are filled with joy.

SECOND READING   PHILIPPIANS 1:4-6, 8-11

Brothers and sisters:
I pray always with joy in my every prayer for all of you,
    because of your partnership for the gospel
    from the first day until now.
I am confident of this,
    that the one who began a good work in you
    will continue to complete it
    until the day of Christ Jesus.
God is my witness,
    how I long for all of you with the affection of Christ Jesus.
And this is my prayer:
    that your love may increase ever more and more
    in knowledge and every kind of perception,
    to discern what is of value,
    so that you may be pure and blameless for the day of Christ,
    filled with the fruit of righteousness
    that comes through Jesus Christ
    for the glory and praise of God.

For the next two weeks, our second reading will come from Philippians. Paul wrote this letter to the community at Philippi while he was imprisoned (1:7; perhaps while under house arrest in Rome, ca. 61–63 CE). Today we read Paul's opening prayer of thanksgiving. He writes confidently that God will continue to "complete" or make whole the community's "good work" or ethical conduct until Christ's return. He expresses faith in how the community continues to progress and grow in union with Christ. This growth brings wisdom, which is grounded in a deep understanding of Christ's death and resurrection. The final verse reminds readers that all righteousness comes from God, is rooted in God, and manifests fully in union with Jesus Christ.

GOSPEL   LUKE 3:1-6

In the fifteenth year of the reign of Tiberius Caesar,
    when Pontius Pilate was governor of Judea,
    and Herod was tetrarch of Galilee,
    and his brother Philip tetrarch of the region of Ituraea
        and Trachonitis,
    and Lysanias was tetrarch of Abilene,
    during the high priesthood of Annas and Caiaphas,
    the word of God came to John the son of Zechariah in
        the desert.
John went throughout the whole region of the Jordan,
    proclaiming a baptism of repentance for the forgiveness of sins,
    as it is written in the book of the words of the prophet Isaiah:
    A voice of one crying out in the desert:
    "Prepare the way of the Lord,
        make straight his paths.
    Every valley shall be filled
        and every mountain and hill shall be made low.
    The winding roads shall be made straight,
        and the rough ways made smooth,
    and all flesh shall see the salvation of God."

Our Gospel reading introduces us to John the Baptist and sets the stage for next Sunday, when we will focus on John's ministry. The text begins with a careful dating scheme that includes a number of important religious and political leaders from the end of the first century BCE through the beginning of the first century CE. Tiberius Caesar was the second Roman emperor who reigned between 14 and 37 CE. Pontius Pilate served under him as governor of the province of Judea between 26 and 36 CE. Herod Antipas ruled Galilee as "tetrarch" (meaning "ruler of a quarter") until his death (ca. 4 BCE–39 CE), while his half-brother Philip ruled the area north of Galilee until his death in 34 CE. Lysanias was a ruler of Rome from 25 CE to 30

CE. Annas was high priest between 6 CE and 15 CE, until the Romans deposed him; he was followed by his son Eleazar, then by his son-in-law Caiaphas between 18 CE and 36 CE. This dating may not be exact for situating John's ministry, but it is significant. It is a scathing critique of the political and religious establishment around the time of Jesus. The word of God bypasses all these important figures for John, who comes to proclaim a symbolic "baptism of repentance," or spiritual cleansing. This cleansing signifies the forgiveness of sins and the people's return to God. John quotes from Isaiah (40:3-5) to announce the coming of the Messiah.

Ponder

In our first reading from Baruch, God leads Israel home from exile in "mercy and justice." Mercy and justice: these divine attributes radiate through the reading. God transforms Jerusalem from a grieving widow into the manifestation of divine glory. God remembers the people and brings them home from where they have been banished and displaced. As Baruch promises his readers, he also promises us divine mercy, justice, healing, and restoration. Similar to Baruch, Paul promises the Philippians that God will continue to "complete" or transform them. As we prepare for the coming of Christ, how do we need God's transformation? In what ways do we long to be healed?

The Gospel presents us with two paths to walk: the way of our current society, with its dominant power structures, and the way of God's salvation. Now as in John's time, we can choose either path. We can view the current system and all of its problems, inequalities, and sufferings as true and entrenched reality, thus orienting ourselves to live passively according to that vision. Or we can orient ourselves toward a different reality: the promise that we will all see the "salvation of God." This second orientation calls us to continual conversion and hope. This Advent season, which orientation are we choosing in our minds, hearts, and actions?

Third Sunday of Advent (Gaudete Sunday)

FIRST READING   ZEPHANIAH 3:14-18a

Shout for joy, O daughter Zion![1]
  Sing joyfully, O Israel!
Be glad and exult with all your heart,
  O daughter Jerusalem!
The LORD has removed the judgment against you,
  he has turned away your enemies;
the King of Israel, the LORD, is in your midst,
  you have no further misfortune to fear.
On that day, it shall be said to Jerusalem:
  Fear not, O Zion, be not discouraged!
The LORD, your God, is in your midst,
  a mighty savior;
he will rejoice over you with gladness,
  and renew you in his love,
he will sing joyfully because of you,
  as one sings at festivals.

Zephaniah (whose name means "the Lord has stored up" or "the Lord has hidden") is a short prophetic book of three chapters. It is set during the time of King Josiah in the eighth century BCE, when Josiah instituted religious reforms and tried to establish political independence from the Assyrian Empire (see 2 Kings 16–23 for his story). The book was likely edited after the Babylonian exile, perhaps as late as the fifth century BCE, as evidenced by Zephaniah's concern for the exiles' return to Judah at the very end of the book (including our reading). The book begins by announcing the "Day of the Lord" and contains powerful imagery of divine judgment that has captured the imagination of its readers and interpreters. For example, a Jewish text from the first century CE, the *Apocalypse of Zephaniah*, imagines

---

1. "Zion" is a religious term that is used interchangeably with "Jerusalem" and can refer to God's Holy City, Israel as a whole, or God's people.

Zephaniah's visits to hell and heaven. A thirteenth-century-CE Christian hymn called the *Dies Irae* (or "Day of Wrath") is included in the Mass for the Dead and draws from Zephaniah's language of the Day of the Lord. Finally, the term *shoah* (*šōʾâ* , the Hebrew word for "disaster" or "ruin") in Zephaniah 1:15 became a synonym for the devastation of European Jews during the Holocaust. Despite the ongoing import of Zephaniah's imagery, we hear from the prophet only twice during our lectionary cycle (including weekday liturgies). Our reading comes from the book's end, in which judgment shifts to rejoicing and the promise of salvation. The prophet depicts Jerusalem as a daughter. Her God is a great king and warrior. The prophet calls her to shout and sing for joy, just as God will "rejoice" and "sing joyfully" because of her.

RESPONSORIAL PSALM   ISAIAH 12:2-3, 4, 5-6

Cry out with joy and gladness: for among you is the great and
Holy One of Israel.

SECOND READING   PHILIPPIANS 4:4-7

Brothers and sisters:
Rejoice in the Lord always.
I shall say it again: rejoice!
Your kindness should be known to all.
The Lord is near.
Have no anxiety at all, but in everything,
    by prayer and petition, with thanksgiving,
    make your requests known to God.
Then the peace of God that surpasses all understanding
    will guard your hearts and minds in Christ Jesus.

These exhortations to the Philippian community are among Paul's final sentiments in his letter. In prison and uncertain about his future, Paul focuses instead on Christ's return. He tells the community to keep this promise of return always in mind. Rejoice. Be kind. Remember that the Lord is near. Have no anxiety about anything.

For Paul, God's peace is like a watchman who stands guard over the community's hearts and minds. Why does this peace "[surpass] all understanding"? Perhaps it is because the ordinary human mind can't comprehend it, or perhaps because such remarkable peace surpasses all human efforts to attain it.

GOSPEL   LUKE 3:10-18

The crowds asked John the Baptist,
  "What should we do?"
He said to them in reply,
  "Whoever has two cloaks
  should share with the person who has none.
And whoever has food should do likewise."
Even tax collectors came to be baptized and they said to him,
  "Teacher, what should we do?"
He answered them,
  "Stop collecting more than what is prescribed."
Soldiers also asked him,
  "And what is it that we should do?"
He told them,
  "Do not practice extortion,
  do not falsely accuse anyone,
  and be satisfied with your wages."

Now the people were filled with expectation,
  and all were asking in their hearts
  whether John might be the Christ.
John answered them all, saying,
  "I am baptizing you with water,
  but one mightier than I is coming.
I am not worthy to loosen the thongs of his sandals.
He will baptize you with the Holy Spirit and fire.
His winnowing fan is in his hand to clear his threshing floor
  and to gather the wheat into his barn,
  but the chaff he will burn with unquenchable fire."
Exhorting them in many other ways,
  he preached good news to the people.

Last Sunday our Gospel reading ended with Luke 3:6. This week we skip over 3:7-9, where John calls the crowds a "brood of vipers" and warns them that they won't get a free pass simply because their ancestor is Abraham. The ax is "at the root of the trees," he says, about to cut down all trees (i.e., the people) that do not bear fruit. Rather than reacting defensively to John's indictment, today's reading picks up with the people's honest response, "What should we do?" John then offers practical advice: share clothes and food, be honest and fair in positions of power. These teachings must have held incredible appeal, because the people begin to wonder if John is the Christ. No, John says, clarifying that his baptism is merely a symbol ("water") in preparation for the one to come. Though his final statements about "fire" and "winnowing" may seem harsh to us, in fact Luke states that John's words are heard as "good news" (gospel) to the people.

Ponder

Gaudete Sunday takes its name from the Latin *gaudete* ("rejoice"), a key word from our Philippians reading. Paul exhorts the community to "[r]ejoice in the Lord always" and to "have no anxiety" about anything as they await Christ's return. Perhaps Paul's expectation was that Christ's coming was so imminent, so joyful, that it simply overpowered all other concerns and sufferings. Similarly, in the Gospel, the people are "filled with expectation" and hear John's prophecy of the coming of the Messiah not as indictment but as "good news." What does this joy, this hopeful expectation, mean for us practically today, in the midst of life's uncertainties and difficulties?

According to Zephaniah, joy is not one-sided. In fact, it begins with God rejoicing over and through us, which God does "with gladness." Our joy therefore begins with God, yet it is also deeply relational and involves our openness to allowing God to encounter us and suffuse us with this joy. As Pope Francis wrote in The Joy of the Gospel, "I invite all Christians, everywhere . . . to a renewed personal encounter with Jesus Christ, or at least an openness to letting him encounter them; I ask all of you to do this unfailingly each day. No one should think that this invitation is not meant for him or her, since no one is excluded from the joy brought by the Lord."[2] In these remaining days of Advent, how can we open ourselves to allow Christ, our deepest Joy, to encounter us?

2. Pope Francis, *Evangelii Gaudium*, 3.

Fourth Sunday of Advent

Thus says the LORD:
You, Bethlehem-Ephrathah
   too small to be among the clans of Judah,
from you shall come forth for me
   one who is to be ruler in Israel;
whose origin is from of old,
   from ancient times.
Therefore the Lord will give them up, until the time
   when she who is to give birth has borne,
and the rest of his kindred shall return
   to the children of Israel.
He shall stand firm and shepherd his flock
   by the strength of the LORD,
   in the majestic name of the LORD, his God;
and they shall remain, for now his greatness
   shall reach to the ends of the earth;
   he shall be peace.

Micah prophesied around the time of the fall of the northern kingdom of Israel to Assyria (ca. 720 BCE), a period that included mass deportations of the people, possible immigration waves of northern refugees south to Judah, and the continued threat of the Assyrian Empire to Judah. Micah was from a small town south of Jerusalem, close to Bethlehem. He reminds his audience that their greatest king, David, came from one of the smallest clans of Judah and that his line will one day reemerge powerfully from the same insignificant clan. For Micah, the return of the line of David is a political yearning that will manifest in a "messiah" or "anointed one" who will come in power and victory to save the people. This messiah will not only bring peace to Judah but "shall be peace" himself, meaning that he will bring harmony and wholeness to the entire known world. According to the New Testament, Jesus is this great "ruler" born in Bethlehem. This is our only reading from Micah during the three-year Sunday lectionary cycle.

RESPONSORIAL PSALM   PSALM 80:2-3, 15-16, 18-19

Lord, make us turn to you; let us see your face and we shall
    be saved.

SECOND READING   HEBREWS 10:5-10

Brothers and sisters:
When Christ came into the world, he said:
    "Sacrifice and offering you did not desire,
        but a body you prepared for me;
    in holocausts and sin offerings[1] you took no delight.
    Then I said, 'As is written of me in the scroll,
    behold, I come to do your will, O God.' "

First he says, "Sacrifices and offerings,
    holocausts and sin offerings,
    you neither desired nor delighted in."
These are offered according to the law.
Then he says, "Behold, I come to do your will."
He takes away the first to establish the second.
By this "will," we have been consecrated
    through the offering of the body of Jesus Christ once for all.

In the verse directly preceding our reading, the author of Hebrews claims it is impossible for animal sacrifices to take away sin once and for all (10:4). What follows in our reading is a reinterpretation of Psalm 40:7-9a in light of Christ as this "once for all" sacrifice. According to Psalm 40, God prefers obedience to sacrifice. The psalm does not reject sacrifice but regards it as meaningless without the right intention. The author of Hebrews reinterprets the psalm to state that Israelite sacrifice is indeed replaced by Jesus's obedience to God and his right intention in voluntarily sacrificing his own body. The word "will" in the last verse refers to God's will that Jesus offer up the body that God gave him.

---

1. "Holocausts" (literally "burnt offerings") were regular offerings of service and dedication to God, while "sin offerings" made reparations for a particular sin.

GOSPEL   LUKE 1:39-45

Mary set out
    and traveled to the hill country in haste
    to a town of Judah,
    where she entered the house of Zechariah
    and greeted Elizabeth.
When Elizabeth heard Mary's greeting,
    the infant leaped in her womb,
    and Elizabeth, filled with the Holy Spirit,
    cried out in a loud voice and said,
    "Blessed are you among women,
    and blessed is the fruit of your womb.
And how does this happen to me,
    that the mother of my Lord should come to me?
For at the moment the sound of your greeting reached my ears,
    the infant in my womb leaped for joy.
Blessed are you who believed
    that what was spoken to you by the Lord
    would be fulfilled."

Between December 19 and 24, we hear of the events leading up to
the birth of Jesus according to Luke. The Gospel of Luke contains
many details of the Christmas story and the people within it that the
church holds dear, including Zechariah and Elizabeth, the *Benedictus*
(Canticle of Zechariah), the angel Gabriel, the relationship between
Mary and Elizabeth, the *Magnificat* (Canticle of Mary), and the details of Jesus's birth in humble circumstances in Bethlehem. In this
text, Elizabeth is "filled with the Holy Spirit" when the unborn John
recognizes the unborn Jesus. The power of the Holy Spirit is already
at work in the women's wombs. After John's silent affirmation of
Jesus, Elizabeth is the first person in the Gospel to state verbally that
Jesus is Lord. Joy underlies the text in the intimacy between John
and Jesus, Elizabeth and Mary. This joy is particularly striking given
that Elizabeth's and Mary's lives were, we can imagine, quite difficult.
None of the Gospels describes how these relationships unfold after
the births of John and Jesus. The *Magnificat*, Mary's prophetic song
of praise, directly follows our text.

Ponder

Micah said the Messiah would come from Bethlehem, the birth-place of King David and a small, insignificant town. Similarly, in the Gospel, Elizabeth and Mary nurture John and Jesus into being in a small and seemingly insignificant place: Elizabeth's home. During their few months of seclusion, nobody knew what was happening in this ordinary place where Elizabeth and Mary were living out their daily lives. This week, we are invited to imagine this setting, this time of seclusion, and the power of places that are unimportant by society's standards. We are invited to experience the bravery of these women and the paradox of greatness that often emerges from what seems small and insignificant.

The second reading from Hebrews states that God "prepared" a body for Christ, who willingly offered it as a once-and-for-all sacrifice. Mary's body was also prepared, in a sense, and she is a powerful example of a courageous, consenting offering. We, too, have bodies prepared for us to offer back to God's service. As we meditate upon Christ's coming this Christmas, consider how God has worked through you and how God continues to seek your consent to become incarnate through your own life and body.

The Nativity of the Lord (Christmas) (Mass During the Night)[1]

FIRST READING   ISAIAH 9:1-6

The people who walked in darkness
    have seen a great light;
upon those who dwelt in the land of gloom
    a light has shone.
You have brought them abundant joy
    and great rejoicing,
as they rejoice before you as at the harvest,
    as people make merry when dividing spoils.
For the yoke that burdened them,
    the pole on their shoulder,
and the rod of their taskmaster
    you have smashed, as on the day of Midian.
For every boot that tramped in battle,
    every cloak rolled in blood,
    will be burned as fuel for flames.
For a child is born to us, a son is given us;
    upon his shoulder dominion rests.
They name him Wonder-Counselor, God-Hero,
    Father-Forever, Prince of Peace.
His dominion is vast
    and forever peaceful,
from David's throne, and over his kingdom,
    which he confirms and sustains
by judgment and justice,
    both now and forever.
The zeal of the LORD of hosts will do this!

---

1. Christmas Mass readings are the same each year throughout the three-year lectionary cycle. See *Ponder: Year A* for commentary on the readings for the Vigil Mass and *Ponder: Year B* for commentary on the readings for the Mass During the Day.

In our lectionary cycle, Isaiah is the most frequently used text from the Hebrew Bible. This reading is one of the best-known texts in Isaiah, and for Christians it is a powerful allusion to Christ. Isaiah is the longest of the prophetic texts (66 chapters), and it was composed in stages. The first portion (Isa 1–39) was written by the prophet Isaiah himself (whose name means "the Lord saves") in the latter half of the eighth century BCE in Judah. This was a time of invasion and crisis; the northern kingdom of Israel eventually fell to Assyria in 720 BCE, while the southern kingdom of Judah survived until the Babylonian exile of 586 BCE. In chapters 1–39, Isaiah prophesies a period of punishment for Judah as well as a time of restoration. The above verses are a song of thanksgiving found in the midst of Isaiah's prophecies of destruction and punishment. The song anticipates God's restoration of a righteous ruler from the line of David. God smashes the "yoke," "pole," and "rod" of the foreign oppressor. Isaiah prophesies the birth of a new king, which likely refers to King Hezekiah (born ca. 739 BCE). Historically, Hezekiah was remembered as a just and righteous king who reestablished a period of peace and justice in Judah.

RESPONSORIAL PSALM   PSALM 96:1-2, 2-3, 11-12, 13 (LUKE 2:11)

Today is born our Savior, Christ the Lord.

SECOND READING   TITUS 2:11-14

Beloved:
The grace of God has appeared, saving all
    and training us to reject godless ways and worldly desires
    and to live temperately, justly, and devoutly in this age,
    as we await the blessed hope,
    the appearance of the glory of our great God
    and savior Jesus Christ,
    who gave himself for us to deliver us from all lawlessness
    and to cleanse for himself a people as his own,
    eager to do what is good.

The letter to Titus is addressed to Paul's coworker who, according to the letter, was commissioned to build up the early Christian community on the island of Crete. Titus is remembered as the ideal Gentile convert (Gal 2:3) who played a crucial role in Paul's ministry (e.g., 2 Cor 8:16-17). The letter is short (three chapters) and theologically rich. Today's reading provides the theological reason for leading a reverent life: God's grace has appeared (Greek *epiphainō* or "epiphany") through Jesus Christ and will again appear ("epiphany") in Christ's Second Coming. The letter also contains one of the strongest statements of Jesus as God in the New Testament in the expression, "the glory of our great God and savior Jesus Christ." Christ will "deliver" or literally "buy back" the people from lawlessness or slavery to become a people "as his own," a reference to the biblical promise to Israel as God's people (e.g., Exod 3:7; 19:5).

GOSPEL   LUKE 2:1-14

In those days a decree went out from Caesar Augustus
    that the whole world should be enrolled.
This was the first enrollment,
    when Quirinius was governor of Syria.
So all went to be enrolled, each to his own town.
And Joseph too went up from Galilee from the town of Nazareth
    to Judea, to the city of David that is called Bethlehem,
    because he was of the house and family of David,
    to be enrolled with Mary, his betrothed, who was with child.
While they were there,
    the time came for her to have her child,
    and she gave birth to her firstborn son.
She wrapped him in swaddling clothes and laid him in a manger,
    because there was no room for them in the inn.

Now there were shepherds in that region living in the fields
    and keeping the night watch over their flock.
The angel of the Lord appeared to them
    and the glory of the Lord shone around them,
    and they were struck with great fear.

The angel said to them,
  "Do not be afraid;
  for behold, I proclaim to you good news of great joy
  that will be for all the people.
For today in the city of David
  a savior has been born for you who is Christ and Lord.
And this will be a sign for you:
  you will find an infant wrapped in swaddling clothes
  and lying in a manger."
And suddenly there was a multitude of the heavenly host with
    the angel,
  praising God and saying:
  "Glory to God in the highest
  and on earth peace to those on whom his favor rests."

This is one of two Gospel accounts of Jesus's birth; the other is Matthew 1:18-25 (which is read at the Vigil Mass). Caesar Augustus was the Roman ruler between 27 BCE and 14 CE; he was hailed as "Lord" and "Savior of the World" because his rule marked a time of peace known as the "Pax Romana" ("Roman peace") or the "Pax Augusta." We know from sources outside the Bible that there were general censuses of Roman citizens in the years 28 BCE, 8 BCE, and 14 CE, but none are recorded from the time of Jesus's birth. Bethlehem was King David's hometown, a place that links Jesus to David through Joseph. Shepherds are also reminiscent of both David, who was a shepherd (1 Sam 16:11), and rulers in general, including God as the ultimate shepherd and ruler (see Ezek 34). God appears as an angel throughout the Bible, and the "glory" of God signifies God's awesome presence (Exod 24:16-17; Isa 40:5). The angel calls Jesus "savior," "Christ" (*Christos* in Greek, translating from *Messiah* in Hebrew), and "Lord" (*Kyrios*). These are the primary titles for Jesus according to Christian belief, and they subvert Roman authority by transferring the titles "Lord" and "savior" from Caesar to Jesus. The scene presents a remarkable juxtaposition between divine glory and human vulnerability in the humble scene of Jesus's birth. "[S]waddling clothes" were used for commoner and king alike (see Wis 7:4-5).

Ponder

The mystery of Christmas comes to us in contradictions: darkness and dawn, suffering and hope, divine glory and human vulnerability. Isaiah sets the stage in a poem that celebrates the end of a time of terrible suffering, when light will infuse the darkness, pain will lead to rejoicing, and hope will dawn with a righteous leader. In the Gospel, Jesus is this light infusing the darkness, divine power born through tiny human fragility, God's glory and the heavenly host breaking into a scene of humility and poverty.

Like our texts, our contemporary Christmas season also comes to us in contradictions. For many, it is a time of celebration, of family and comfort and joy. But we celebrate Jesus's birth in the midst of societal brokenness and suffering. This is a time when suicide rates increase and loneliness, grief, and poverty are experienced more acutely. As people of faith, the Christmas mystery invites us to hold these contradictions together. Jesus is born into our suffering, our pain, our community. He is found in the places of greatest need. This is the gift of Christ, born to walk with us, to sustain us, to be intimately present with us in the reality of our lives.

Yet the daring hope and promise of Christ is that suffering and brokenness do not have the last word. The light shines and will shine in the darkness. Jesus's birth is a promise of healing, transformation, and, ultimately, resurrection. May we all celebrate and live into this daring hope as we hold and sustain each other as a community, today and every day.

The Holy Family
of Jesus, Mary, and Joseph[1]

FIRST READING   1 SAMUEL 1:20-22, 24-28 (ALT. SIR 3:2-6, 12-14)

In those days Hannah conceived, and at the end of her term bore
    a son
    whom she called Samuel, since she had asked the LORD for him.
The next time her husband Elkanah was going up
    with the rest of his household
    to offer the customary sacrifice to the LORD and to fulfill
        his vows,
    Hannah did not go, explaining to her husband,
    "Once the child is weaned,
    I will take him to appear before the LORD
    and to remain there forever;
    I will offer him as a perpetual nazirite."

Once Samuel was weaned, Hannah brought him up with her,
    along with a three-year-old bull,
    an ephah[2] of flour, and a skin of wine,
    and presented him at the temple of the LORD in Shiloh.
After the boy's father had sacrificed the young bull,
    Hannah, his mother, approached Eli and said:
    "Pardon, my lord!
As you live, my lord,
    I am the woman who stood near you here, praying to the LORD.
I prayed for this child, and the LORD granted my request.
Now I, in turn, give him to the LORD;
    as long as he lives, he shall be dedicated to the LORD."
Hannah left Samuel there.

Hannah is one of several examples in the Hebrew Bible of women
who conceive with God's help. Her name derives from the Hebrew

---

1. The readings used here are the optional readings for Year C. For the alternative readings from Sirach and Colossians, see *Ponder: Year A*.
2. One ephah was about 23 liters.

ḥānan and means "favor" or "grace." The temple in Shiloh was an important northern sanctuary and the home of the ark of the covenant (see, e.g., 1 Sam 3:3). In her customary yearly visit to this temple, Hannah prays silently and fervently for a son, promising to dedicate the child to God if her prayer is answered (1 Sam 1:11). The term "nazirite" comes from the Hebrew *nāzar*, which means "to dedicate" or "to consecrate" and refers to men and women who set themselves apart to serve God for a particular amount of time (Num 6:1-21). Seeing her pray, the prophet Eli first thinks Hannah is drunk, so fervent are her prayers and so uncommon was it to pray silently in the temple. When Eli realizes his mistake, he promises that Hannah will give birth to a son. After three years, the customary time for weaning, Hannah and her husband Elkanah dedicate Samuel as promised. The sacrifices are either offerings to God in gratitude for Samuel's birth or offerings made along with the nazirite vow (Num 6:14-17). This story may have originally been *Saul's* birth story, for the root of Saul's name is "to ask" (*šāʾal*), and the story contains a number of wordplays on his name. The name Samuel means "God hears" (from the Hebrew root *šāmaʿ*, meaning "to hear," plus the name *El* for God).

RESPONSORIAL PSALM   PSALM 84:2-3, 5-6, 9-10

Blessed are they who dwell in your house, O Lord.

SECOND READING   1 JOHN 3:1-2, 21-24 (ALT. COL 3:12-21)

Beloved:
See what love the Father has bestowed on us
    that we may be called the children of God.
And so we are.
The reason the world does not know us
    is that it did not know him.
Beloved, we are God's children now;
    what we shall be has not yet been revealed.
We do know that when it is revealed we shall be like him,
    for we shall see him as he is.

Beloved, if our hearts do not condemn us,
　　we have confidence in God and receive from him whatever
　　　　we ask,
　　because we keep his commandments and do what pleases him.
And his commandment is this:
　　we should believe in the name of his Son, Jesus Christ,
　　and love one another just as he commanded us.
Those who keep his commandments remain in him, and he
　　in them,
　　and the way we know that he remains in us
　　is from the Spirit he gave us.

In 1 John, God's commandments are rooted in two essential traits: belief and love. These two terms (along with "beloved" as a derivation of "love") repeat throughout the letter. Today's reading describes how "love" (*agapē*) flows from God through those who believe in God, thus transforming believers into God's children. The "love the Father has bestowed on us" is the gift of Jesus Christ. This love makes adoption and inheritance as children of God possible as both a present reality and a future promise. Failure to love is the clearest sign of sin. One must therefore act in love and guard the commandments, behavior that allows believers to remain or abide in and with God. (For more information on the broader context of this reading, see the commentary on 1 John in the Second through Sixth Sundays of Easter in *Ponder: Year B*.)

GOSPEL　　　　　　　　　　　　　　　　　　LUKE 2:41-52

Each year Jesus' parents went to Jerusalem for the feast
　　of Passover,
　　and when he was twelve years old,
　　they went up according to festival custom.
After they had completed its days, as they were returning,
　　the boy Jesus remained behind in Jerusalem,
　　but his parents did not know it.
Thinking that he was in the caravan,
　　they journeyed for a day
　　and looked for him among their relatives and acquaintances,

> but not finding him,
> they returned to Jerusalem to look for him.
> After three days they found him in the temple,
>   sitting in the midst of the teachers,
>   listening to them and asking them questions,
>   and all who heard him were astounded
>   at his understanding and his answers.
> When his parents saw him,
>   they were astonished,
>   and his mother said to him,
>   "Son, why have you done this to us?
> Your father and I have been looking for you with great anxiety."
> And he said to them,
>   "Why were you looking for me?
> Did you not know that I must be in my Father's house?"
> But they did not understand what he said to them.
> He went down with them and came to Nazareth,
>   and was obedient to them;
>   and his mother kept all these things in her heart.
> And Jesus advanced in wisdom and age and favor
>   before God and man.

This story of Jesus in the temple is unique to Luke. The setting is the family's yearly Passover pilgrimage to the Jerusalem temple, a custom relayed in Deuteronomy 16:5-6. The story may also be related to that of the prophet Samuel (see 1 Sam 1–3) and is meant to highlight Jesus's natural authority and home in the temple. The conversation between Jesus and his parents is a learning experience for Mary and Joseph, who must come to understand that Jesus's ultimate home and identity are connected not with them but with God. Jesus offers a challenge to his parents in this honest reminder that he is not bound to normal household expectations, yet he remains obedient and respectful to them. As in Luke 2:19, Mary guards all of this in her heart. This is the last we hear of Jesus the child before the beginning of his adult ministry.

Ponder

This feast was established in 1893 as an optional celebration, and it became a feast of the universal church under Benedict XV in 1921. At the time, it was a call to remember and preserve the holiness of family life in the midst of the immense social changes of the nineteenth century. Yet in one sense, our readings demonstrate more of a disruption of family units than their preservation. In 1 Samuel, Hannah dedicates her young child wholeheartedly to serve God in the temple, which becomes the child's home. Mary similarly gives Jesus away wholeheartedly when she says "yes" to God, even as she slowly grows into a full understanding of what this means throughout Jesus's life. Both family units are disrupted for a broader vision of family in relation to God's kingdom. In this reality, we are all "children" of God united in love (1 John 3:1). Given your own unique experiences of family, how do these readings push you to disrupt, and then reenvision, what "family" means to you?

Jesus remains in the temple rather than following his parents home from Jerusalem. His disappearance costs them two additional days of hard travel, yet when they find him, he does not apologize, and they do not seem angry. We hear only that they searched for him with "great anxiety" and that they were "astonished" when they heard his wisdom in the temple. This Gospel gently reminds us of the pain that comes from letting go of those we love as they follow their life paths. The Gospel can also be read as a cautionary tale about tensions between our faith lives and our blood families. How do you practice full belonging and care for family and community while also listening for the call of a higher authority?

Solemnity of Mary,
the Holy Mother of God

The LORD said to Moses:
   "Speak to Aaron and his sons and tell them:
   This is how you shall bless the Israelites.
Say to them:
   The LORD bless you and keep you!
   The LORD let his face shine upon
     you, and be gracious to you!
   The LORD look upon you kindly and
     give you peace!
So shall they invoke my name upon the Israelites,
   and I will bless them."

The book of Numbers is the fourth book of the Torah or Pentateuch (the first five books of the Hebrew Bible). It is a compilation of sources that includes old stories, folk traditions, and legal material. The above text is an ancient priestly blessing that all priests were required to bestow upon the people (see also Lev 9:22-23). It is a three-part blessing, each part slightly longer than the previous, to evoke God's overflowing mercy and favor. The Hebrew words in each blessing contain a wealth of meanings. For example, in the first blessing, to "keep you" literally means to "guard you" (*šāmar*, often translated as "protect"). This is the same word used in God's admonitions to the people to "guard" or "keep" the commandments (Exod 19:5), and it is the command given to Adam to "keep" the Garden of Eden (Gen 2:15; NRSV). In the second blessing, to "let [one's] face shine" upon another is to deal kindly or with compassion toward them. In the last of the three blessings, the literal translation of "The LORD look upon you kindly" is "The LORD lift up his face upon you." Finally, "peace" (Hebrew *šālôm*) means wholeness and completeness. Old amulets (small ornaments or pieces of jewelry worn for protection) inscribed with this blessing have been discovered in Israel dating as far back as the First Temple period (sixth century BCE or earlier). People wore these amulets as a way of continually invoking God's name.

RESPONSORIAL PSALM   PSALM 67:2-3, 5, 6, 8

> May God bless us in his mercy.

SECOND READING   GALATIANS 4:4-7

> Brothers and sisters:
> When the fullness of time had come, God sent his Son,
>   born of a woman, born under the law,
>   to ransom those under the law,
>   so that we might receive adoption as sons.
> As proof that you are sons,
>   God sent the Spirit of his Son into our hearts,
>   crying out, "Abba, Father!"
> So you are no longer a slave but a son,
>   and if a son then also an heir, through God.

For background information on Paul's letter to the Galatians, see notes for the Ninth Sunday in Ordinary Time. In this section of his letter, Paul compares the giving of the Jewish law with Christ's coming and the Gentiles' adoption as children of God through faith (3:1–4:31). His argument contrasts being a "slave" (to the cosmic forces of evil) with adoption as a child or "son" and "heir" into the household of faith. In today's text, Paul stresses that Jesus was both human ("born of a woman") and Jewish ("born under the law"), sent as God's Son both to liberate his own people ("those under the law") and to adopt the Gentiles. Through faith, Jews and Gentiles become equal heirs and children of God. A key to understanding Paul is to remember that he was a devout Jew who kept the commandments and did not believe that the law in itself was bad. Elsewhere, he reminds his readers that "the law is holy, and the commandment is holy and righteous and good" (Rom 7:12). However, in Paul's view, the human person is subject to sin and is ultimately incapable of holding to the standards of the law. True liberation comes through Christ, who embodies the law and is the eternal High Priest, able to remove all sins for all time (Heb 9:11-15).

GOSPEL   LUKE 2:16-21

The shepherds went in haste to Bethlehem and found Mary
    and Joseph,
    and the infant lying in the manger.
When they saw this,
    they made known the message
    that had been told them about this child.
All who heard it were amazed
    by what had been told them by the shepherds.
And Mary kept all these things,
    reflecting on them in her heart.
Then the shepherds returned,
    glorifying and praising God
    for all they had heard and seen,
    just as it had been told to them.

When eight days were completed for his circumcision,
    he was named Jesus, the name given him by the angel
    before he was conceived in the womb.

This Sunday's reading from Luke draws us back to Jesus's birth. The
newborn Jesus lies in a manger in Bethlehem. An angel of God comes
to a group of shepherds and reveals that the Messiah has been born.
The shepherds hurry to find Mary and Joseph and relay the information to others. We read this text today because it conveys the
relationship between Christ and his mother, Mary, the "God-bearer"
(Greek *theotokos*). It also describes Mary as the first true disciple,
the one who heard the shepherds' words and "kept" (or "treasured";
NRSV) these things, "reflecting on them" in her heart. Mary also
"kept all these things in her heart" after she and Joseph lost Jesus in
the temple after the Passover, a story we read last Sunday (Luke 2:41-
52). The Greek term for "reflect," which also translates as "ponder," is
symballō, which means literally "to throw together." In other words,
Mary holds together the entire story of Christ within herself.

Ponder

At its core, "peace" in Hebrew means wholeness and complete-ness. This is a peace that only God can give. Our reading from Numbers is a prayer for God's peace that was regularly invoked in worship and later worn on amulets. Each year on January 1, the church joins with many in the world to pray for world peace. Yet from an ancient perspective, true peace is only possible when all people turn to God and live a life rooted in God. In our contem-porary, pluralistic context, what does it mean to pray for world peace? As you pray with the first reading, rest in this prayer for you and for all people: "The LORD bless you and keep you! / The LORD let his face shine upon you, and be gracious to you! / The LORD look upon you kindly and give you peace!"

According to Paul, God sent the Spirit of the Son "into our hearts." In the Gospel, when the shepherds recount what they have been told about Jesus, Mary holds their message "in her heart." When we are quiet and attentive, it is in the heart that we experience Christ deep within us. It is in the heart that we all become "God-bearers." (Greek *theotokos*, meaning "God-bearer," is the term that the Council of Ephesus bestowed upon Mary in 431 CE.) Today we celebrate Mary as the "God-bearer," and we recognize the great gift of God within each of us, more intimate to us than our own flesh. Our readings and this Sunday's feast are invitations to ponder Mary's role in the divine promise as well as our own roles as God-bearers in the world around us.

The Epiphany of the Lord

Rise up in splendor, Jerusalem! Your light has come,
   the glory of the Lord shines upon you.
See, darkness covers the earth,
   and thick clouds cover the peoples;
but upon you the LORD shines,
   and over you appears his glory.
Nations shall walk by your light,
   and kings by your shining radiance.
Raise your eyes and look about;
   they all gather and come to you:
your sons come from afar,
   and your daughters in the arms of their nurses.

Then you shall be radiant at what you see,
   your heart shall throb and overflow,
for the riches of the sea shall be emptied out before you,
   the wealth of nations shall be brought to you.
Caravans of camels shall fill you,
   dromedaries from Midian and Ephah;
all from Sheba shall come
   bearing gold and frankincense,
   and proclaiming the praises of the LORD.

Isaiah 56–66 (often called "Third Isaiah") likely dates to the early Persian period (late sixth–early fourth centuries BCE) during Judah's era of restoration after the Babylonian exile (for more information on the exile, see next Sunday's notes on Isaiah 40). The above reading begins a long poem in Isaiah 60–62 addressed to Jerusalem. Written after the Persians had defeated Babylon (ca. 538 BCE) and a remnant of Judeans were already returning from exile, the prophetic voice imagines Jerusalem's continued restoration and glory. The Holy City will become home to a righteous nation that includes not only Judeans but all Gentiles who universally recognize the God of Israel. The "nations" approach as in procession to Zion alongside the Judeans. In earlier chapters of Isaiah (and in other prophetic texts), God uses the "nations" as a tool for Israel's punishment. Now, however, the nations will give praise to the God of Israel and help sustain Jerusalem.

RESPONSORIAL PSALM   PSALM 72:1-2, 7-8, 10-11, 12-13

Lord, every nation on earth will adore you.

SECOND READING   EPHESIANS 3:2-3a, 5-6

Brothers and sisters:
You have heard of the stewardship[1] of God's grace
    that was given to me for your benefit,
    namely, that the mystery was made known to me
        by revelation.
It was not made known to people in other generations
    as it has now been revealed
    to his holy apostles and prophets by the Spirit:
    that the Gentiles are coheirs, members of the same body,
and copartners in the promise in Christ Jesus through the gospel.

Unity between Jews and Gentiles is a key theme in Paul's letter to the Ephesians. Likely, one of Paul's Jewish-Christian followers (rather than Paul himself) wrote this letter in the late first century CE, perhaps during a time when Jewish-Christians and Gentiles were splitting off into separate communities, or perhaps during a time of Roman persecution. One of the letter's concerns is the continued unity of the growing church community as the Body of Christ. The "mystery" spoken of here is the union of Jewish and Gentile believers into a single community.

---

1. The Greek *oikonomia* is often used in the sense of "stewardship" or "task." Here it refers to God's plan realized through Paul. (An alternative translation is "commission.")

GOSPEL   MATTHEW 2:1-12

When Jesus was born in Bethlehem of Judea,
    in the days of King Herod,
    behold, magi from the east arrived in Jerusalem, saying,
    "Where is the newborn king of the Jews?
We saw his star at its rising
    and have come to do him homage."
When King Herod heard this,
    he was greatly troubled,
    and all Jerusalem with him.
Assembling all the chief priests and the scribes of the people,
    he inquired of them where the Christ was to be born.
They said to him, "In Bethlehem of Judea,
    for thus it has been written through the prophet:
    And you, Bethlehem, land of Judah,
        are by no means least among the rulers of Judah;
    since from you shall come a ruler,
        who is to shepherd my people Israel."
Then Herod called the magi secretly
    and ascertained from them the time of the star's appearance.
He sent them to Bethlehem and said,
    "Go and search diligently for the child.
When you have found him, bring me word,
    that I too may go and do him homage."
After their audience with the king they set out.
And behold, the star that they had seen at its rising preceded them,
    until it came and stopped over the place where the child was.
They were overjoyed at seeing the star,
    and on entering the house
    they saw the child with Mary his mother.
They prostrated themselves and did him homage.
Then they opened their treasures
    and offered him gifts of gold, frankincense, and myrrh.
And having been warned in a dream not to return to Herod,
    they departed for their country by another way.

Historically, the word "magi" designated both a priestly Persian class
and all those with supernatural knowledge or abilities (not unlike our
modern word "magician"). But in this text, the word "magi" refers to

those with astrological knowledge and, more importantly, to Gentiles from the east (Mesopotamia) who have come to worship Jesus. This story therefore demonstrates that Gentiles are included in Jesus's mission from the very beginning. Both Matthew's and Luke's Gospels include stories of Jesus's birth, but while Luke places the Jewish poor at the birth scene, Matthew puts the Gentiles first. (Note that Luke was a Gentile Christian, while Matthew was a Jewish-Christian, yet each of them places the other community first.) This story of the magi also asserts that Jesus is the Jewish Messiah, for Bethlehem is the place of King David's birth according to 1 Samuel, and the passage includes various texts from the Hebrew Bible that connect Jesus to the line of David (Mic 5:1-3; 2 Sam 5:2).

Ponder

Isaiah offers a striking contrast between the darkness covering the earth and the splendor, light, and radiance of God and the Holy City, Jerusalem. For many of us, the threat of darkness in our lives, our communities, and our world is all too real. Yet our readings remind us of God's light, which brings hope into the midst of darkness. This light makes our hearts "throb" and "overflow," according to Isaiah. It manifests as a star shining above a baby in a manger, according to Matthew. On this feast day, how do you live into the promise of God's radiance overflowing into the world? Where and how do you expect to see the rising of a star?

"Epiphany" comes from the Greek *epiphaneia*, meaning "radiance" or "manifestation." Our readings are filled with God's manifestation to the Gentiles. In Isaiah, God's light becomes a beacon for all nations. In Ephesians, Paul describes the great "mystery" that leads to the union of all people as the Body of Christ. And in Matthew, foreigners first witness God's light manifest over and in the baby Jesus. Unity is God's ultimate wish and plan for our world. As humans, divisiveness and exclusion are the easy way out. What takes far more courage and creativity is cooperation with the divine will. This feast day invites us to ponder how we embrace and cooperate with the great mystery and promise of the union of the Body of Christ.

The Baptism of the Lord[1]

FIRST READING   ISAIAH 40:1-5, 9-11 (ALT. 42:1-4, 6-7)

Comfort, give comfort to my people,
  says your God.
Speak tenderly to Jerusalem, and proclaim to her
   that her service is at an end,
  her guilt is expiated;
indeed, she has received from the hand of the Lord
  double for all her sins.

A voice cries out:
In the desert prepare the way of the Lord!
  Make straight in the wasteland a highway for our God!
Every valley shall be filled in,
  every mountain and hill shall be made low;
the rugged land shall be made a plain,
  the rough country, a broad valley.
Then the glory of the Lord shall be revealed,
  and all people shall see it together;
  for the mouth of the Lord has spoken.

Go up onto a high mountain,
  Zion, herald of glad tidings;
cry out at the top of your voice,
  Jerusalem, herald of good news!
Fear not to cry out
  and say to the cities of Judah:
  Here is your God!
Here comes with power
  the Lord God,
  who rules by a strong arm;
here is his reward with him,
  his recompense before him.

---

1. The readings used here are the optional readings for Year C. For the alternative readings from Isaiah and Acts, see *Ponder: Year A.*

Like a shepherd he feeds his flock;
in his arms he gathers the lambs,
carrying them in his bosom,
and leading the ewes with care.

For Christians, this is one of the better-known texts in the Hebrew Bible. It begins what is often called "Second Isaiah" (Isaiah 40–55), written by an anonymous prophet(s) toward the end of the Babylonian exile (ca. 586–536 BCE). The likely historical setting is around 539 BCE, when the Persian Empire overthrew Babylon. The overarching goal of Second Isaiah is to give hope to the exiled Judeans as they await return to Judah. The author emphasizes the permanence of God's covenant and the promise that Judah will be restored to its former glory. God's intimacy and care for the people flow through the chapters, as we see in the first verse of our reading, which opens Second Isaiah: "Comfort, give comfort to my people, / says your God" ("comfort," from the Hebrew verb *niham*, signifies deep emotion, care, and compassion). Envisioning the return to Judah and the restoration of the Holy City, Jerusalem (also called Zion), our reading invokes the exodus in its call to the people to prepare the "way" of God out of the wilderness (Babylon) and home to Zion. Once the way has been cleared, God's "glory" will be revealed to all people. Different voices interweave throughout: the prophet, God, an unknown "voice," and finally, the Holy City itself. Our reading also contains two seemingly paradoxical images for God: the storm God who comes in power and might, and the shepherd who cares tenderly for the flock.

RESPONSORIAL PSALM   PSALM 104:1b-2, 3-4, 24-25, 27-28, 29-30

O bless the Lord, my soul.

SECOND READING   TITUS 2:11-14; 3:4-7 (ALT. ACTS 10:34-38)

Beloved:
The grace of God has appeared, saving all
    and training us to reject godless ways and worldly desires
    and to live temperately, justly, and devoutly in this age,
    as we await the blessed hope,

the appearance of the glory of our great God
and savior Jesus Christ,
who gave himself for us to deliver us from all lawlessness
and to cleanse for himself a people as his own,
eager to do what is good.
When the kindness and generous love
of God our savior appeared,
not because of any righteous deeds we had done
but because of his mercy,
he saved us through the bath of rebirth
and renewal by the Holy Spirit,
whom he richly poured out on us
through Jesus Christ our savior,
so that we might be justified by his grace
and become heirs in hope of eternal life.

For general context on the letter of Titus and verses 2:11-14, see notes for The Nativity of the Lord in this volume. Titus 3:4-7 draws from the final section of the letter (3:1-11), which calls the early church community to be submissive and perform good works in expectation of Jesus's return. The "bath of rebirth and renewal" refers to baptism, which leads to transformation in the present and a promise of resurrection in the future through Jesus Christ.

GOSPEL   LUKE 3:15-16, 21-22

The people were filled with expectation,
and all were asking in their hearts
whether John might be the Christ.
John answered them all, saying,
"I am baptizing you with water,
but one mightier than I is coming.
I am not worthy to loosen the thongs of his sandals.
He will baptize you with the Holy Spirit and fire."

After all the people had been baptized
and Jesus also had been baptized and was praying,
heaven was opened and the Holy Spirit descended upon him
in bodily form like a dove.

And a voice came from heaven,
"You are my beloved Son;
with you I am well pleased."

We begin at the conclusion of John the Baptist's short ministry in Luke (see also notes to the Gospel reading for the Third Sunday of Advent). John first calls the people to repent, pointing away from himself by quoting our first reading from Isaiah: "Prepare the way of the Lord" (3:3-6). He calls the people a "brood of vipers" and gives practical instructions for salvation (e.g., share your clothes and food, do not extort, be satisfied with your wages; 3:7-14). The people are then "filled with expectation." We skip over John's final proclamations and imprisonment (3:17-20) and go straight to the scene after Jesus is baptized, though Luke does not state by whom (unlike Mark and Matthew). Luke also alludes to John's baptizing "all the people" before (or along with?) Jesus. In the Bible, the dove is a symbol of Israel (e.g., Ps 68:13; Hos 11:11); the Holy Spirit therefore comes upon Jesus as a dove to identify him as the chosen one of Israel.

Ponder

St. Catherine of Siena once wrote, "It is the nature of love to love as much as we feel we are loved and to love whatever the one we love loves."[2] God's love saturates our readings. In Isaiah, God comforts a broken people, cradling them gently as a shepherd cradles beloved lambs. Titus describes God's great kindness and love in gifting us richly with new life through Christ. And in the Gospel, God calls Jesus the "beloved Son" and pours the Spirit upon Jesus, just as Jesus's very life will proclaim God's love pouring itself out on all people. Take several moments, lingering in prayer, to imagine God, imagine Christ, pouring love upon you, calling you "beloved" and saying, "I am well pleased with you."

Watching baptisms is both ordinary and extraordinary. We do not see doves descending or hear voices booming from the sky. And yet there is a remarkable solidarity in the experience, for baptisms collapse space and time. As we witness the baptism before us, we are also witnessing and reliving our own baptism. Celebrating the baptism of Jesus this week similarly collapses space and time. It is a celebration of the entire Christian mystery that will lead through Jesus's ministry to his death and resurrection. It is therefore also a celebration of the promise of our own resurrection: Christ's Spirit descending upon us and simultaneously drawing us back to him. We live and die within the water of our baptismal promises. How do those promises shape our lives in the reality of this world? How do they shape our understanding of death?

2. St. Catherine of Siena, *The Letters of Catherine of Siena*, vol. 3, trans. Suzanne Noffke (Tempe, AZ: Arizona Center for Medieval and Renaissance Studies, 2000), 163, Letter T299.

First Sunday of Lent

FIRST READING   DEUTERONOMY 26:4-10

Moses spoke to the people, saying:
"The priest shall receive the basket from you
and shall set it in front of the altar of the LORD, your God.
Then you shall declare before the LORD, your God,
'My father was a wandering Aramean
who went down to Egypt with a small household
and lived there as an alien.
But there he became a nation
great, strong, and numerous.
When the Egyptians maltreated and oppressed us,
imposing hard labor upon us,
we cried to the LORD, the God of our fathers,
and he heard our cry
and saw our affliction, our toil, and our oppression.
He brought us out of Egypt
with his strong hand and outstretched arm,
with terrifying power, with signs and wonders;
and bringing us into this country,
he gave us this land flowing with milk and honey.
Therefore, I have now brought you the firstfruits
of the products of the soil
which you, O LORD, have given me.'
And having set them before the LORD, your God,
you shall bow down in his presence."

Our reading describes the background for the annual wheat harvest
(Jewish Shavuot and Christian Pentecost). This was a time when Jews
made pilgrimage to the Jerusalem temple to offer the first fruits of
their harvests in thanksgiving to God. Shavuot also marks the time
when Israel received the Torah on Mount Sinai. Contextually, the
reading is embedded in Moses's final sermon to the people as they are
poised to enter the Promised Land after forty years of traveling from
Egypt. In the sermon, Moses retells the exodus story, the central story
of Israelite religion, and reminds the people of the reverence they

should have for God. Moses explains how God has brought them out of Egypt through a series of "signs and wonders" and has given them the great gift of the land of Israel. The people are therefore to serve this great God with thanksgiving and gratitude. The reference to a "wandering Aramean" may refer to Jacob in order to connect these verses to the stories of the patriarchs and matriarchs who came from Aram (see Gen 24:10; 31:20).

RESPONSORIAL PSALM   PSALM 91:1-2, 10-11, 12-13, 14-15

Be with me, Lord, when I am in trouble.

SECOND READING   ROMANS 10:8-13

Brothers and sisters:
What does Scripture say?
The word is near you,
  in your mouth and in your heart
—that is, the word of faith that we preach—,
for, if you confess with your mouth that Jesus is Lord
and believe in your heart that God raised him from the dead,
you will be saved.
For one believes with the heart and so is justified,
  and one confesses with the mouth and so is saved.
For the Scripture says,
No one who believes in him will be put to shame.
For there is no distinction between Jew and Greek;
  the same Lord is Lord of all,
  enriching all who call upon him.
For "everyone who calls on the name of the Lord will be saved."

In this passage from his letter to the Romans, Paul is in the middle of arguing that true "righteousness" is rooted in faith in Christ, not in adherence to particular rules or precepts. He quotes from Deuteronomy 30:14 ("The word is near you, / in your mouth and in your heart"), Isaiah 28:16 ("No one who believes in him will be put to shame"), and Joel 3:5 ("everyone who calls on the name of the Lord will be saved") to describe devotion and reverence to the God of Israel and to Jesus as Lord. For Paul, devotion begins in the heart and manifests in a spoken confession of belief (a confession that could be difficult as well as dangerous in the first-century context of early Christianity). While our first reading focuses on the particular relationship between God and Israel as the chosen people, Paul shifts the perspective to identify the chosen people as all who believe, whether Jew or Gentile, and who call "on the name of the Lord" (Christ).

GOSPEL   LUKE 4:1-13

Filled with the Holy Spirit, Jesus returned from the Jordan
    and was led by the Spirit into the desert for forty days,
    to be tempted by the devil.
He ate nothing during those days,
    and when they were over he was hungry.
The devil said to him,
    "If you are the Son of God,
    command this stone to become bread."
Jesus answered him,
    "It is written, *One does not live on bread alone.*"
Then he took him up and showed him
    all the kingdoms of the world in a single instant.
The devil said to him,
    "I shall give to you all this power and glory;
    for it has been handed over to me,
    and I may give it to whomever I wish.
All this will be yours, if you worship me."
Jesus said to him in reply,
    "It is written:
    You shall worship the Lord, your God,
        and him alone shall you serve."
Then he led him to Jerusalem,
    made him stand on the parapet of the temple, and said to him,
    "If you are the Son of God,
    throw yourself down from here, for it is written:
    He will command his angels concerning you, to guard you,
    and:
    With their hands they will support you,
        lest you dash your foot against a stone."

Jesus said to him in reply,
  "It also says,
  You shall not put the Lord, your God, to the test."
When the devil had finished every temptation,
  he departed from him for a time.

Luke's account of Jesus's temptation begins with a reminder of his baptism, which has just taken place (3:21-22). In the opening verse of today's reading, Luke creates an intentional link between the two events—Jesus is first baptized and then, filled with the Holy Spirit, is sent out to undergo a series of tests. He remains in the desert for forty days (a number in the Bible that symbolizes completion and alludes to the Israelites' forty years in the desert). Each of Jesus's responses to the devil comes from the book of Deuteronomy. First, Jesus states that sustenance comes only from the word of God (Deut 8:3). Then, he makes a declaration of loyalty to God alone (Deut 6:13). Finally, Jesus declares adherence to the commandments (Deut 6:16). According to first-century Judaism, the world was a space of duality between evil and good, in which angels fought on God's side against evil spirits. In the final days, good would defeat evil through a great test of strength. This great test of strength is what Luke describes here. Note that while angels appear in Mark's account of Jesus's temptation to aid him in his struggles (1:13), in Luke's account, there are no angels—Jesus defeats the devil alone.

Ponder

Our readings from Deuteronomy and Luke take place in deserts, which are spaces of liminality and preparation. In Deuteronomy, the Israelites prepare to enter the Promised Land after forty years in the desert. In Luke, Jesus is sent out into the desert for forty days to prepare for ministry. He is tested with wealth, power, fame, and supernatural abilities. The devil then departs from him "for a time," a phrase that reminds us that Jesus will continue to be tempted throughout his life. As you begin this Lenten season, can you relate to the sense of being in the desert, a space of liminality and preparation? What tempts you, and what is your source of strength?

Our readings describe single-minded devotion and gratitude to the God who is devoted to us. Deuteronomy recalls the exodus story and expresses deep gratitude for a God of the oppressed, a God who claims a people in need and carries them from slavery to the Promised Land. Paul describes Christ's overwhelming offer of salvation regardless of religious background or social distinction. In Luke's Gospel, we witness Jesus's faithful adherence to God throughout his time in the desert. Our Lenten practice calls us to similar adherence and devotion. May we have the courage to strip away, or perhaps take on, whatever might be necessary to reorient ourselves in service and gratitude to God this Lenten season.

Second Sunday of Lent

FIRST READING   GENESIS 15:5-12, 17-18

The Lord God took Abram outside and said,
   "Look up at the sky and count the stars, if you can.
Just so," he added, "shall your descendants be."
Abram put his faith in the LORD,
   who credited it to him as an act of righteousness.

He then said to him,
   "I am the LORD who brought you from Ur of the Chaldeans
   to give you this land as a possession."
"O Lord GOD," he asked,
   "how am I to know that I shall possess it?"
He answered him,
   "Bring me a three-year-old heifer, a three-year-old she-goat,
   a three-year-old ram, a turtledove, and a young pigeon."
Abram brought him all these, split them in two,
   and placed each half opposite the other;
   but the birds he did not cut up.
Birds of prey swooped down on the carcasses,
   but Abram stayed with them.
As the sun was about to set, a trance fell upon Abram,
   and a deep, terrifying darkness enveloped him.

When the sun had set and it was dark,
   there appeared a smoking fire pot and a flaming torch,
   which passed between those pieces.
It was on that occasion that the LORD made a covenant
    with Abram,
   saying: "To your descendants I give this land,
   from the Wadi of Egypt to the Great River, the Euphrates."

In the stories of Abraham and Sarah, God continually promises the childless couple that they will have many descendants. In today's reading, Abram (whom God renames "Abraham" in Genesis 17 as part of a new covenantal identity, while Sarai becomes "Sarah") puts his faith in God without trying to understand how this miracle will come about. Abram then performs a covenant ceremony in order to seal God's promise to him. The ceremony reflects an ancient practice in which participants in a covenant made an oath by passing through the dismembered parts of an animal (see Jer 34:18). The expression in Hebrew of "making a covenant" is literally "cutting a covenant." In this case, it is not Abram but God who "makes" or "cuts" a covenant by passing between the pieces in the form of a smoking fire pot and a flaming torch. It is a strange image and suggests that God's form is ultimately beyond comprehension. God then gifts the land of Israel to Abram's descendants.

RESPONSORIAL PSALM   PSALM 27:1, 7-8, 8-9, 13-14

The Lord is my light and my salvation.

SECOND READING   PHILIPPIANS 3:17–4:1 [OR 3:20–4:1]

Join with others in being imitators of me, brothers and sisters,
    and observe those who thus conduct themselves
    according to the model you have in us.
For many, as I have often told you
    and now tell you even in tears,
    conduct themselves as enemies of the cross of Christ.
Their end is destruction.
Their God is their stomach;
    their glory is in their "shame."
Their minds are occupied with earthly things.
But our citizenship is in heaven,
    and from it we also await a savior, the Lord Jesus Christ.
He will change our lowly body
    to conform with his glorified body
    by the power that enables him also
    to bring all things into subjection to himself.

Therefore, my brothers and sisters,
    whom I love and long for, my joy and crown,
    in this way stand firm in the Lord.

Paul alludes to Jesus's "glorified body" in order to describe our transformation in Christ from human or "lowly" bodies into resurrected bodies. He exhorts the Philippians to stand firm in their belief in "the cross," meaning both crucifixion and resurrection. He mentions the "enemies of the cross," those who call themselves Christians but do not accept the reality of the cross. While these "enemies" are focused on worldly things, true Christian "citizenship" belongs in heaven. In using the word "citizenship," Paul makes a pointed statement about ultimate political loyalty: are the Philippians ultimately citizens of Rome or citizens of Christ? Those who place their trust in the cross and in Jesus's resurrection will be transformed to conform with or become part of Christ's glorified body.

GOSPEL   LUKE 9:28b-36

Jesus took Peter, John, and James
    and went up the mountain to pray.
While he was praying his face changed in appearance
    and his clothing became dazzling white.
And behold, two men were conversing with him, Moses
        and Elijah,
    who appeared in glory and spoke of his exodus
    that he was going to accomplish in Jerusalem.
Peter and his companions had been overcome by sleep,
    but becoming fully awake,
    they saw his glory and the two men standing with him.
As they were about to part from him, Peter said to Jesus,
    "Master, it is good that we are here;
    let us make three tents,
    one for you, one for Moses, and one for Elijah."
But he did not know what he was saying.
While he was still speaking,
    a cloud came and cast a shadow over them,
    and they became frightened when they entered the cloud.
Then from the cloud came a voice that said,
    "This is my chosen Son; listen to him."
After the voice had spoken, Jesus was found alone.
They fell silent and did not at that time
    tell anyone what they had seen.

Each year on the Second Sunday of Lent, we read a Gospel account of the transfiguration. In the account, Jesus and the disciples go up a mountain to pray, as Moses did to receive the commandments in Exodus and as Elijah did to hear the "voice of thin silence" in 1 Kings 19.[1] Mountains are places of encounter with the Divine. Moses and Elijah represent the two great prophets of Jewish tradition. The dazzling white clothes may represent the apocalyptic glory of a martyr (e.g., Rev 3:5, 18). In Mark's version of the transfiguration, Peter calls Jesus "Rabbi," and the disciples are terrified (9:2-8). In Luke's account, Peter calls Jesus "Master," and there is no such terror. The disciples then hear God's voice declaring that Jesus is the "chosen Son." According to Mark, Jesus commands the disciples to remain silent about the event. In Luke's account, the disciples remain quiet of their own accord. Yet the disciples do not fully understand what they have witnessed, for in the very next episode, they are unable to perform a miracle, and Jesus calls them, shockingly, part of the "faithless and perverse generation" (9:37-43).

1. In Hebrew, the phrase is *qôl dĕmāmâ daqqâ*, which translates literally as "a voice of thin silence" (1 Kgs 19:12). However, the weight and significance of each Hebrew term leaves the phrase open to many possible translations. For example, the NABRE translates it as "a light silent sound," the NRSV as "a sound of sheer silence," the JPS (Jewish Publication Society) as "a soft murmuring sound," the KJV as "a still small voice," and the Douay-Rheims as "a whistling of a gentle air."

Ponder

God's promises can overwhelm the senses and understanding. In Genesis, the promise to Abram is sealed through a contractual covenant. God appears to Abram as a smoking pot and a flaming torch in the midst of overwhelming darkness. In the Gospel, the dazzling sights and sounds are equally overwhelming. Like the disciples and like Abram, we may not yet fully understand the power of God's promise to us. And what is this promise? It is the full reality of the cross, according to Paul. It is the promise that, through Jesus's crucifixion and resurrection, the reality of resurrection also belongs to us. We are in the process of being transformed, and we will be transformed. As you pray with these readings, what does God's promise mean to you today? How do you experience it?

The call of transfiguration is the call to listen and observe in order to follow. In the Gospel, despite the overwhelming sights, God does not tell the disciples to "look" but rather to "listen" to Jesus. Paul tells the Philippians to "observe" in order to be "imitators" of Christ. Why listen and observe? Because both mean attentiveness and openness in seeing and experiencing Christ all around us, in the seeming ordinariness of our lives. It is the call to listen and observe that leads to our transformation and the transformation of "all things," as Paul says, into Christ. How are you actively listening and observing today?

Third Sunday of Lent

FIRST READING   EXODUS 3:1-8a, 13-15

Moses was tending the flock of his father-in-law Jethro,
   the priest of Midian.
Leading the flock across the desert, he came to Horeb,
   the mountain of God.
There an angel of the LORD appeared to Moses in fire
   flaming out of a bush.
As he looked on, he was surprised to see that the bush,
   though on fire, was not consumed.
So Moses decided,
   "I must go over to look at this remarkable sight,
   and see why the bush is not burned."

When the LORD saw him coming over to look at it more closely,
   God called out to him from the bush, "Moses! Moses!"
He answered, "Here I am."
God said, "Come no nearer!
Remove the sandals from your feet,
   for the place where you stand is holy ground.
I am the God of your fathers," he continued,
   "the God of Abraham, the God of Isaac, the God of Jacob."
Moses hid his face, for he was afraid to look at God.
But the LORD said,
   "I have witnessed the affliction of my people in Egypt
   and have heard their cry of complaint against their
      slave drivers,
   so I know well what they are suffering.
Therefore I have come down to rescue them
   from the hands of the Egyptians
   and lead them out of that land into a good and spacious land,
   a land flowing with milk and honey."

Moses said to God, "But when I go to the Israelites
   and say to them, 'The God of your fathers has sent me to you,'
   if they ask me, 'What is his name?' what am I to tell them?"
God replied, "I am who am."

Then he added, "This is what you shall tell the Israelites:
I AM sent me to you."

God spoke further to Moses, "Thus shall you say to the Israelites:
The LORD, the God of your fathers,
the God of Abraham, the God of Isaac, the God of Jacob,
has sent me to you.

"This is my name forever;
thus am I to be remembered through all generations."

In this story, the God of Israel appears to Moses in the burning bush. God claims ownership over the people of Israel and promises to rescue them from Egypt, the land of slavery.[1] When Moses asks for God's personal name, the reply is "I AM," or in Hebrew, *'ehyeh 'ăšer 'ehyeh*. This phrase can translate as past, present, and future: "I was who I was," "I am who I am," and "I will be who I will be." In other words, God is active and unbound by time or any other human concept. This sacred name became YHWH in Hebrew, drawing from the root consonants of the verb "to be" (*hāyâ*). Our translation of YHWH in English Bibles is "LORD," a poor match to the mystical quality and literal meaning of the Hebrew. Some scholars and others will pronounce the name as "Yahweh," though the lack of vowels in Hebrew emphasizes that God's personal name is too awesome to speak aloud.

RESPONSORIAL PSALM   PSALM 103:1-2, 3-4, 6-7, 8, 11

The Lord is kind and merciful.

---

1. Contemporary readers may take issue with the idea of God claiming "ownership" over us or "possessing" us. (Paul uses the latter expression in his letter to the Philippians; see the Fifth Sunday of Lent.) We may think of these terms as akin to slavery or bondage, yet in the ancient context, they meant just the opposite. According to the Hebrew Bible, ancient Israel understood God's "ownership" or "possession" of them in the sense of liberation and a deep, covenantal relationship. This relationship required something of them in return, yet they took on the challenge of covenant living with joy, pride, and free will.

SECOND READING   1 CORINTHIANS 10:1-6, 10-12

I do not want you to be unaware, brothers and sisters,
  that our ancestors were all under the cloud
  and all passed through the sea,
  and all of them were baptized into Moses
  in the cloud and in the sea.
All ate the same spiritual food,
  and all drank the same spiritual drink,
  for they drank from a spiritual rock that followed them,
  and the rock was the Christ.
Yet God was not pleased with most of them,
  for they were struck down in the desert.

These things happened as examples for us,
  so that we might not desire evil things, as they did.
Do not grumble as some of them did,
  and suffered death by the destroyer.
These things happened to them as an example,
  and they have been written down as a warning to us,
  upon whom the end of the ages has come.
Therefore, whoever thinks he is standing secure
  should take care not to fall.

Believe it or not, the broader context of this reading is Paul's concern about idolatry, specifically eating meat that comes from pagan sacrifices. Paul's argument is full of symbols and allusions to stories from the exodus and wilderness traditions in the Hebrew Bible (e.g., Exod 16:4-35). Paul also incorporates ideas connected to divine Wisdom in early Judaism (e.g., according to the Wisdom of Solomon, Wisdom herself led the people out of Egypt; Wis 10:18–11:4). Paul replaces the focus on "Wisdom" with a focus on "Christ" and warns the community to avoid temptations.

GOSPEL   LUKE 13:1-9

Some people told Jesus about the Galileans
   whose blood Pilate had mingled with the blood of
      their sacrifices.
Jesus said to them in reply,
   "Do you think that because these Galileans suffered in this way
   they were greater sinners than all other Galileans?
By no means!
But I tell you, if you do not repent,
   you will all perish as they did!
Or those eighteen people who were killed
   when the tower at Siloam fell on them—
   do you think they were more guilty
   than everyone else who lived in Jerusalem?
By no means!
But I tell you, if you do not repent,
   you will all perish as they did!"

And he told them this parable:
   "There once was a person who had a fig tree planted in
      his orchard,
   and when he came in search of fruit on it but found none,
   he said to the gardener,
   'For three years now I have come in search of fruit on this
      fig tree
   but have found none.
So cut it down.
Why should it exhaust the soil?'
He said to him in reply,
   'Sir, leave it for this year also,
   and I shall cultivate the ground around it and fertilize it;
   it may bear fruit in the future.
If not you can cut it down.' "

In the ancient world, physical suffering was widely viewed as a direct consequence of sin and was associated with God's judgment. Jesus counters this problematic theological view. Simultaneously and somewhat confusingly, he uses examples of unmerited suffering to warn those who fail to repent or turn from their wrongdoing. He counsels the people to learn from the unexpected death of others and repent now in order to be ready for judgment at any time. He then shifts to the parable of the fig tree (compare with Matt 21:18-19 and Mark 11:12-14), a parable that serves as both medicine and mirror. As medicine, the parable comforts those who continue to stumble along as they try to follow the way of Jesus. As mirror, it compels complacent or lukewarm Christians to take stock of who they are. The parable shows that Jesus is both compassionate and demanding. He expects full repentance and emphasizes the reality of judgment, and he is also deeply merciful. As long as his disciples are open to him, Christ will continue to "cultivate" and "fertilize" them to follow him more faithfully.

Ponder

According to our Exodus reading, God's nature is uncontainable, indescribable, and utterly beyond human comprehension. Luke's parable underscores this reality by depicting God's nature as paradox: God is both compassion and judgment. For the disciple who is open and trying, however, both readings ultimately lean on the side of compassion. They remind us that God has claimed us and that God's power works through and with human weakness. For example, if you read the broader call story of Moses (Exod 3:1–4:17), you will notice that Moses is reluctant and flawed. And Jesus's disciples are not so different in Luke's Gospel! Yet all disciples are transformed by grace. Use this week's readings as a mirror for self-examination. What are your weaknesses and strengths? How is God calling you to conversion while shaping and transforming you?

Paul built his life upon the reality of the crucified and resurrected Christ. In our second reading, he beseeches the Corinthians to do the same and stand secure in Christ, their rock. It is this rock that will help strengthen them against the temptation of idolatry. Each of us also builds our life upon something; the question is what. Paul calls to us through our second reading, asking us to examine what is at the center of our lives and in what we stand secure.

Fourth Sunday of Lent (Laetare Sunday)

FIRST READING   JOSHUA 5:9a, 10-12

The LORD said to Joshua,
   "Today I have removed the reproach of Egypt from you."

While the Israelites were encamped at Gilgal on the plains
    of Jericho,
   they celebrated the Passover
   on the evening of the fourteenth of the month.
On the day after the Passover,
   they ate of the produce of the land
   in the form of unleavened cakes and parched grain.
On that same day after the Passover,
   on which they ate of the produce of the land, the
    manna ceased.
No longer was there manna for the Israelites,
   who that year ate of the yield of the land of Canaan.

In the book of Joshua, the Israelites enter the Promised Land after a forty-year journey from Egypt. Those desert years involved many religious changes. One was the institution of the Passover festival (from the story of God "passing over" the homes of the Israelites in the final plague prior to liberation from Egypt; Exod 12:27). In the desert, God provided daily sustenance for the people with manna (similar to wafers) that rained down miraculously from the sky. The above reading initiates the change that the people had dreamed of during those long years. They enter the Promised Land, celebrate the Passover for the first time there, and finally have nourishment from the land itself. The reference to "reproach" in the first verse of the reading comes from the Hebrew root *gālal* and is a play on words with the place name "Gilgal." Contextually, these verses come from a longer section that focuses on the circumcision of the new generation of Israelites in the land, a practice they had not kept during the wilderness period.

RESPONSORIAL PSALM   PSALM 34:2-3, 4-5, 6-7

Taste and see the goodness of the Lord.

SECOND READING   2 CORINTHIANS 5:17-21

Brothers and sisters:
Whoever is in Christ is a new creation:
   the old things have passed away;
   behold, new things have come.
And all this is from God,
   who has reconciled us to himself through Christ
   and given us the ministry of reconciliation,
   namely, God was reconciling the world to himself in Christ,
   not counting their trespasses against them
   and entrusting to us the message of reconciliation.
So we are ambassadors for Christ,
   as if God were appealing through us.
We implore you on behalf of Christ,
   be reconciled to God.
For our sake he made him to be sin who did not know sin,
   so that we might become the righteousness of God in him.

For Paul, crucifixion and resurrection begin a new period of human history in which guilt is wiped away through God's mercy and Jesus's obedience (see Rom 5:10). In this new period, humans are reconciled with God as if they had never committed sin. The Greek word translated here as "new" (*kainē*) means complete reorientation. Christ's redemptive activity is therefore a promise of radical transformation or reorientation for all who are open to it. Yet reconciliation can be abused or lost if believers become closed to it, no longer allowing Christ to exercise this redemptive activity through them. The meaning of "being sin" in the last verse likely refers to Jesus becoming a sin offering or sacrifice for sin in his crucifixion.

Tax collectors and sinners were all drawing near to listen to Jesus,
    but the Pharisees and scribes began to complain, saying,
    "This man welcomes sinners and eats with them."
So to them Jesus addressed this parable:
"A man had two sons, and the younger son said to his father,
    'Father give me the share of your estate that should come to me.'
So the father divided the property between them.
After a few days, the younger son collected all his belongings
    and set off to a distant country
    where he squandered his inheritance on a life of dissipation.
When he had freely spent everything,
    a severe famine struck that country,
    and he found himself in dire need.
So he hired himself out to one of the local citizens
    who sent him to his farm to tend the swine.
And he longed to eat his fill of the pods on which the swine fed,
    but nobody gave him any.
Coming to his senses he thought,
    'How many of my father's hired workers
    have more than enough food to eat,
    but here am I, dying from hunger.
I shall get up and go to my father and I shall say to him,
    "Father, I have sinned against heaven and against you.
I no longer deserve to be called your son;
    treat me as you would treat one of your hired workers." '
 So he got up and went back to his father.
While he was still a long way off,
    his father caught sight of him, and was filled with compassion.
He ran to his son, embraced him and kissed him.
His son said to him,
    'Father, I have sinned against heaven and against you;
    I no longer deserve to be called your son.'
But his father ordered his servants,
    'Quickly bring the finest robe and put it on him;
    put a ring on his finger and sandals on his feet.
Take the fattened calf and slaughter it.
Then let us celebrate with a feast,
    because this son of mine was dead, and has come to life again;

he was lost, and has been found.'
Then the celebration began.
Now the older son had been out in the field
and, on his way back, as he neared the house,
he heard the sound of music and dancing.
He called one of the servants and asked what this might mean.
The servant said to him,
'Your brother has returned
and your father has slaughtered the fattened calf
because he has him back safe and sound.'
He became angry,
and when he refused to enter the house,
his father came out and pleaded with him.
He said to his father in reply,
'Look, all these years I served you
and not once did I disobey your orders;
yet you never gave me even a young goat to feast on with
my friends.
But when your son returns
who swallowed up your property with prostitutes,
for him you slaughter the fattened calf.'
He said to him,
'My son, you are here with me always;
everything I have is yours.
But now we must celebrate and rejoice,
because your brother was dead and has come to life again;
he was lost and has been found.' "

The parable of the two brothers (often called the parable of the Prodigal Son) is unique to Luke's Gospel. It is the last of three parables of mercy in Luke 15 and is directed at the pious and religious elite, who will likely relate to the older brother. Five things to note about this parable: (1) We have no idea to what extent the younger son is repentant for his actions. He has lived a "life of dissipation" (literally "reckless living"; Greek *zōn asōtōs*) until he hit rock bottom and was forced to care for pigs, the most unclean animal according to Jewish tradition. At this point, he realizes that he would lead a better life by returning home to become one of his father's servants. (2) The younger son greets his father respectfully ("Father"), unlike the older son at the end of the parable. (3) The father, not the sons, is the central focus of this passage. He demonstrates extravagant mercy, reaching out and loving both sons regardless of whether either son merits it. (4) The father twice alludes to death and resurrection in relation to the younger son, which recalls Jesus's crucifixion and resurrection ("was dead, and has come to life again" and "was lost and has been found"; vv. 24, 32). (5) Although we may especially relate to one of the characters in the story, the more fruitful approach may be to discover ourselves in all three.

Ponder

Our readings invite us to a new way of being in the world. In Joshua, the Israelites lose their daily allotment of manna that nourished them in the desert. In place of manna, God calls the people to a better form of nourishment from the land itself. This physical nourishment becomes a symbol of inner renewal and transformation, marked outwardly by the first Passover celebration in the Promised Land. In Luke's Gospel, both sons are also called to transformation, or what Paul calls becoming a "new creation." Ponder this theme of transformation. What kind of transformation do you need right now, and how would inward transformation manifest tangibly in your daily life and actions?

This Sunday is a day of celebration called Laetare Sunday (*laetare* is Latin for "rejoice"). We might also call it Reconciliation Sunday based on our readings. These readings are about both literal and spiritual journeys, about wandering far afield and eventually coming home. We are all on this journey of change and transformation that at times is marked by suffering, disorientation, and sin. Yet our journey is also marked by complete freedom, both on our part and on the part of the Divine. We have freedom in our choices, and God has freedom in the offer of salvation. The question is whether we trust in the promise of salvation and reconciliation. Do you believe that this process of salvation, this return and reconciliation with God and with each other, is possible for you and for all people?

Fifth Sunday of Lent

FIRST READING   ISAIAH 43:16-21

Thus says the LORD,
  who opens a way in the sea
  and a path in the mighty waters,
who leads out chariots and horsemen,
  a powerful army,
till they lie prostrate together, never to rise,
  snuffed out and quenched like a wick.
Remember not the events of the past,
  the things of long ago consider not;
see, I am doing something new!
  Now it springs forth, do you not perceive it?
In the desert I make a way,
  in the wasteland, rivers.
Wild beasts honor me,
  jackals and ostriches,
for I put water in the desert
  and rivers in the wasteland
  for my chosen people to drink,
the people whom I formed for myself,
  that they might announce my praise.

The exodus is the central story of Israel's history. In it, the God of Israel brings the people out of slavery and claims them. In the above reading, the prophet alludes to the great miracle of God parting the sea in the exodus story, then states (shockingly!) that Israel should no longer focus on that past miracle but instead look to the future. In our second reading last Sunday, Paul referred to those in Christ as a "new creation" (2 Cor 5:17); the above reading similarly states that the Lord is "doing something new." In the context of the book of Isaiah, this "new" miracle is God bringing the people home to Judah after the Babylonian exile (ca. 536 BCE). The prophet describes this return metaphorically in terms of the natural world: a wasteland becomes fertile, and wild animals praise the God of Israel.

RESPONSORIAL PSALM   PSALM 126:1-2, 2-3, 4-5, 6

The Lord has done great things for us; we are filled with joy.

SECOND READING   PHILIPPIANS 3:8-14

Brothers and sisters:
I consider everything as a loss
    because of the supreme good of knowing Christ Jesus my Lord.
For his sake I have accepted the loss of all things
    and I consider them so much rubbish,
    that I may gain Christ and be found in him,
    not having any righteousness of my own based on the law
    but that which comes through faith in Christ,
    the righteousness from God,
    depending on faith to know him and the power of
        his resurrection
    and the sharing of his sufferings by being conformed to
        his death,
    if somehow I may attain the resurrection from the dead.

It is not that I have already taken hold of it
    or have already attained perfect maturity,
    but I continue my pursuit in hope that I may possess it,
    since I have indeed been taken possession of by Christ Jesus.
Brothers and sisters, I for my part
    do not consider myself to have taken possession.
Just one thing: forgetting what lies behind
    but straining forward to what lies ahead,
    I continue my pursuit toward the goal,
    the prize of God's upward calling, in Christ Jesus.

Paul writes his letter to the Philippians from jail, uncertain of his future. Yet his letter brims with joy and hope. It is a call to unity. Here Paul describes his life prior to being "taken possession of by Christ" as meaningless or "rubbish" (literally "excrement" in Greek). The fact that Paul is a devout Jew—a leader of his community from a prominent lineage—means nothing in relation to what it means to "gain" Christ. Christ is the totality of everything—the "supreme good" and the righteousness of God. Paul describes his search to "know" Christ and to "be found in him," with the ultimate goal of being conformed to the crucified Christ and sharing in his resurrection. Paul is clear: it is Christ who has taken possession of him, not him of Christ. He continues to pursue the hope that he may one day know the risen Christ, thus attaining resurrection himself to be part of the living Christ. This pursuit is described in terms of running or Greek footraces, yet the "goal" and "prize" is Christ.

GOSPEL   JOHN 8:1-11

Jesus went to the Mount of Olives.
But early in the morning he arrived again in the temple area,
    and all the people started coming to him,
    and he sat down and taught them.
Then the scribes and the Pharisees brought a woman
    who had been caught in adultery
    and made her stand in the middle.
They said to him,
    "Teacher, this woman was caught
    in the very act of committing adultery.
Now in the law, Moses commanded us to stone such women.
So what do you say?"
They said this to test him,
    so that they could have some charge to bring against him.
Jesus bent down and began to write on the ground with
        his finger.
But when they continued asking him,
    he straightened up and said to them,
    "Let the one among you who is without sin
    be the first to throw a stone at her."
Again he bent down and wrote on the ground.
And in response, they went away one by one,
    beginning with the elders.
So he was left alone with the woman before him.
Then Jesus straightened up and said to her,
    "Woman, where are they?
Has no one condemned you?"
She replied, "No one, sir."
Then Jesus said, "Neither do I condemn you.
Go, and from now on do not sin any more."

This story leaves much to the imagination. After leaving the Jerusalem temple the previous night, Jesus returns in the morning. Crowds flock to him and he teaches them, though we do not know what he is teaching. The focus then shifts to those who test Jesus with legal concerns, the subject being the punishment for adultery. It is important to note that the Torah laws regarding adultery are unclear: Deuteronomy 22:23-24 decrees stoning for a betrothed young woman who commits adultery. Deuteronomy 22:22 and Leviticus 20:10 prescribe death for an adulterous spouse, yet without specifying the manner of execution. More importantly, we do not know to what extent these punishments were actually put into practice; they serve as extreme cases and literary devices to make a point in the Torah (as a comparison, the Sermon on the Mount does not require us literally to chop off our hand, as described in Matt 5:30!). As such, it is unclear just how the religious elite are attempting to trap Jesus. The woman brought before Jesus is unnamed. We do not know how she feels, nor do we know how Jesus feels about the disturbance. Is he annoyed or bored by yet another attempt to test him, or does he radiate loving-kindness? Jesus bends down to write on the ground, then stands up and issues his infamous statement about throwing stones. He then bends down to write on the ground again. We do not know what he is writing—is it something profound, or could it be doodling? But we do know this: something about what Jesus says, how he says it, or what he writes on the ground has a powerful effect. Not a single person remains to accuse the woman.

Ponder

In Isaiah, God is "doing something new." This "something" is as miraculous as God's deliverance of the people from Egypt to take possession of them. This promise of "newness" is a promise given specifically to the people whom God chose and "formed" as a prized possession. Similarly, in our second reading, Christ took "possession" of Paul to create him anew. In return, Paul seeks to follow or pursue Christ. Consider the language of "possessing" and "pursuit" as metaphors for your faith journey. Can you relate to the experience of being possessed by God? What holds you back from following or pursuing God wholeheartedly in return?

"Go, and from now on do not sin any more." Jesus invites us all to be liberated from our pasts into new, or renewed, commitments to God. Like the characters in the Gospel passage, each of us has sinned, yet none of us is condemned. This gospel message has no qualifications or boundaries. It is therefore an impossible concept for the mind to fully grasp, and it is certainly not our societal ideal (consider our criminal justice system, with its emphasis on punishment over rehabilitation). This message is also the Easter promise and invitation: the promise is our liberation, and the invitation is transformation into Christ. From what do you need liberation today?

Palm Sunday of the Passion of the Lord

The Lord GOD has given me
  a well-trained tongue,
that I might know how to speak to the weary
  a word that will rouse them.
Morning after morning
  he opens my ear that I may hear;
and I have not rebelled,
  have not turned back.
I gave my back to those who beat me,
  my cheeks to those who plucked my beard;
my face I did not shield
  from buffets and spitting.

The Lord GOD is my help,
  therefore I am not disgraced;
I have set my face like flint,
  knowing that I shall not be put to shame.

The above reading draws from the third of four "Suffering Servant" poems in Second Isaiah (for more context on Second Isaiah, see commentary on Isaiah 40 from The Baptism of the Lord). We will read from the fourth Suffering Servant poem on Good Friday. The third poem combines two voices: the servant's (vv. 4-9) and God's (vv. 10-11). Twice the servant equates himself with a disciple or "one who is taught," a phrase that is translated as "well-trained" in the first sentence of the above reading but is lost in translation in the second sentence (the literal translation of the second sentence is: "Morning by morning he wakens—wakens my ear to listen as those who are taught. The Lord GOD has opened my ear, and I have not rebelled, have not turned back"). The servant listens before he speaks; he then speaks directly to the weary and afflicted. His words make him a physical target, yet he suffers nonviolently and acclaims God through his words. The servant is male but anonymous. He has been identified with numerous figures, including the prophet Isaiah or another unknown prophet, the exiled

Judeans, Zion, or a future savior figure. Christian tradition views the servant as Jesus. Part of the power of these servant poems is the mystery of the servant's identity, which allows the servant to stand for all those who have suffered injustice yet stand peaceful and firm in their commitment to God and in their vision of a just world.

RESPONSORIAL PSALM   PSALM 22:8-9, 17-18, 19-20, 23-24

My God, my God, why have you abandoned me?

SECOND READING   PHILIPPIANS 2:6-11

Christ Jesus, though he was in the form of God,
    did not regard equality with God
    something to be grasped.
Rather, he emptied himself,
    taking the form of a slave,
    coming in human likeness;
    and found human in appearance,
    he humbled himself,
    becoming obedient to the point of death,
    even death on a cross.
Because of this, God greatly exalted him
    and bestowed on him the name
    which is above every name,
    that at the name of Jesus
    every knee should bend,
    of those in heaven and on earth and under the earth,
    and every tongue confess that
    Jesus Christ is Lord,
    to the glory of God the Father.

The hymn in today's reading from Philippians is one of the oldest texts in the New Testament. It describes the entire mystery of Christ, who was in the physical "form" (*morphē*) of God and was hence equal to God, yet who did not regard this equality as something to be "grasped" (the Greek term *harpagmos* is rare and may mean to be held onto by force or to be exploited in some way). According to traditional biblical scholarship, the hymn describes how Christ self-empties, not of his divinity but of his status of glory. He then humbles, or literally "humiliates," himself through incarnation and crucifixion. The humble one is then exalted (literally "superexalted") and adored by the entire universe in his new title as Lord (*Kyrios*).

GOSPEL   LUKE 22:14–23:56 OR 23:1-49 (HERE 23:39-49)

Now one of the criminals hanging there reviled Jesus, saying,
   "Are you not the Christ?
   Save yourself and us."
The other, however, rebuking him, said in reply,
   "Have you no fear of God,
   for you are subject to the same condemnation?
And indeed, we have been condemned justly,
   for the sentence we received corresponds to our crimes,
   but this man has done nothing criminal."
Then he said,
   "Jesus, remember me when you come into your kingdom."
He replied to him,
   "Amen, I say to you,
   today you will be with me in Paradise."

It was now about noon and darkness came over the whole land
   until three in the afternoon
   because of an eclipse of the sun.
Then the veil of the temple was torn down the middle.
Jesus cried out in a loud voice,
   "Father, into your hands I commend my spirit";
   and when he had said this he breathed his last.

The centurion who witnessed what had happened glorified God
      and said,
   "This man was innocent beyond doubt."
When all the people who had gathered for this spectacle
saw what had happened,
   they returned home beating their breasts;
   but all his acquaintances stood at a distance,
   including the women who had followed him from Galilee
   and saw these events.

Our long reading (excerpted here) draws us into the passion. In his conversation with the two criminals, which is recounted only in Luke, Jesus states that the thief who asks Jesus to "remember" him will be with Jesus in paradise and will share in his glory that very day. These are Jesus's last words to another person before he dies. At noon, the powers of darkness cover the earth because "the sun's light failed" (according to a literal reading of the Greek). The veil of the temple that hangs between the holy place and the holy of holies, the most sacred place in the temple, is torn in two. Jesus then quotes from Psalm 31:6 (unlike in Mark and Matthew, where he quotes from Psalm 22: "My God, my God, why have you abandoned me?"). In Mark and Matthew, the centurion states that Jesus was the "Son of God"; here, the centurion calls him a "just" or "righteous" man (a literal translation from the Greek), meaning that he was innocent of any crime against the state. In beating their breasts, Luke shows that the crowd is already partly converted.

Ponder

The anonymity of Isaiah's servant gives him a universal application and allows each of us to name the servant from our own experiences. It also prompts us to see aspects of ourselves reflected in each character: we are the suffering and the weary, we are the persecutors, and we are the servant standing up for the least among us. The long account of Christ's passion similarly invites us to see ourselves mirrored in the cast of characters. As you meditate with these texts, with whom do you identify today?

Our readings juxtapose human praise and condemnation, suffering and glory, a triumphant procession and crucifixion. Despite human inconstancy and at great cost, the servant who suffers for all of us remains steady and constant throughout. Our readings and our entry into Holy Week call us to ponder the juxtapositions and the inconstancy of our own lives and our world, the inevitability of suffering in human life, and above all, Jesus Christ, our model for discipleship.

Easter Sunday of the Resurrection of the Lord

FIRST READING   ACTS 10:34a, 37-43

Peter proceeded to speak and said:
  "You know what has happened all over Judea,
  beginning in Galilee after the baptism
  that John preached,
  how God anointed Jesus of Nazareth
  with the Holy Spirit and power.
He went about doing good
  and healing all those oppressed by the devil,
  for God was with him.
We are witnesses of all that he did
  both in the country of the Jews and in Jerusalem.
They put him to death by hanging him on a tree.
This man God raised on the third day and granted that he
    be visible,
  not to all the people, but to us,
  the witnesses chosen by God in advance,
  who ate and drank with him after he rose from the dead.
He commissioned us to preach to the people
  and testify that he is the one appointed by God
  as judge of the living and the dead.
To him all the prophets bear witness,
  that everyone who believes in him
  will receive forgiveness of sins through his name."

On weekdays and Sundays throughout the Easter season, we read from the Acts of the Apostles. Acts is the sequel to Luke's Gospel, and we refer to the author of both books as "Luke" (even though the author is not identified by name in either book). Acts recounts the time from Jesus's ascension until Paul's arrival in Rome, focusing on the Jerusalem church, the missionary activity of Peter and Paul, and the continuity between Judaism and the early Christian community. The author describes the ideal Gentile convert as one who practices Jewish acts of piety like almsgiving and prayer (see 10:2) and other practices that maintain association with Jews (in other words, avoiding practices that were detestable to Jews, such as eating meat sacrificed to idols; see 15:20). Today's reading comes from a key story in which God directs Peter to include the Gentiles in his gospel mission. The story deals with the conversion of Cornelius, a Gentile officer in the Roman army, who sends for Peter after receiving a vision from God. Peter simultaneously receives a vision in which God dissolves Jewish dietary regulations. Here, Peter travels to Cornelius's house where a group of Gentiles are assembled, and he tells those gathered the story of Jesus's life, death, and resurrection. While he is proclaiming that Jesus forgives the sins of those who believe, Peter witnesses the Holy Spirit being poured out upon those assembled, and he orders that they be baptized (10:44-48).

RESPONSORIAL PSALM   PSALM 118:1-2, 16-17, 22-23

This is the day the Lord has made; let us rejoice and be glad.
  or: Alleluia.

SECOND READING   COLOSSIANS 3:1-4 (ALT. 1 COR 5:6b-8)[1]

Brothers and sisters:
If then you were raised with Christ, seek what is above,
  where Christ is seated at the right hand of God.
Think of what is above, not of what is on earth.
For you have died, and your life is hidden with Christ in God.
When Christ your life appears,
  then you too will appear with him in glory.

We will read semi-continuously through Colossians from the Fifteenth through Eighteenth Sundays in Ordinary Time. A primary argument of Colossians is that baptism (which is akin to death and resurrection) makes one full or complete in Christ. It changes one's

---

1. For commentary on the alternative reading from 1 Corinthians, see *Ponder: Year B.*

reality and way of being irrevocably. This notion of change lies behind today's reading; through baptism, the early community has been raised with Christ and is complete in Christ. They are therefore to put off their old lives and act in accordance with the reality of what lies above and within: the kingdom of God. The last verse speaks to Christ's return or "appearance," which will glorify all those who have been baptized in Christ.

GOSPEL   LUKE 24:1-12 (ALT. JOHN 20:1-9)[2]

At daybreak on the first day of the week
    the women who had come from Galilee with Jesus
    took the spices they had prepared
    and went to the tomb.
They found the stone rolled away from the tomb;
    but when they entered,
    they did not find the body of the Lord Jesus.
While they were puzzling over this, behold,
    two men in dazzling garments appeared to them.
They were terrified and bowed their faces to the ground.
They said to them,
    "Why do you seek the living one among the dead?
He is not here, but he has been raised.
Remember what he said to you while he was still in Galilee,
    that the Son of Man must be handed over to sinners
    and be crucified, and rise on the third day."
And they remembered his words.
Then they returned from the tomb
    and announced all these things to the eleven
    and to all the others.
The women were Mary Magdalene, Joanna, and Mary the
        mother of James;
    the others who accompanied them also told this to
        the apostles,

---

2. This is the Gospel reading for the Easter Vigil in Year C. For commentary on John 20:1-9, the Gospel for the Mass of Easter Day, see *Ponder: Year B.*

but their story seemed like nonsense
and they did not believe them.
But Peter got up and ran to the tomb,
bent down, and saw the burial cloths alone;
then he went home amazed at what had happened.

We read Luke's account of the resurrection during the Easter Vigil, and it is also an option for Easter Sunday. According to Mark's account (16:1-7), which is likely the earliest Gospel witness, three women go to the tomb to prepare Jesus for burial (Mary Magdalene; James's mother, Mary; and Salome). They encounter a young man in white within the tomb, who tells them that Jesus has risen and orders them to inform the disciples. They flee from the tomb and, according to the Gospel's original ending, tell no one about their experience (16:8). In comparison, Luke's version has a multitude of women at the tomb, only three of whom are identified. The women encounter not one but two men in dazzling garments, who are later identified as angels (24:23). They are similarly terrified as in Mark's version, yet they run instantly to tell the disciples. The story then leads into the account of Jesus's appearance on the road to Emmaus beginning in verse 13. In John's Gospel, only Mary Magdalene goes to the tomb. When she sees the stone removed, she runs to get Simon Peter and the "disciple whom Jesus loved," and they all return to the tomb together (20:1-3). The disciples then go home while Mary stays at the tomb weeping, and she is the first person to whom Jesus appears.

Ponder

Luke's Gospel pulls us deeply into the account of Christ's resurrection to stand alongside the early disciples. We are left at the empty tomb to experience this great, remarkable, and disorienting mystery as if for the first time. We are the disciples on Sunday morning, trying to understand what it means that Jesus has risen from the grave. In the Acts reading, Peter begins his speech to the crowds with the words "You know what has happened." He then recounts the entire story of Jesus, from baptism through resurrection. Today, Peter speaks to us. Do we know what has happened—not as a historical event, but as something happening right now?

"[Y]our life is hidden with Christ in God." Our reading from Colossians signals a tension: we have already been raised with Christ, yet the full reality of resurrection has not yet been revealed to us. We must continually orient ourselves toward and trust in the "already" and the "not yet." Today we are drawn into this resurrection reality: first Christ's and then our own. By gathering alongside the early converts in our Acts reading, we renew ourselves in the ongoing reality of our own baptisms. As we recall and live into our baptisms in Christ, the gates of our new reality burst open for us. Allow yourself to rest in this resurrection experience. What does it feel like for you today?

Second Sunday of Easter (or Sunday of Divine Mercy)

FIRST READING   ACTS 5:12-16

Many signs and wonders were done among the people
   at the hands of the apostles.
They were all together in Solomon's portico.
None of the others dared to join them, but the people
   esteemed them.
Yet more than ever, believers in the Lord,
   great numbers of men and women, were added to them.
Thus they even carried the sick out into the streets
   and laid them on cots and mats
   so that when Peter came by,
   at least his shadow might fall on one or another of them.
A large number of people from the towns
   in the vicinity of Jerusalem also gathered,
   bringing the sick and those disturbed by unclean spirits,
   and they were all cured.

Our reading takes as its departure the story of Ananias and Sapphira (5:1-11), who hoard their resources rather than contribute them to the communal needs of the early Christian community (and then lie about it). When Peter confronts Ananias and Sapphira, first one then the other, they drop dead. Today's reading then stresses the implications of belief in Jesus and the ideals of the early Christian community as described prior to the story of Ananias and Sapphira. Our reading details all the "signs and wonders" done among the community gathered at Solomon's portico, an area on the east side of the temple (see Acts 3:11). "None of the others" refers to nonbelievers that the Christian community nonetheless treats with respect.

RESPONSORIAL PSALM   PSALM 118:2-4, 13-15, 22-24

Give thanks to the Lord for he is good, his love is everlasting.
  or: Alleluia.

SECOND READING   REVELATION 1:9-11a, 12-13, 17-19

I, John, your brother, who share with you
    the distress, the kingdom, and the endurance we have in Jesus,
    found myself on the island called Patmos
    because I proclaimed God's word and gave testimony to Jesus.
I was caught up in spirit on the Lord's day
    and heard behind me a voice as loud as a trumpet, which said,
    "Write on a scroll what you see."
Then I turned to see whose voice it was that spoke to me,
    and when I turned, I saw seven gold lampstands
    and in the midst of the lampstands one like a son of man,
    wearing an ankle-length robe, with a gold sash around
        his chest.

When I caught sight of him, I fell down at his feet as though dead.
He touched me with his right hand and said, "Do not be afraid.
I am the first and the last, the one who lives.
Once I was dead, but now I am alive forever and ever.
I hold the keys to death and the netherworld.
Write down, therefore, what you have seen,
    and what is happening, and what will happen afterwards."

This Easter season, we read from the book of Revelation, the book
that closes the New Testament canon with intense, apocalyptic imagery of Christ's return. The author, John, is likely a different person
than the author of the Fourth Gospel. Revelation was written in the
late first/early second century CE in response to Roman persecution
of early Christians and immense social instability. Its apocalyptic,
end-of-the-world imagery offered hope to early Christians in the
promise that Christ would soon return to overturn the world order
and end their suffering. We begin this Sunday with John's first vision
on the island of Patmos (in the southern Aegean Sea, west of Anatolia
or modern-day Turkey). Like the prophet Ezekiel (e.g., Ezek 2:2), he

is "caught up in [the] spirit" of God, who commands him to write down his visions on a scroll. The seven gold lampstands signify seven churches located in seven prominent cities of western Anatolia, listed in verse 11b (not included in our reading). In the midst of these lampstands, John has a vision of Christ. In the Greco-Roman world, it was believed that the keys to Hades (the underworld) were held by the Greek goddess Hecate. In John's vision, it is Christ who controls or holds "the keys to death and the netherworld" (literally "Hades") because he now lives forever and has power over life and death.

GOSPEL   JOHN 20:19-31

On the evening of that first day of the week,
    when the doors were locked, where the disciples were,
    for fear of the Jews,
    Jesus came and stood in their midst
    and said to them, "Peace be with you."
When he had said this, he showed them his hands and his side.
The disciples rejoiced when they saw the Lord.
Jesus said to them again, "Peace be with you.
As the Father has sent me, so I send you."
And when he had said this, he breathed on them and said
    to them,
    "Receive the Holy Spirit.
Whose sins you forgive are forgiven them,
    and whose sins you retain are retained."

Thomas, called Didymus, one of the Twelve,
    was not with them when Jesus came.
So the other disciples said to him, "We have seen the Lord."
But he said to them,
    "Unless I see the mark of the nails in his hands
    and put my finger into the nailmarks
    and put my hand into his side, I will not believe."

Now a week later his disciples were again inside
    and Thomas was with them.
Jesus came, although the doors were locked,
    and stood in their midst and said, "Peace be with you."

> Then he said to Thomas, "Put your finger here and see my hands,
>   and bring your hand and put it into my side,
>   and do not be unbelieving, but believe."
> Thomas answered and said to him, "My Lord and my God!"
> Jesus said to him, "Have you come to believe because you have
>   seen me?
> Blessed are those who have not seen and have believed."
>
> Now Jesus did many other signs in the presence of his disciples
>   that are not written in this book.
> But these are written that you may come to believe
>   that Jesus is the Christ, the Son of God,
>   and that through this belief you may have life in his name.

According to John, after the resurrection, Jesus first appears to Mary Magdalene (20:11-18) and then to the disciples. The disciples are still living in the shock and fear of the crucifixion, locking their doors in fear of those who had sought Jesus's death. "Peace be with you" is a traditional Jewish greeting (see John 14:27). Jesus shows the disciples his pierced body to prove he is not a ghost, and they rejoice. Jesus then commissions the disciples and breathes the Spirit on them. The Greek word for "breathe" (*emphysaō*) is used only here and in the Greek translation of Ezekiel 37:9, where God breathes upon the bones of the dead to bring them back to life. In both Greek and Hebrew, "breath" is synonymous with "wind" and "spirit." According to Catholic tradition, Jesus's words here about forgiving and retaining sins provide the origins of the sacrament of reconciliation. Note Jesus's gentleness with Thomas, whereas elsewhere in the book of John, Jesus is sharply critical of those who demand signs (2:15-18; 4:48; 6:2, 26). Jesus complies with Thomas's request, and Thomas calls Jesus his "Lord" and "God" (Greek *Kyrios Theos*), a translation of the Hebrew name for the "Lord God" (*Yahweh Elohim*). We do not know whether Thomas touches Jesus, but we do know that he makes the most complete affirmation of Christ's true nature of anyone in the Gospel. Jesus's words in response transcend the scene and speak to Christians across time.

Ponder

Our readings are filled with extraordinary visions, signs, and wonders that are meant to console and empower followers of Christ to a life of active faith. Written within the context of first-century Roman rule, underlying these readings is the recognition that a life committed to Christ comes at great cost. That world may seem far removed from ours. Yet resurrection reminds us that signs and wonders are real and ongoing, and the cost of discipleship is still high. Dietrich Bonhoeffer once said that when Christ calls someone, he is calling them to "come and die."[1] Through dying, Christ also bids us to come and live. This week, open yourself to the "signs and wonders" working around you and through you, subtle though they may seem. As Christ calls you to become a conduit for such signs and wonders, what is the cost? What is the gain?

"Blessed are those who have not seen and have believed." Jesus's words transcend the Gospel scene and speak directly to us. But what do these words mean to us today? Surely they acknowledge our lack of physical evidence for Jesus's resurrection; unlike the early disciples, we cannot physically see and touch the wounds on Jesus's hands or feet. However, one cannot have faith without seeing or experiencing to some extent. To follow Christ is to have experienced the great mercy and love of God, at least in some small way. Perhaps, then, Jesus is calling us to two things: first, to faith that extends beyond tangible evidence; and second, to become tangible witnesses of God's love and mercy to others so they might come to "see" and believe.

1. Dietrich Bonhoeffer, *The Cost of Discipleship,* 2nd rev. and unabridged edition, trans. R. H. Fuller and Irmgard Booth (New York: The Macmillan Company, 1959), 79.

Third Sunday of Easter

FIRST READING   ACTS 5:27-32, 40b-41

When the captain and the court officers had brought the
     apostles in
  and made them stand before the Sanhedrin,
  the high priest questioned them,
  "We gave you strict orders, did we not,
  to stop teaching in that name?
Yet you have filled Jerusalem with your teaching
  and want to bring this man's blood upon us."
But Peter and the apostles said in reply,
  "We must obey God rather than men.
The God of our ancestors raised Jesus,
  though you had him killed by hanging him on a tree.
God exalted him at his right hand as leader and savior
  to grant Israel repentance and forgiveness of sins.
We are witnesses of these things,
  as is the Holy Spirit whom God has given to those who
     obey him."

The Sanhedrin ordered the apostles
  to stop speaking in the name of Jesus, and dismissed them.
So they left the presence of the Sanhedrin,
  rejoicing that they had been found worthy
  to suffer dishonor for the sake of the name.

Just prior to this account, the apostles are arrested for the second time and placed in prison (5:17-18). An angel of God opens the prison doors in the middle of the night, and the apostles return to the temple area to continue teaching about Jesus. As we read here, the captain and court officers then realize the apostles have escaped and return to the temple area to bring them before the Sanhedrin, the assembly of Jewish leaders. The leaders try to stop the apostles from teaching about Jesus, and Peter and the apostles respond with a concise theological summary of Jesus's death, resurrection, and glorification. The section left out of our reading (vv. 33-40a) is crucial for understanding the whole. In these verses, Gamaliel, one of the Jewish leaders, convinces the council to let the apostles go. He tells them that "if this endeavor or this activity is of human origin, it will destroy itself. But if it comes from God, you will not be able to destroy them; you may even find yourselves fighting against God" (vv. 38-39). Convinced, the council releases the disciples after first flogging them. The disciples rejoice in their suffering for Jesus.

RESPONSORIAL PSALM   PSALM 30:2, 4, 5-6, 11-12, 13

I will praise you, Lord, for you have rescued me.
or: Alleluia.

SECOND READING   REVELATION 5:11-14

I, John, looked and heard the voices of many angels
    who surrounded the throne
    and the living creatures and the elders.
They were countless in number, and they cried out in a
        loud voice:
        "Worthy is the Lamb that was slain
            to receive power and riches, wisdom and strength,
            honor and glory and blessing."
Then I heard every creature in heaven and on earth
    and under the earth and in the sea,
    everything in the universe, cry out:
        "To the one who sits on the throne and to the Lamb
            be blessing and honor, glory and might,
            forever and ever."
The four living creatures answered, "Amen,"
    and the elders fell down and worshiped.

We skip forward from chapter 1 (last Sunday) to the middle of chapter 5 in Revelation. In chapters 4–5, John is invited to ascend to heaven to behold visions of God. The visions in these chapters draw upon apocalyptic imagery from the books of Ezekiel and Daniel. John sees the throne of God, upon which sits the glory of God, described in terms of precious gems (4:1-3). Around the throne of

God are twenty-four additional thrones, which likely symbolize the twelve tribes of Israel plus the twelve disciples, upon which sit the "elders," or attendants, of God (4:4). Around the throne are four "living creatures" (see Ezek 1) who have the appearance of different animals (4:6-9). In our reading, John hears the voices of the angels who surround the throne of God and praise Christ, the sacrificial Lamb. Everyone—every single creature in the universe, including the four living creatures and the elders—worships God and the Lamb (Christ) as equal in majesty.

GOSPEL   JOHN 21:1-19 [OR 21:1-14]

At that time, Jesus revealed himself again to his disciples at the
    Sea of Tiberias.
He revealed himself in this way.
Together were Simon Peter, Thomas called Didymus,
    Nathanael from Cana in Galilee,
    Zebedee's sons, and two others of his disciples.
Simon Peter said to them, "I am going fishing."
They said to him, "We also will come with you."
So they went out and got into the boat,
    but that night they caught nothing.
When it was already dawn, Jesus was standing on the shore;
    but the disciples did not realize that it was Jesus.
Jesus said to them, "Children, have you caught anything to eat?"
They answered him, "No."
So he said to them, "Cast the net over the right side of the boat
    and you will find something."
So they cast it, and were not able to pull it in
    because of the number of fish.
So the disciple whom Jesus loved said to Peter, "It is the Lord."
When Simon Peter heard that it was the Lord,
    he tucked in his garment, for he was lightly clad,
    and jumped into the sea.
The other disciples came in the boat,
    for they were not far from shore, only about a hundred yards,
    dragging the net with the fish.
When they climbed out on shore,
    they saw a charcoal fire with fish on it and bread.

Jesus said to them, "Bring some of the fish you just caught."
So Simon Peter went over and dragged the net ashore
    full of one hundred fifty-three large fish.
Even though there were so many, the net was not torn.
Jesus said to them, "Come, have breakfast."
And none of the disciples dared to ask him, "Who are you?"
    because they realized it was the Lord.
Jesus came over and took the bread and gave it to them,
    and in like manner the fish.
This was now the third time Jesus was revealed to his disciples
    after being raised from the dead.

When they had finished breakfast, Jesus said to Simon Peter,
    "Simon, son of John, do you love me more than these?"
Simon Peter answered him, "Yes, Lord, you know that I love you."
Jesus said to him, "Feed my lambs."
He then said to Simon Peter a second time,
    "Simon, son of John, do you love me?"
Simon Peter answered him, "Yes, Lord, you know that I love you."
Jesus said to him, "Tend my sheep."
Jesus said to him the third time,
    "Simon, son of John, do you love me?"
Peter was distressed that Jesus had said to him a third time,
    "Do you love me?" and he said to him,
    "Lord, you know everything; you know that I love you."
Jesus said to him, "Feed my sheep.
Amen, amen, I say to you, when you were younger,
    you used to dress yourself and go where you wanted;
    but when you grow old, you will stretch out your hands,
    and someone else will dress you
    and lead you where you do not want to go."
He said this signifying by what kind of death he would glorify God.
And when he had said this, he said to him, "Follow me."

Our reading draws from the epilogue of John's Gospel (John 21), likely a later addition that depicts a post-resurrection experience found only in John. As in other resurrection accounts, the disciples do not recognize Jesus at first. When "the disciple whom Jesus loved" declares, "It is the Lord," Peter immediately jumps into the water to go to him. Peter's actions are particularly powerful given his recent denial of Jesus. Jesus's subsequent conversation with the disciples involves a simple communal meal in which the description of Jesus "taking" and "giving" is reminiscent of the Eucharist. Jesus then asks Peter three times whether he loves him (echoing Peter's threefold denial of Jesus in John 18). The first two times, when Jesus asks whether Peter "loves" (*agapaō*) him, Peter responds that he does "love" (*phileō*) Jesus. The Greek verb *agapaō* refers to self-sacrificial love; it is a self-emptying love that is fully oriented toward the other. The Greek *phileō* denotes friendship and personal attachment as a feeling or sentiment; it is a conditional love. The third time, Jesus changes his question to the verb *phileō*. Some commentators think that Jesus is therefore meeting Peter in his current, limited understanding of Jesus's request. Others argue that the Gospel writer is simply varying his vocabulary, as he does throughout this scene. The story prefigures Peter's eventual martyrdom.

Ponder

In the book of Acts, "the name" is key. The high priest orders the apostles to stop teaching "in that name." The apostles refuse, and they continue to live and act "for the sake of the name." Throughout the book of Acts, the early apostles demonstrate absolute dedication to this name, Jesus Christ, in their mission to grow the early Christian community. In distinct ways, our readings this Sunday all depict single-mindedness of worship and orientation toward Jesus. They invite us to probe our own inner orientation that guides our thoughts, desires, and actions. If we were to give a "name" to our ultimate orientation, what would it be?

Pope Francis once said that God "invites us to strip ourselves of our many idols and to worship him alone; to proclaim, to witness, to adore."[1] In the Gospel reading, Peter demonstrates this "stripping" by jumping instantly into the water to follow Christ. He is able to swim because, as the text says, he is "lightly clad." In other words, very little holds him back. And yet Peter may still have a ways to go, as demonstrated in his dialogue with Jesus. He loves Jesus, yet this love may still be conditional. Peter's journey is our journey. We follow Christ as best we can and in fits and starts. Yet the promise of Easter is that Jesus meets us where we are, drawing us gently and lovingly toward him until nothing holds us back.

1. Pope Francis, Homily at Basilica of Saint Paul Outside-the-Walls, Third Sunday of Easter, April 14, 2013.

Fourth Sunday of Easter

FIRST READING   ACTS 13:14, 43-52

Paul and Barnabas continued on from Perga
    and reached Antioch in Pisidia.
On the sabbath they entered the synagogue and took their seats.
Many Jews and worshipers who were converts to Judaism
    followed Paul and Barnabas, who spoke to them
    and urged them to remain faithful to the grace of God.

On the following sabbath almost the whole city gathered
    to hear the word of the Lord.
When the Jews saw the crowds, they were filled with jealousy
    and with violent abuse contradicted what Paul said.
Both Paul and Barnabas spoke out boldly and said,
    "It was necessary that the word of God be spoken to you first,
    but since you reject it
    and condemn yourselves as unworthy of eternal life,
    we now turn to the Gentiles.
For so the Lord has commanded us,
    I have made you a light to the Gentiles,
    that you may be an instrument of salvation
    to the ends of the earth."

The Gentiles were delighted when they heard this
    and glorified the word of the Lord.
All who were destined for eternal life came to believe,
    and the word of the Lord continued to spread
    through the whole region.
The Jews, however, incited the women of prominence who
        were worshipers
    and the leading men of the city,
    stirred up a persecution against Paul and Barnabas,
    and expelled them from their territory.
So they shook the dust from their feet in protest against them,
    and went to Iconium.
The disciples were filled with joy and the Holy Spirit.

The focus of our reading is Paul's first trip to Antioch in Syria. The account is part of the inauguration of his mission to the Gentiles that extends from Acts 10:1–15:35, which we read throughout the weekday lectionary. On the Sabbath, Paul and his companions go to the synagogue as usual. In verses 15-32, which are excluded from today's reading, the synagogue officials tell Paul to stand up and preach to the people. He uses the occasion to recount all of salvation history leading up to Christ, after which the people urge Paul and Barnabas to return and preach again the following Sabbath. Paul's words clearly captivate those in attendance, for it seems many are either persuaded or are in the process of being persuaded by his message. The next week, however, the people become "filled with jealousy" when they see the "whole city" gather to hear Paul and Barnabas. Paul responds to their aggression by proclaiming the inclusion of the Gentiles in his message of salvation, quoting from Isaiah's message of inclusion of the nations (Isa 49:6). The reference to those who are "destined" for eternal life refers in some sense to a determined future, though this idea does not undermine the notion of free will as seen consistently throughout the Bible (including Acts).

RESPONSORIAL PSALM   PSALM 100:1-2, 3, 5

We are his people, the sheep of his flock.
or: Alleluia.

SECOND READING   REVELATION 7:9, 14b-17

I, John, had a vision of a great multitude,
    which no one could count,
    from every nation, race, people, and tongue.
They stood before the throne and before the Lamb,
    wearing white robes and holding palm branches in their hands.

Then one of the elders said to me,
    "These are the ones who have survived the time of
        great distress;
    they have washed their robes
    and made them white in the blood of the Lamb.

"For this reason they stand before God's throne
and worship him day and night in his temple.
The one who sits on the throne will shelter them.
They will not hunger or thirst anymore,
nor will the sun or any heat strike them.
For the Lamb who is in the center of the throne
will shepherd them
and lead them to springs of life-giving water,
and God will wipe away every tear from their eyes."

Today's reading from Revelation draws from a series of visions in 6:1–8:5 in which the "Lamb" (Christ) opens seven seals. The number seven repeats throughout Revelation and is a symbolic number that signifies completion (among other things). There are four seals of destruction (6:1-8) and three of judgment (6:9–8:1). In an interlude between the sixth and seventh seals, John has two visions of divine protection and salvation of the faithful in the end times. The vision described here breaks down any perceived boundaries—national, racial, cultural, linguistic—to describe the "great multitude" of the faithful who come together to worship Christ. Christ is both the "Lamb" and, paradoxically, the "shepherd," who promises eternal shelter and protection. Christ's blood does not stain but cleanses, washing clothes white (a color that symbolizes victory, purity, and innocence). The Lamb and God act together to care lovingly and tenderly for the faithful.

GOSPEL   JOHN 10:27-30

Jesus said:
"My sheep hear my voice;
I know them, and they follow me.
I give them eternal life, and they shall never perish.
No one can take them out of my hand.
My Father, who has given them to me, is greater than all,
and no one can take them out of the Father's hand.
The Father and I are one."

The Fourth Sunday of Easter is known as "Good Shepherd Sunday" because the Gospel reading draws from John 10:1-21, which describes Jesus as the "good" or "noble" (Greek *kalos*) shepherd. Our Gospel this Sunday mirrors the final verse from our second reading: Jesus (the Lamb) acts as shepherd to his sheep. Just prior to this passage, the people gather around Jesus and ask him, "How long are you going to keep us in suspense? If you are the Messiah, tell us plainly" (v. 24), and Jesus answers, "I told you and you do not believe . . . . you do not believe, because you are not among my sheep" (vv. 25-26). In contrast, Jesus's true followers (his sheep) hear his voice and follow him. The promise is abundant life: death cannot take them from Jesus or from the Father, both of whom have power over death. Subsequent to our reading, the people pick up rocks to stone Jesus (v. 31)—stoning was the penalty for blasphemy.

Ponder

Saint Gregory the Great once said, "I assure you that it is not by faith that you will come to know him, but by love; not by mere conviction, but by action." Our readings describe action that is rooted in a belief so strong, so full-hearted, that it exudes from one's actions. From the disciples to the early Christians who "hear" and "follow" the shepherd, these followers of Christ lived for a promise far beyond their earthly pain and suffering. They acted toward the vision of standing one day before Christ's throne with the promise of God holding them and wiping away their tears. As Gregory the Great exhorted his listeners: "Turn now to consider how these words of our Lord imply a test for yourselves also. Ask yourselves whether you belong to his flock, whether you know him, whether the light of his truth shines in your minds."[1]

"I, John, had a vision of a great multitude." This vision of inclusion is strikingly beautiful. It describes the collapse of those perceived barriers that so often divide us. To be a person of faith is to live by this vision of unity. It is to be "catholic," which means "universal" or, literally, "in respect of the whole" (from the Greek *katholikos*). And yet our readings carry a tension between inclusion and exclusion, as described most explicitly in the reading from Acts. We want to include and be included, but at the same time, the tendency to exclude exerts a strong pull on us. As Christians, to be included is to be one of the sheep who hears Christ and follows. It is to be part of the Body of Christ. How expansive is this Body? As you pray with the readings this week, take time to examine your own tendencies to include and exclude, and ultimately rest in the arms of the God who loves you and all people.

1. Gregory the Great, from a homily on the Gospels (Hom. 14. 3–6: PL 76, 1129–30).

Fifth Sunday of Easter

FIRST READING   ACTS 14:21-27

After Paul and Barnabas had proclaimed the good news to
    that city
    and made a considerable number of disciples,
    they returned to Lystra and to Iconium and to Antioch.
They strengthened the spirits of the disciples
    and exhorted them to persevere in the faith, saying,
    "It is necessary for us to undergo many hardships
    to enter the kingdom of God."
They appointed elders for them in each church and,
    with prayer and fasting, commended them to the Lord
    in whom they had put their faith.
Then they traveled through Pisidia and reached Pamphylia.
After proclaiming the word at Perga they went down to Attalia.
From there they sailed to Antioch,
    where they had been commended to the grace of God
    for the work they had now accomplished.
And when they arrived, they called the church together
    and reported what God had done with them
    and how he had opened the door of faith to the Gentiles.

This Sunday's reading carefully details Paul and Barnabas's journey throughout Asia Minor (modern-day Turkey) as they continue to minister to the Gentiles and support the early Christian communities. The verses directly prior to our reading recount an event in which Paul is stoned and left for dead outside Lystra (vv. 19-20), which reminds us how difficult the disciples' journey was. Yet the above reading focuses not on the difficulties but rather on the disciples' strengthening, encouraging, and building up of the communities they had helped to create. They finally return to Antioch, where Barnabas and Paul first began their two-person ministry and where the disciples were first called "Christians" (11:25-26). There, the two describe all that had taken place in the meantime, including the radical decision to extend the message of salvation to the Gentiles.

RESPONSORIAL PSALM   PSALM 145:8-9, 10-11, 12-13

I will praise your name forever, my king and my God.
   or: Alleluia.

SECOND READING   REVELATION 21:1-5a

Then I, John, saw a new heaven and a new earth.
The former heaven and the former earth had passed away,
   and the sea was no more.
I also saw the holy city, a new Jerusalem,
   coming down out of heaven from God,
   prepared as a bride adorned for her husband.
I heard a loud voice from the throne saying,
   "Behold, God's dwelling is with the human race.
He will dwell with them and they will be his people
   and God himself will always be with them as their God.
He will wipe every tear from their eyes,
   and there shall be no more death or mourning, wailing or pain,
   for the old order has passed away."

The One who sat on the throne said,
   "Behold, I make all things new."

Our reading comes from the extensive imagery of the "new" Jerusalem at the end of the book of Revelation. John's vision of the
renewal of creation in the form of a "new heaven and a new earth"
draws from the Hebrew Bible (e.g., Isa 65:17; 66:22) and from other
important early Jewish texts outside of the biblical canon (including
Jubilees 1:29; 4:26; and 1 Enoch 91:16). According to early Judaism, the final eschatological event would include God's renewal and
transformation of all creation. In the new creation there would be no
sea, which was often perceived as a force of power and chaos in the
ancient Middle East (see Gen 1:2). The image of the eschatological
Jerusalem as a bride contrasts with Rome as the "whore of Babylon"
(see Rev 17–18). Like last week's reading, God is depicted as a loving
parent who wipes away tears and consoles. Paradoxically, in this new
world God is both seated on a high throne and firmly entrenched
among the people.

GOSPEL   JOHN 13:31-33a, 34-35

When Judas had left them, Jesus said,
  "Now is the Son of Man glorified, and God is glorified in him.
If God is glorified in him,
  God will also glorify him in himself,
  and God will glorify him at once.
My children, I will be with you only a little while longer.
I give you a new commandment: love[1] one another.
As I have loved you, so you also should love one another.
This is how all will know that you are my disciples,
  if you have love for one another."

The Fifth through Seventh Sundays of Easter draw us into the broader context of Jesus's final meal with his disciples (John 13–17). Today's reading takes place after the festival of Passover and Jesus's washing of the disciples' feet. Jesus becomes troubled and tells the disciples that one of them will betray him (13:21). Satan enters Judas, who departs from the scene. Jesus then tells his disciples what will happen to him and reorients their perspective to view his impending death not as a shameful act, but as the occasion when he will be honored by God. His death will be a statement of willing obedience to God. He then speaks tenderly to the disciples, calling them his "children" and exhorting them to love one another. This is the first time we hear a command to love formulated in this way in the New Testament. This commandment is a reminder of what should be at the heart of faith: God's love working through our lives. It repeats throughout 1 and 2 John.

1. "Love": Greek *agapaō*. This is unconditional, selfless love, the love with which Jesus pours himself out for us. See notes on the Gospel reading for the Third Sunday of Easter (John 21:1-19).

Ponder

This week's and last week's readings from Revelation contain beautiful descriptions of God's love for us. God promises to make all things new, to rid the world of pain and suffering, to comfort and "wipe every tear from their eyes." This remarkable depiction of love is both a promise and a calling, a comfort and a challenge. According to Saint Teresa of Calcutta, "Today God is loving the world through you and through me and through all those who are his love and compassion in the world."[2] When we experience God's love, that experience inevitably expands outward. But first we must experience that love personally. As you pray with the readings, can you open to and experience this divine love within and around you?

Paul and Barnabas's journey must have been exhausting. Constantly traveling, without a home or physical security, they never knew what they would encounter in a city or how they would be treated. Yet they continued to witness to Christ and "strengthened the spirits" of early communities of faith. Without Christ's love burning within and through them, it is hard to imagine how they could have kept up this work without mental or physical breakdown. Simply put, Paul and Barnabas were living witnesses to Jesus's commandment to love one another as he loves us. This week, consider praying for the grace to be a conduit of that same love for those around you, particularly in situations that you find most challenging.

2. Mother Teresa, *Where There Is Love, There Is God: A Path to Closer Union with God and Greater Love for Others,* compiled and edited by Brian Kolodiejchuk, M.C. (New York: Doubleday, 2010), 320.

Sixth Sunday of Easter

FIRST READING   ACTS 15:1-2, 22-29

Some who had come down from Judea were instructing
    the brothers,
    "Unless you are circumcised according to the Mosaic practice,
    you cannot be saved."
Because there arose no little dissension and debate
    by Paul and Barnabas with them,
    it was decided that Paul, Barnabas, and some of the others
    should go up to Jerusalem to the apostles and elders
    about this question.

The apostles and elders, in agreement with the whole church,
    decided to choose representatives
    and to send them to Antioch with Paul and Barnabas.
The ones chosen were Judas, who was called Barsabbas,
    and Silas, leaders among the brothers.
This is the letter delivered by them:

"The apostles and the elders, your brothers,
    to the brothers in Antioch, Syria, and Cilicia
    of Gentile origin: greetings.
Since we have heard that some of our number
    who went out without any mandate from us
    have upset you with their teachings
    and disturbed your peace of mind,
    we have with one accord decided to choose representatives
    and to send them to you along with our beloved Barnabas
        and Paul,
    who have dedicated their lives to the name of our Lord
        Jesus Christ.
So we are sending Judas and Silas
    who will also convey this same message by word of mouth:
    'It is the decision of the Holy Spirit and of us
    not to place on you any burden beyond these necessities,
    namely, to abstain from meat sacrificed to idols,
    from blood, from meats of strangled animals,
    and from unlawful marriage.

If you keep free of these,
  you will be doing what is right. Farewell.' "

This is a key text in the book of Acts. Picking up from last Sunday's reading, Paul and Barnabas depart Antioch to join the Jerusalem Council. There they discuss the legitimacy of the mission to the Gentiles with the church apostles and elders. The central question is whether Gentiles must convert to Judaism in order to be saved— more specifically, whether they must be circumcised and "observe the Mosaic law" (v. 5). The resolution is not easy or simple in its historical context, and conflicts emerge later in Acts. Yet the remarkable, radical change that takes place in this meeting cannot be understated. In it, what was once an internal, Jewish mission broadens to include the Gentiles without their having to convert to Judaism. Our reading skips verses 3-21, in which Peter eloquently recounts his mission to the Gentiles. In particular, he explains how he had witnessed the Holy Spirit's descent upon the Gentiles regardless of their full conversion to Judaism. Peter poses a question: if the Spirit had "purified their hearts" by faith, making no distinction between Jew or Gentile (v. 9), then why would the council "[put] God to the test" by placing upon the Gentiles such a difficult burden as the requirement to keep all of the commandments (v. 10)? What saves, he argues, is the grace of Jesus Christ (vv. 10-11).

RESPONSORIAL PSALM   PSALM 67:2-3, 5, 6, 8

O God, let all the nations praise you!
  or: Alleluia.

SECOND READING   REVELATION 21:10-14, 22-23

The angel took me in spirit to a great, high mountain
  and showed me the holy city Jerusalem
  coming down out of heaven from God.
It gleamed with the splendor of God.
Its radiance was like that of a precious stone,
  like jasper, clear as crystal.

It had a massive, high wall,
with twelve gates where twelve angels were stationed
and on which names were inscribed,
the names of the twelve tribes of the Israelites.
There were three gates facing east,
three north, three south, and three west.
The wall of the city had twelve courses of stones as its foundation,
on which were inscribed the twelve names
of the twelve apostles of the Lamb.

I saw no temple in the city
for its temple is the Lord God almighty and the Lamb.
The city had no need of sun or moon to shine on it,
for the glory of God gave it light,
and its lamp was the Lamb.

We continue John's vision of the new Jerusalem with imagery that mirrors the prophet Ezekiel's description of the rebuilt Jerusalem temple (Ezek 40–47). Ezekiel prophesied to the exiled Judean population in Babylon (ca. 586–536 BCE), a community that yearned to return to Jerusalem and rebuild their destroyed temple. They eventually did so under the Persian Empire, the history of which is recounted in the books of Ezra and Nehemiah. Similarly, Revelation offers solace to a primarily Jewish-Christian audience in the wake of the second major destruction of the beloved temple (ca. 70 CE). Our reading describes a "new Jerusalem" in which there is no longer need of a religious structure to mediate between humans and the Divine. The author envisions all of Jerusalem shimmering with the glory of God. The number twelve symbolizes the tribes of Israel and the number of apostles.

GOSPEL   JOHN 14:23-29

Jesus said to his disciples:
"Whoever loves me will keep my word,
and my Father will love him,
and we will come to him and make our dwelling with him.
Whoever does not love me does not keep my words;
yet the word you hear is not mine
but that of the Father who sent me.

"I have told you this while I am with you.
The Advocate, the Holy Spirit,
   whom the Father will send in my name,
   will teach you everything
   and remind you of all that I told you.
Peace I leave with you; my peace I give to you.
Not as the world gives do I give it to you.
Do not let your hearts be troubled or afraid.
You heard me tell you,
   'I am going away and I will come back to you.'
If you loved me,
   you would rejoice that I am going to the Father;
   for the Father is greater than I.
And now I have told you this before it happens,
   so that when it happens you may believe."

Our Gospel reading continues to develop the love commandment from last Sunday. Remember that this long exhortation takes place subsequent to Jesus washing the disciples' feet. As we read last Sunday, Jesus then calls his disciples his "children" and tells them to love one another. Here, Jesus describes the relationship between the one who loves and the risen Christ. Whoever truly "loves" (Greek *agapaō*) Jesus will necessarily act in love ("will keep [his] word") and enter into the dynamic, unifying love of Christ and God. The union of Christ and God will literally come to dwell or make a home in such a person. In the verse immediately following our reading, he tells the disciples to rejoice in the crucifixion, for the union of Jesus with God through his death and resurrection will break the power of this world (see v. 30).

Ponder

"Do not let your hearts be troubled or afraid." Jesus's commandments are daring. First, he commands us to love as God loves us. Yet we humans are so imperfect, hardly capable of loving in this way. Then he tells us not to be troubled or afraid, even to be at peace, teachings that can be difficult to swallow in light of our lived experiences of suffering, pain, and sin. Jesus is not suggesting that we have arrived at some state of perfection in our ability to carry out these commandments. Instead, he is pointing us toward a path beyond what is obvious or visible, an alternative orientation to the glaring self-absorption of this world. In commanding us to follow this path, Jesus promises our transformation. Our task is not to be perfect. Our task is simply to follow the path.

Our readings invite us to ponder the role of religious commandments or laws. According to Acts, they are not to be a "burden" beyond what is "necessary." Yet what is necessary? Our Gospel points to the ultimate necessity, which is Love—not love as a fleeting feeling or emotion, but the Divine outpouring that embraces the world. The reality is that without the movement of the Spirit, without God's grace and our work, this type of love is impossible. It necessarily calls for the implementation of practical guidelines or "laws" to help us shift from self-absorption to a more expansive, outward orientation. What are these necessary laws in your own life?

The Ascension of the Lord[1]

FIRST READING   ACTS 1:1-11

In the first book, Theophilus,
  I dealt with all that Jesus did and taught
  until the day he was taken up,
  after giving instructions through the Holy Spirit
  to the apostles whom he had chosen.
He presented himself alive to them
  by many proofs after he had suffered,
  appearing to them during forty days
  and speaking about the kingdom of God.
While meeting with them,
  he enjoined them not to depart from Jerusalem,
  but to wait for "the promise of the Father
  about which you have heard me speak;
  for John baptized with water,
  but in a few days you will be baptized with the Holy Spirit."

When they had gathered together they asked him,
  "Lord, are you at this time going to restore the kingdom
        to Israel?"
He answered them, "It is not for you to know the times or seasons
  that the Father has established by his own authority.
But you will receive power when the Holy Spirit comes upon you,
  and you will be my witnesses in Jerusalem,
  throughout Judea and Samaria,
  and to the ends of the earth."
When he had said this, as they were looking on,
  he was lifted up, and a cloud took him from their sight.
While they were looking intently at the sky as he was going,
  suddenly two men dressed in white garments stood
        beside them.
They said, "Men of Galilee,
  why are you standing there looking at the sky?

1. In some dioceses in the United States, the solemnity of the Ascension of the Lord is celebrated on a Thursday, while in others, it is celebrated on the following Sunday.

> This Jesus who has been taken up from you into heaven
> will return in the same way as you have seen him going
> into heaven."

The ascension marks the transfer of the locus of Christ's work from Jesus himself to the disciples through the Holy Spirit. Jesus ascends, yet the Spirit will soon descend, and the disciples will become Christ's hands and feet on earth. The above verses link Acts with Luke's Gospel, two books written by the same author. Here the author retells and expands upon essential information from the end of the Gospel (see Luke 24:13-53). In the Gospel, Jesus's resurrection and ascension occur on the same day. But in the Acts account, Jesus lingers among the disciples for a forty-day period (the number of completeness), teaching and preparing them for ministry. After this time, the disciples remain unsure of the future and ask Jesus if the coming of the Spirit will be the moment when he will "restore the kingdom to Israel." He tells them not to focus on this question but instead to focus on their task to be his "witnesses" (Greek *mártys*, meaning "witness" or "martyr"; see the Gospel reading) to the entire world. Four times, the above reading emphasizes that Jesus was "taken up" or "lifted up" into the "heaven[s]" or "sky" (Greek *ouranos*). Both Moses and Elijah are associated with forty-day periods and with ascending into the clouds (Exod 24:18; 1 Kgs 19:8). Also note that at the transfiguration, clouds overshadow Moses and Elijah along with Jesus (Luke 9:34-36). In 2 Kings 2:1-25, Elijah ascends and so transfers his power to Elisha, while Moses shifts his prophetic spirit to Joshua when he dies (Deut 34:9). Perhaps the two men dressed in white in the above reading are to be understood as Elijah and Moses. Like their prophetic shifts of power, Jesus's ascension marks the promise of the Spirit descending on his disciples.

RESPONSORIAL PSALM   PSALM 47:2-3, 6-7, 8-9

God mounts his throne to shouts of joy: a blare of trumpets for the Lord.
or: Alleluia.

SECOND READING   EPHESIANS 1:17-23
                                          (ALT. HEB 9:24-28; 10:19-23)

Brothers and sisters:
May the God of our Lord Jesus Christ, the Father of glory,
    give you a Spirit of wisdom and revelation
    resulting in knowledge of him.
May the eyes of your hearts be enlightened,
    that you may know what is the hope that belongs to his call,
    what are the riches of glory
    in his inheritance among the holy ones,
    and what is the surpassing greatness of his power
    for us who believe,
    in accord with the exercise of his great might,
    which he worked in Christ,
    raising him from the dead
    and seating him at his right hand in the heavens,
    far above every principality, authority, power, and dominion,
    and every name that is named
    not only in this age but also in the one to come.
And he put all things beneath his feet
    and gave him as head over all things to the church,
    which is his body,
    the fullness of the one who fills all things in every way.

This prayer for wisdom and knowledge is one of the richest in Paul's letters. Though deeply monotheistic, it is addressed not to Christ but to God, and the focus is God's work through Christ. The first half of the prayer emphasizes wisdom and hope, while the second half carries the notion of hope further to describe Jesus's dominance over all present and future powers. The passage depends upon the psalms, particularly in its references to Christ sitting "at [the] right hand" of God (Ps 110:1) and putting "all things at his feet" (Ps 8:7). Drawing upon these psalms, Paul depicts Jesus as authoritative and highly exalted, the climax of God's creation and the rightful earthly descendant of King David. The phrase "every principality, authority, power, and dominion" represents all the hostile spiritual powers that Christ subjects to himself (see 1 Cor 15:20-28). In the final verse, Christ is the fullness of all reality and of the cosmos as the head of the church. The church is an expression and embodiment of Christ, and of God's purpose for the world.

GOSPEL   LUKE 24:46-53

Jesus said to his disciples:
  "Thus it is written that the Christ would suffer
  and rise from the dead on the third day
  and that repentance, for the forgiveness of sins,
  would be preached in his name
  to all the nations, beginning from Jerusalem.
You are witnesses of these things.
And behold I am sending the promise of my Father upon you;
  but stay in the city
  until you are clothed with power from on high."

Then he led them out as far as Bethany,
  raised his hands, and blessed them.
As he blessed them he parted from them
  and was taken up to heaven.
They did him homage
  and then returned to Jerusalem with great joy,
  and they were continually in the temple praising God.

This is the earlier and terser version of the account given in our Acts reading. In Luke's account, Jesus's resurrection and ascension occur in a single day. On the day of his resurrection, Jesus encounters two of the disciples who are traveling to Emmaus and reveals himself to them at dinner (24:13-32). The two disciples then return immediately to Jerusalem to recount their experience of the risen Jesus to the other disciples (vv. 33-35). As they are explaining how Jesus was revealed to them in the "breaking of the bread," Jesus appears in their midst (v. 36). He "open[s] their minds" to understand the Scriptures in light of his death and resurrection (v. 45; just preceding our reading) and then commissions them to be his "witnesses" (v. 48; see notes from today's first reading from Acts). The "promise of my Father" is the Holy Spirit, as explained in Acts. Jesus is then "taken up to heaven," or carried upward into the sky (see also the notes from today's first reading).

Ponder

Today we read the ascension story twice: the shorter form in Luke and the longer form in Acts. In Acts, after Jesus is "lifted up," the two men in white ask the disciples, "[W]hy are you standing there looking at the sky?" The disciples are looking for Jesus, like many of us do, somewhere "up there," beyond this life. And why shouldn't we? Our readings emphasize that Jesus ascends into the heavens, "far above" all earthly powers and temptations. Yet our readings stretch us both up and down. Ascension is the promise of the Spirit's "descension" to us. The disciples' "great joy" after Jesus ascends in the Gospel suggests that they understand this promise. Christ is both "far above" and "deep within" us and our world. How do both realities stretch you as you ponder the presence of Christ?

Our readings between now and Pentecost might lead us to imagine the Spirit's coming as a fairytale-like ending to the story, resulting in instantaneous and worldwide conversion to Christ. But of course we know the ending is not so simple. Rather, the promise of Christ's ascension and the Spirit's descension is a promise that our path is a way of growth into the "already" and the "not yet," into full knowledge of Christ. Ephesians offers a breathtaking vision of what such knowledge means. It means that the Spirit will enlighten or literally "give light" to the "eyes of [our] hearts" (Greek *dianoia*, which can also mean "mind," "thought," or "intention") to understand Christ our hope. This promise is not a fairytale; it is happening. Have you experienced it?

Seventh Sunday of Easter

FIRST READING   ACTS 7:55-60

Stephen, filled with the Holy Spirit,
  looked up intently to heaven and saw the glory of God
  and Jesus standing at the right hand of God,
  and Stephen said, "Behold, I see the heavens opened
  and the Son of Man standing at the right hand of God."
But they cried out in a loud voice,
  covered their ears, and rushed upon him together.
They threw him out of the city, and began to stone him.
The witnesses laid down their cloaks
  at the feet of a young man named Saul.
As they were stoning Stephen, he called out,
  "Lord Jesus, receive my spirit."
Then he fell to his knees and cried out in a loud voice,
  "Lord, do not hold this sin against them";
  and when he said this, he fell asleep.

Our reading recounts the story of Stephen, the first martyr of the early church. When Stephen dies, his final words echo those of Jesus in Luke's Gospel: "Father, into your hands I commend my spirit" (Luke 23:46; Ps 31:6). Stephen then asks for forgiveness for his killers, just as Jesus did from the cross ("Father, forgive them, they know not what they do"; Luke 23:34). Stephen's story, which extends from the end of Acts 6 through our reading today, is also powerful in other ways. Stephen retells Israel's salvation history from Abraham through the Babylonian exile, drawing Jesus into this history. The people do not want to hear him and cover their ears to prevent his message from seeping through. Saul is present for Stephen's death and approves of his killing. Directly following his death, a "severe persecution" begins against the church (Acts 8:1), of which Saul is a key instigator (8:3). Yet just one chapter later (Acts 9), Saul will encounter the risen Jesus and will have a remarkable experience of conversion himself.

RESPONSORIAL PSALM   PSALM 97:1-2, 6-7, 9

The Lord is king, the most high over all the earth.
or: Alleluia.

SECOND READING   REVELATION 22:12-14, 16-17, 20

I, John, heard a voice saying to me:
"Behold, I am coming soon.
I bring with me the recompense I will give to each
    according to his deeds.
I am the Alpha and the Omega, the first and the last,
    the beginning and the end."

Blessed are they who wash their robes
    so as to have the right to the tree of life
    and enter the city through its gates.

"I, Jesus, sent my angel to give you this testimony for
        the churches.
I am the root and offspring of David,
    the bright morning star."

The Spirit and the bride say, "Come."
Let the hearer say, "Come."
Let the one who thirsts come forward,
    and the one who wants it receive the gift of life-giving water.

The one who gives this testimony says, "Yes, I am coming soon."
Amen! Come, Lord Jesus!

These are among the final verses of Revelation and part of the book's epilogue, which focuses on warnings and exhortations not to alter the book's teachings or seal it up (i.e., put it away and forget about it), for the end is near. Apocalyptic in perspective, the author of Revelation expects Christ's return at any moment, which we see clearly in these final verses. Christ is God, "the Alpha and the Omega," the first and last letters of the Greek alphabet. These letters symbolize the totality of everything (note that "the Lord God" also claims "the Alpha and the Omega" as a title in Rev 1:8). Simultaneously, Jesus is the Jewish

messiah, the "root and offspring" from the line of King David. Those
who "wash their robes" are those who have been cleansed from sin by
washing their robes in the "blood of the Lamb" (Rev 7:14; see notes
for the Fourth Sunday of Easter). The bride is the new, heavenly Jerusalem mentioned throughout the book, which is imagined as the
Garden of Eden that contains the tree of life (Gen 2:8; see also notes
on Rev 21 from the Sixth Sunday of Easter). The final lines and their
call-and-response format read in the style of communal liturgy.

GOSPEL   JOHN 17:20-26

Lifting up his eyes to heaven, Jesus prayed, saying:
  "Holy Father, I pray not only for them,
  but also for those who will believe in me through their word,
  so that they may all be one,
  as you, Father, are in me and I in you,
  that they also may be in us,
  that the world may believe that you sent me.
And I have given them the glory you gave me,
  so that they may be one, as we are one,
  I in them and you in me,
  that they may be brought to perfection[1] as one,
  that the world may know that you sent me,
  and that you loved them even as you loved me.
Father, they are your gift to me.
I wish that where I am they also may be with me,
  that they may see my glory that you gave me,
  because you loved me before the foundation of the world.
Righteous Father, the world also does not know you,
  but I know you, and they know that you sent me.
I made known to them your name and I will make it known,
  that the love with which you loved me
  may be in them and I in them."

---

1. The verb translated as "brought to perfection" here is the Greek *teleioō*, which
can also translate as "accomplish, fulfill, finish."

John 17 is an extended prayer between Jesus and God; we read a portion of it each year on the Seventh Sunday of Easter (17:1-11a in Year A; 17:11b-19 in Year B). It is also the culmination of Jesus's teachings before his arrest, in which he extends the "new commandment" ("love one another"; 13:34) to its ultimate end: Christian unity and the mystical union of God, Christ, and church. Jesus prays, not only for those who currently believe in him, but also for all believers across time who will believe in him by their "word" (speech, action). Jesus also describes how and when the entire "world" will come to know him: when all Christians are fully unified in Christ. In other words, the church will only perform its essential mission in the world when it is fully unified, through love, in Christ. The church therefore takes the unity of God and Christ as its (our) model and principle. When the church is true to its destiny and lives into unity in love (*agapē*), it becomes the continuation of Christ as mediator and revealer of God in the world. The word "glory" repeated in this passage refers to God's divine presence.

Ponder

After Stephen's death in Acts, severe persecution broke out against the early church. Given the violence and religious schism this reading depicts, it is a fruitful text to ponder in relation to Jesus's prayer for unity in the Gospel. Allow yourself to sink into this prayer. It is radically hopeful, its vision perhaps difficult to imagine in our contemporary divided church and world. Right now, what would it look like—practically, tangibly—for the church to live into Jesus's standards, placing the goal of unity at the forefront of our lives? What would it look like for you personally to live into these standards?

This last Sunday of Easter before Pentecost, a charged expectation runs through our readings: something, *someone*, is coming to reorient our world, and we must be ready. Our readiness is dependent upon our love, here and now—our willingness to give ourselves completely, as Stephen did. In our Gospel reading, Jesus states that we are God's "gift" to him in order to make him known in this world. By living authentic lives of faith, we bear witness to and become Christ's gift. This week, ponder Jesus's statement that you are a gift to him. What does this mean to you? How does it impel you to respond in love, leaning into the promise that Christ is coming, with your help, to reorient and reconcile our world?

Pentecost Sunday[1]

FIRST READING   ACTS 2:1-11

When the time for Pentecost was fulfilled,
   they were all in one place together.
And suddenly there came from the sky
   a noise like a strong driving wind,
   and it filled the entire house in which they were.
Then there appeared to them tongues as of fire,
   which parted and came to rest on each one of them.
And they were all filled with the Holy Spirit[2]
   and began to speak in different tongues,
   as the Spirit enabled them to proclaim.

Now there were devout Jews from every nation under heaven
     staying in Jerusalem.
At this sound, they gathered in a large crowd,
   but they were confused
   because each one heard them speaking in his own language.
They were astounded, and in amazement they asked,
   "Are not all these people who are speaking Galileans?
Then how does each of us hear them in his native language?
We are Parthians, Medes, and Elamites,
   inhabitants of Mesopotamia, Judea and Cappadocia,
   Pontus and Asia, Phrygia and Pamphylia,
   Egypt and the districts of Libya near Cyrene,
   as well as travelers from Rome,
   both Jews and converts to Judaism, Cretans and Arabs,
   yet we hear them speaking in our own tongues
   of the mighty acts of God."

Pentecost (Greek for "fiftieth") occurs fifty days after Passover during the yearly barley festival (*Shavuot* in Hebrew), which celebrates the giving of the Torah on Mount Sinai. Historically, it was one of three

---

1. The readings used here are the optional readings for Year C. For the alternative readings from 1 Corinthians and John, see *Ponder: Year A.*
2. "Spirit": Greek *pneuma*—wind, breath, spirit, Spirit.

pilgrimage festivals that attracted devout Jews to Jerusalem. Yet the Jews in the above reading are "staying," or literally "residing" (from the Greek *katoikeō*) in Jerusalem, not simply visiting from afar (v. 5). The Spirit descending echoes the divine presence descending in fire in Exodus 19:16-18 to impart the commandments to Israel. It also parallels Jesus receiving the Spirit in Luke 3:21-22. The image of "tongues as of fire" is common in the Hebrew Bible (e.g., Isa 5:24), and both fire and wind symbolize divine presence (e.g., Gen 1:2; Exod 3:2; 14:24). Every known nation is listed here, foreshadowing the spread of Christianity. Unlike Paul's discussion of the incomprehensibility of those "speaking in tongues" in 1 Corinthians 14:6-19, the languages spoken here are understood by everyone: speakers from Iran (Parthians, Medes, Elamites), Turkey (Cappadocia, Pontus, Asia, Phrygia, Pamphylia), northern Africa, and Rome. In the Tower of Babel (Gen 11:1-9), God divided humans by creating different languages after they attempted to cross the divine-human boundary (the story explains the origin of diverse languages and cultures). Here, the diversity of speech is a cause not for division but for unification.

RESPONSORIAL PSALM   PSALM 104:1, 24, 29-30, 31, 34

Lord, send out your Spirit, and renew the face of the earth.
or: Alleluia.

SECOND READING   ROMANS 8:8-17 (ALT. 1 COR 12:3b-7, 12-13)

Brothers and sisters:
Those who are in the flesh cannot please God.
But you are not in the flesh;
    on the contrary, you are in the spirit,
    if only the Spirit of God dwells in you.
Whoever does not have the Spirit of Christ does not belong to him.
But if Christ is in you,
    although the body is dead because of sin,
    the spirit is alive because of righteousness.
If the Spirit of the one who raised Jesus from the dead dwells
        in you,
    the one who raised Christ from the dead

will give life to your mortal bodies also,
    through his Spirit that dwells in you.
Consequently, brothers and sisters,
    we are not debtors to the flesh,
    to live according to the flesh.
For if you live according to the flesh, you will die,
    but if by the Spirit you put to death the deeds of the body,
    you will live.

For those who are led by the Spirit of God are sons of God.
For you did not receive a spirit of slavery to fall back into fear,
    but you received a Spirit of adoption,
    through whom we cry, "Abba, Father!"
The Spirit himself bears witness with our spirit
    that we are children of God,
    and if children, then heirs,
    heirs of God and joint heirs with Christ,
    if only we suffer with him
    so that we may also be glorified with him.

Romans 8 concludes Paul's long explanation of the meaning of God's righteousness (Rom 1:18–8:39). In this explanation, Paul first indicts all humanity, stating that no one is righteous (3:9-20). Yet through Christ, God's righteousness repairs the divine-human relationship and justifies all who believe, Jews and Gentiles alike (3:21–5:21). This remarkable gift of (re)unification with God crucifies the old self and sets one free of sin, to be "slaves" not of sin but of righteousness (6:1-23). To be set free from sin is to be liberated from trying to live in accordance with the law, the highest spiritual standard that no one living in the "flesh" can successfully follow (7:1-25). For Paul, "flesh" is not the body itself, which is a "temple of the holy Spirit" (1 Cor 6:19). Rather, the "flesh" is the person controlled by passions and human weakness. In Romans 8:1-17, Paul juxtaposes living according to the "flesh" with living according to the Spirit through death and resurrection, which leads to spiritual "adoption" (Greek *hyiothesía*) as children of God. Paul uses the same expression in Romans 9:4 to describe Israel as chosen or "adopted" by God. He also draws closely from the Hebrew Bible's metaphors of Israel's adoption as God's son (e.g., Deut 14:1; Hos 11:1). According to Paul, through the Holy Spirit and the presence of Christ within, Gentiles become equal or "joint" heirs of the promises given to Abraham. Paul speaks of the dynamic relationship between believers and God when stating that the Spirit communicates intimately to believers that they are God's children, which results in them crying out to "Abba" or "Father" as an expression of joy and confidence. He also acknowledges the reality and necessity of suffering in this world in order that we may have a stake in, and hope for, the glory to come.

GOSPEL   JOHN 14:15-16, 23b-26 (ALT. JOHN 20:19-23)

Jesus said to his disciples:
  "If you love me, you will keep my commandments.
And I will ask the Father,
    and he will give you another Advocate to be with you always.

"Whoever loves me will keep my word,
    and my Father will love him,
    and we will come to him and make our dwelling with him.
Those who do not love me do not keep my words;
    yet the word you hear is not mine
    but that of the Father who sent me.

"I have told you this while I am with you.
The Advocate, the Holy Spirit whom the Father will send in
      my name,
    will teach you everything
    and remind you of all that I told you."

After Jesus tells the disciples that he is "going to the Father" (John 14:12), he challenges them to continue to guard the commandments, which are encapsulated in the commandment to love (see the Gospel notes for the Fifth through Seventh Sundays of Easter). He then promises that he will send the "Advocate" (Greek *paraklētos*) to help them. Only in John's Gospel do we find this expression for the Holy Spirit. The Greek word means literally "to call alongside" and is a term drawn from the legal world to designate one who advocates for, encourages, or stands in support of another. Several verses of our reading (vv. 23-26) coincide with the Gospel reading from the Sixth Sunday of Easter (see notes there for further context).

Ponder

No single image encapsulates the great mystery of Pentecost. The coming of the Holy Spirit is as powerful as a "strong driving wind" and "tongues as of fire," as intimate as Christ breathing into us, and as personal as our own life-giving breath. The Spirit advocates for and walks alongside each of us, manifesting through the diversity of our languages, cultures, and gifts. To walk with the Spirit is to walk the path of unification in the oneness of Christ through our diversity. This path is not easy or simple, as Paul reminds us. It is the path of love—love that is not a passing feeling but love-in-action. It is a love that invites us to embrace the possibility of suffering. It is a love that can be countercultural in advocating for each human being—indeed all of life and creation—while calling each of us to the highest standards of life in Christ. May we be open to walking this path, each of us in our individual way, that we may allow the Spirit to act for us and through us to heal our broken and divided world.

What began with ashes ends with fire. Today marks the end of a cycle that begins with death (Good Friday) leading to new life (Easter) and letting go (Ascension) in order to receive and live into the new (Pentecost). The disciples would not have been able to live into their new reality without letting go of what they knew before. This process of letting go to live into the new is Pentecost. It is an ongoing, mysterious process that we are also called to live into daily. You are already a new creation. Yet what do you need to let go of—or embrace—in order to live fully into this reality?

The Most Holy Trinity

FIRST READING   PROVERBS 8:22-31

Thus says the wisdom of God:
"The LORD possessed me, the beginning of his ways,
    the forerunner of his prodigies of long ago;
from of old I was poured forth,
    at the first, before the earth.
When there were no depths I was brought forth,
    when there were no fountains or springs of water;
before the mountains were settled into place,
    before the hills, I was brought forth;
while as yet the earth and fields were not made,
    nor the first clods of the world.

"When the Lord established the heavens I was there,
    when he marked out the vault over the face of the deep;
when he made firm the skies above,
    when he fixed fast the foundations of the earth;
when he set for the sea its limit,
    so that the waters should not transgress his command;
then was I beside him as his craftsman,
    and I was his delight day by day,
playing before him all the while,
    playing on the surface of his earth;
    and I found delight in the human race."

In the Hebrew Bible, wisdom is not about book knowledge or intelligence but about knowledge or understanding of God. Such knowledge is rooted in awe and reverence toward God, which is encapsulated in the Hebrew term "fear" (*yir'â*; see Prov 1:7). In Proverbs 1–9, this wisdom is embodied or personified by a woman ("Lady Wisdom"), who entices one to follow her path that leads to God and life. The language used here to describe wisdom may remind us of God's questioning of Job, "Where were you when I founded the earth? / Tell me, if you have understanding" (Job 38:4). In Job, God's questions are meant to remind Job of his limited comprehension as a human. In contrast, Wisdom in Proverbs promises to guide humans into all understanding. Elsewhere in the Hebrew Bible, wisdom is associated with the Torah, the essence of God's "teaching" or law revealed to Israel (Sir 24). In Christianity, wisdom becomes associated with Christ, as we see in the first verses of John's Gospel, where the notion of "Wisdom" is identified with "the Word" ("In the beginning was the Word, / and the Word was with God . . ."). The Holy Spirit is similarly linked with divine Wisdom, as we see in today's Gospel. Jesus says to his disciples and so to us, "I have much more to tell you, but you cannot bear it now. But when he comes, the Spirit of truth, he will guide you to all truth."

RESPONSORIAL PSALM   PSALM 8:4-5, 6-7, 8-9

O Lord, our God, how wonderful your name in all the earth!

SECOND READING   ROMANS 5:1-5

Brothers and sisters:
Therefore, since we have been justified by faith,
    we have peace with God through our Lord Jesus Christ,
    through whom we have gained access by faith
    to this grace in which we stand,
    and we boast in hope of the glory of God.
Not only that, but we even boast of our afflictions,
    knowing that affliction produces endurance,
    and endurance, proven character,
    and proven character, hope,
    and hope does not disappoint,
    because the love of God has been poured out into our hearts
    through the Holy Spirit that has been given to us.

In today's reading from Romans, "justification" is the reparation ("repair" or reconciliation) of the divine-human relationship that makes all people righteous before God through faith. Such justification stems from God's righteousness as manifest in Christ, through whom believers gain access to God. According to Jewish tradition,

God's "glory" or divine presence was taken from Adam after his sin; here, Paul states that future salvation will restore it (see also Rom 3:23). To "boast" is not to boast in one's own works but rather in God's power. Paul consoles and strengthens the suffering community, reminding them that God is their source of unending hope through the promise of resurrection and through the divine love that is "poured" into them through the Holy Spirit. For additional commentary on the book of Romans, see notes for Pentecost Sunday.

GOSPEL   JOHN 16:12-15

Jesus said to his disciples:
   "I have much more to tell you, but you cannot bear it now.
But when he comes, the Spirit of truth,
   he will guide you to all truth.
He will not speak on his own,
   but he will speak what he hears,
   and will declare to you the things that are coming.
He will glorify me,
   because he will take from what is mine and declare it to you.
Everything that the Father has is mine;
   for this reason I told you that he will take from what is mine
   and declare it to you."

Throughout the Easter season, we read through Jesus's final discourse to his disciples (John 13–17). On Pentecost Sunday, we read from John 14, in which Jesus explains his continued union with the disciples after his death through the "Advocate" or "helper" (Greek *paraklētos*; the Holy Spirit). Jesus promises that this Spirit will teach the disciples "everything" (14:26). In today's reading, Jesus refers to the Holy Spirit as the "Spirit of truth" who will guide the disciples into all understanding and will work through the disciples to continue Christ's witness in the world. Jesus emphasizes the unity of the Father, Son, and Spirit, as well as the truth and wisdom that will come when the Spirit leads the disciples into "all truth." When Jesus states that the Spirit "will glorify me," this glorification will be manifest through the Body of Christ: the church.

Ponder

In our first reading, Wisdom has its beginning in God and is God's companion. God delights in Wisdom. Yet Wisdom delights not in God but in humans! The mystery of this dynamic relationship of "delight" between God, Wisdom, and humanity is reflected in the Trinity. Far from an abstract concept, the Trinity is about relationship with and in the divine. God has extended the divine relationship to us and, through us, into the world. Our own care for creation is a reflection of this partnership we have with God (see today's psalm). Through God's grace and presence, we can and will transform our world. What sense do you have of the Trinity working through you in this way, calling you into relationship, calling you to care for what God has made?

"I have much more to tell you, but you cannot bear it now," Jesus tells his disciples. In some ways, we are like the disciples, having walked with Jesus through the mysteries of death and resurrection, ascension and Pentecost. As we move into Ordinary Time, we celebrate two transitional Sundays: Trinity Sunday and Corpus Christi. These Sundays invite us to reflect on where we go from here and how we continue to grow into this great gift of union and participation with God. Jesus tells us that the way forward will slowly become clear if we orient ourselves toward the Holy Spirit. The Spirit will slowly guide us into what we do not yet see or understand: complete knowledge of the mysteries of God. All we must do is remain attentive and open, praying for the grace to cultivate and guard the essential call to become active participants in God's love.

The Most Holy Body and Blood of Christ (Corpus Christi)

In those days, Melchizedek, king of Salem, brought out bread
    and wine,
and being a priest of God Most High,
he blessed Abram with these words:
"Blessed be Abram by God Most High,
the creator of heaven and earth;
and blessed be God Most High,
who delivered your foes into your hand."
Then Abram gave him a tenth of everything.

This story contains one of only two references in the Hebrew Bible to Melchizedek, king and priest of Salem (which was later renamed Jerusalem). Melchizedek means "my king is righteous," and he appears in the story without context or lineage. Yet he is clearly important, as demonstrated by his name and memory in biblical tradition. In the story, Abram (later renamed Abraham) rescues his nephew Lot from the kings of Sodom and Gomorrah. Melchizedek then blesses Abram by *El Elyon* (God Most High), the Canaanite god who was worshiped in pre- and early Israelite times. Eventually, the name *El Elyon* was subsumed into the name of the God of Israel, who is also called "God Most High." This blessing creates a link between the line of Abraham and Jerusalem. Melchizedek's offering of bread and wine and Abram's return offering create a solemn alliance between the two parties and legitimate the later tithing of ten percent to Jerusalem's priests. Psalm 110:4 honors Melchizedek by suggesting that the royal Davidic line in Jerusalem is linked forever to this righteous king and priest (see today's psalm). Early Christian theology views this priesthood as fulfilled in Christ as the eternal mediator between God and humanity through his sacrifice, his body and blood (see Heb 7), symbolism that carries into eucharistic theology.

RESPONSORIAL PSALM   PSALM 110:1, 2, 3, 4

You are a priest forever, in the line of Melchizedek.

SECOND READING   1 CORINTHIANS 11:23-26

Brothers and sisters:
I received from the Lord what I also handed on to you,
    that the Lord Jesus, on the night he was handed over,
    took bread, and, after he had given thanks,
    broke it and said, "This is my body that is for you.
Do this in remembrance of me."
In the same way also the cup, after supper, saying,
    "This cup is the new covenant in my blood.
Do this, as often as you drink it, in remembrance of me."
For as often as you eat this bread and drink the cup,
    you proclaim the death of the Lord until he comes.

This is the earliest written description of Jesus's Last Supper (Gospel accounts of the meal were written later). In the broader context of 1 Corinthians 11, Paul expresses concern over divisions in the community between the "haves" and the "have-nots." This division was particularly clear at the community's celebrations of the Lord's Supper, the very place where the Corinthians should have been most capable of understanding the unity of the Body of Christ. First, Paul notes that there are factions among the community when they gather together as a church (11:17-19). He tells them that when they come together, "it is not really to eat the Lord's supper" (11:20; NRSV). Rather, when the time comes to share the Body and Blood of Christ, each one goes ahead with their own meal, "and one goes hungry while another gets drunk" (11:21). Paul's description of the meals also serves as a historical reminder that in the early Christian community, the community gathered for an actual meal to recreate Jesus's Last Supper. Yet some had little food with which to partake of the meal, while others became drunk from their abundance. Paul then reminds the community why they are gathered, using the words that we recognize as the eucharistic words of institution. Note that the bread is broken before the meal but the cup is consecrated after the meal (traditionally, this is the third of four cups in the Passover

Seder). What follows in 11:27-28 is a key aspect of Paul's teaching on the Eucharist, even though it is not included in Sunday's reading. In these verses, Paul reminds the community that the Body and Blood of Christ are not to be consumed without prior self-examination of one's heart and actions.

GOSPEL   LUKE 9:11b-17

Jesus spoke to the crowds about the kingdom of God,
   and he healed those who needed to be cured.
As the day was drawing to a close,
   the Twelve approached him and said,
   "Dismiss the crowd
   so that they can go to the surrounding villages and farms
   and find lodging and provisions;
   for we are in a deserted place here."
He said to them, "Give them some food yourselves."
They replied, "Five loaves and two fish are all we have,
   unless we ourselves go and buy food for all these people."
Now the men there numbered about five thousand.
Then he said to his disciples,
   "Have them sit down in groups of about fifty."
They did so and made them all sit down.
Then taking the five loaves and the two fish,
   and looking up to heaven,
   he said the blessing over them, broke them,
   and gave them to the disciples to set before the crowd.
They all ate and were satisfied.
And when the leftover fragments were picked up,
   they filled twelve wicker baskets.

This account is one of but a few stories from Jesus's ministry that is attested in all four Gospels. His blessing over the food anticipates the Last Supper, yet the story also points to a deeper lesson about unity in the Christian community (literally, the unity of the Body of Christ). Like Paul's discussion in our second reading, Jesus is showing his disciples and the people what this unity means: an orientation toward communal responsibility and the common good. When one goes hungry, the community is divided. The disciples may have been well-meaning in their suggestion that the people be dismissed to find food and lodging, but Jesus takes the opportunity to feed them himself, thereby making a radical statement about the nature of our responsibility in caring for others. Later, at the Last Supper, Jesus will acknowledge that his life is not his own—it is given to him by God to be poured out for others. Here he reminds the disciples that their lives are similarly to be given in service of others.

Ponder

Our readings today deal less with abstract ideas about the Eucharist and more with the practical reality of how the Eucharist is related to caring for others. In the Gospel, before Jesus fed the people, he taught and healed. The disciples then tried to dismiss the crowds because there was not enough food. Yet Jesus reminded them that it was not enough to provide for people spiritually. They needed physical nourishment. In today's world, countless people lack sufficient resources. Jesus reminds us that we, like the disciples, are not to turn our backs on others, thinking the problems are too great or the resources too scarce. As a eucharistic people, we are called to greater hope, imagination, and resourcefulness in providing nourishment for others. What small steps might you take to follow this call more fully?

In the ancient world, the common meal of bread and wine created covenants and bound people together through the hospitality of shared meals. This "binding" is also at the heart of the Eucharist. In the words of institution, Jesus tells us that his life is not his own—it is given to him by God, to be poured out for others. To "remember" this reality is not simply to call it to mind but to make it present, and to "do this" is to follow Jesus's whole manner of life and being. The Eucharist is a powerful reminder that our lives—our whole selves—are gifts from God, to be poured out for others. How do you allow Christ to be present in you, to live out this truth, day to day?

Second Sunday in Ordinary Time

FIRST READING   ISAIAH 62:1-5

For Zion's sake I will not be silent,
    for Jerusalem's sake I will not be quiet,
until her vindication[1] shines forth like the dawn
    and her victory[2] like a burning torch.

Nations shall behold your vindication,
    and all the kings your glory;
you shall be called by a new name
    pronounced by the mouth of the LORD.
You shall be a glorious crown in the hand of the LORD,
    a royal diadem held by your God.
No more shall people call you "Forsaken,"
    or your land "Desolate,"
but you shall be called "My Delight,"
    and your land "Espoused."
For the LORD delights in you
    and makes your land his spouse.
As a young man marries a virgin,
    your Builder shall marry you;
and as a bridegroom rejoices in his bride
    so shall your God rejoice in you.

Our reading comes from the last portion of the book of Isaiah ("Third Isaiah"; see notes for The Epiphany of the Lord). The setting is Judah in a postexilic context, after 536 BCE. The focus is renewal and hope with a twofold focus: God's love for Jerusalem, and the inclusion of all people into the divine covenant with Israel. Our passage lies at the center of this message of hope. The prophet speaks on behalf of God to prophesy Jerusalem's renewal, a time when the Holy City will become the physical manifestation of God's glory. In the passage, Jerusalem is a city as well as a people in whom God will delight.

---

1. "Vindication" translates more literally as "righteousness" (Hebrew ṣedek).
2. "Victory" translates more literally as "salvation" (Hebrew yĕšuʿâ).

The relationship and love between God and Jerusalem is expressed as a marriage. In our English translations, we miss the sound play in Hebrew between the terms "forsaken" (*ʿăzûbâ*) and "my delight" (*ḥefṣî-bâ*), "desolate" (*šěmāmâ*) and "espoused" (*běʿûlâ*).

RESPONSORIAL PSALM   PSALM 96:1-2, 2-3, 7-8, 9-10

Proclaim his marvelous deeds to all the nations.

SECOND READING   1 CORINTHIANS 12:4-11

Brothers and sisters:
There are different kinds of spiritual gifts but the same Spirit;
    there are different forms of service but the same Lord;
    there are different workings but the same God
    who produces all of them in everyone.
To each individual the manifestation of the Spirit
    is given for some benefit.
To one is given through the Spirit the expression of wisdom;
    to another, the expression of knowledge according to the
        same Spirit;
    to another, faith by the same Spirit;
    to another, gifts of healing by the one Spirit;
    to another, mighty deeds;
    to another, prophecy;
    to another, discernment of spirits;
    to another, varieties of tongues;
    to another, interpretation of tongues.
But one and the same Spirit produces all of these,
    distributing them individually to each person as he wishes.

As we enter into Ordinary Time, we begin a semi-continuous reading through 1 Corinthians 12–15. In today's reading, Paul contextualizes the gift of glossolalia (speaking in tongues) within the different and varying gifts that together create unity within the Christian community. Paul orders the nine named gifts from the greatest (wisdom) to the least (tongues): wisdom, knowledge, faith, healing, mighty deeds, prophecy, discernment of spirits, tongues and their interpretation.

The Spirit distributes these gifts through God's power and according to God's desire, so it would be ridiculous for any person to boast of the gifts they have received by God's grace. These gifts have their beginning and their completion in God, and their purpose is service to God through the common good.

GOSPEL   JOHN 2:1-11

There was a wedding at Cana in Galilee,
   and the mother of Jesus was there.
Jesus and his disciples were also invited to the wedding.
When the wine ran short,
   the mother of Jesus said to him,
   "They have no wine."
And Jesus said to her,
   "Woman, how does your concern affect me?
My hour has not yet come."
His mother said to the servers,
   "Do whatever he tells you."
Now there were six stone water jars there for Jewish
    ceremonial washings,
   each holding twenty to thirty gallons.
Jesus told them,
   "Fill the jars with water."
So they filled them to the brim.
Then he told them,
   "Draw some out now and take it to the headwaiter."
So they took it.
And when the headwaiter tasted the water that had become wine,
   without knowing where it came from
   —although the servers who had drawn the water knew—,
   the headwaiter called the bridegroom and said to him,
   "Everyone serves good wine first,
   and then when people have drunk freely, an inferior one;
   but you have kept the good wine until now."
Jesus did this as the beginning of his signs at Cana in Galilee
   and so revealed his glory,
   and his disciples began to believe in him.

Next week we will return to the Gospel of Luke, but this week we make a brief sojourn into John's Gospel. Jesus and his mother (Mary is never named in this Gospel) are at a wedding in which a family's honor is at stake. The festivities may also have taxed their resources (not unlike today's weddings!). Mary challenges Jesus with a request, and at first it seems that he does not wish to respond. He calls her "woman," a name that some would argue conveys disrespect and downplays their blood ties. When Jesus tells her that his "hour has not come," he reveals for the first time who he is. Although his time is "not yet," it is nevertheless anticipated. Despite his enigmatic response, Mary demonstrates remarkable insight into Jesus's identity by telling the servers to do "whatever he tells" them. Strangely (considering his previous rebuke), her statement prompts Jesus to act, and the quantity of water-turned-wine is excessive to the extreme. This passage is the first of Jesus's "signs" in John's Gospel that reveal "his glory" and elicit faith.

Ponder

In Isaiah, God "marries" Jerusalem, "delights" in Jerusalem, and reveals Jerusalem's "glory." In our Gospel reading, a wedding becomes the occasion for the Gospel's first sign of Jesus's divinity. This week as we return to Ordinary Time, our readings invite us to ponder the wedding imagery of celebration and rejoicing. They also encourage us to extend our imagination to consider how God delights in us and invites us into a marriage or covenant relationship. How do you respond to this invitation?

There is something important about this first sign of Jesus's divinity in John's Gospel. On one level, the story demonstrates Jesus's response to a need, though the need may seem fairly inconsequential. At a deeper level, the story contains themes that weave through all the signs in John's Gospel: transformation from one element to another (i.e., water to wine) or from one way of being to another, divine love that permeates and embraces human life, divisions between those who can read signs and those who cannot, the reversal of expectations, and the promise of great celebration. Of course, the ultimate sign is Jesus himself, the true bridegroom. As you pray with the Gospel, which theme resonates with you the most?

Third Sunday in Ordinary Time
(Sunday of the Word of God)

FIRST READING NEHEMIAH 8:2-4a, 5-6, 8-10

Ezra the priest brought the law before the assembly,
   which consisted of men, women,
   and those children old enough to understand.
Standing at one end of the open place that was before the
    Water Gate,
   he read out of the book from daybreak till midday,
   in the presence of the men, the women,
   and those children old enough to understand;
   and all the people listened attentively to the book of the law.
Ezra the scribe stood on a wooden platform
   that had been made for the occasion.
He opened the scroll
   so that all the people might see it
   —for he was standing higher up than any of the people—;
   and, as he opened it, all the people rose.
Ezra blessed the LORD, the great God,
   and all the people, their hands raised high, answered,
   "Amen, amen!"
Then they bowed down and prostrated themselves before
    the LORD,
   their faces to the ground.
Ezra read plainly from the book of the law of God,
   interpreting it so that all could understand what was read.
Then Nehemiah, that is, His Excellency, and Ezra the priest-scribe
   and the Levites who were instructing the people
   said to all the people:
   "Today is holy to the LORD your God.
Do not be sad, and do not weep"—
   for all the people were weeping as they heard the words of
    the law.
He said further: "Go, eat rich foods and drink sweet drinks,
   and allot portions to those who had nothing prepared;
   for today is holy to our LORD.

Do not be saddened this day,
    for rejoicing in the LORD must be your strength!"

The book of Nehemiah is a postexilic text, meaning that it focuses on the Judeans' return to Judah after the Babylonian exile (ca. 586–536 BCE) and the restoration of the community in Judah. This restoration includes the rebuilding of the temple and the transformation of the liturgical traditions. Our reading describes the first public reading of the "law" or Torah in this returned community. This public reading begins a new liturgical practice that has echoes in Jewish and Christian liturgical traditions today in its focus on Scripture readings over sacrifices. In this orientation toward the Scriptures, God's presence can be experienced in local congregations or assemblies rather than in rituals that must be performed in a single Jerusalem temple. In this reading, when the people hear the Torah read aloud, they weep. Perhaps they are overwhelmed by the moment, or perhaps they find the content of the readings overwhelming (or even indicting).

RESPONSORIAL PSALM   PSALM 19:8, 9, 10, 15

Your words, Lord, are Spirit and life.

SECOND READING   1 CORINTHIANS 12:12-30 [OR 12:12-14, 27]

Brothers and sisters:
As a body is one though it has many parts,
    and all the parts of the body, though many, are one body,
    so also Christ.
For in one Spirit we were all baptized into one body,
    whether Jews or Greeks, slaves or free persons,
    and we were all given to drink of one Spirit.

Now the body is not a single part, but many.
If a foot should say,
    "Because I am not a hand I do not belong to the body,"
    it does not for this reason belong any less to the body.
Or if an ear should say,
    "Because I am not an eye I do not belong to the body,"
    it does not for this reason belong any less to the body.

If the whole body were an eye, where would the hearing be?
If the whole body were hearing, where would the sense of
    smell be?
But as it is, God placed the parts,
    each one of them, in the body as he intended.
If they were all one part, where would the body be?
But as it is, there are many parts, yet one body.
The eye cannot say to the hand, "I do not need you,"
    nor again the head to the feet, "I do not need you."
Indeed, the parts of the body that seem to be weaker
    are all the more necessary,
    and those parts of the body that we consider less honorable
    we surround with greater honor,
    and our less presentable parts are treated with greater propriety,
    whereas our more presentable parts do not need this.
But God has so constructed the body
    as to give greater honor to a part that is without it,
    so that there may be no division in the body,
    but that the parts may have the same concern for one another.
If one part suffers, all the parts suffer with it;
    if one part is honored, all the parts share its joy.

Now you are Christ's body, and individually parts of it.
Some people God has designated in the church
    to be, first, apostles; second, prophets; third, teachers;
    then, mighty deeds;
    then gifts of healing, assistance, administration,
    and varieties of tongues.
Are all apostles? Are all prophets? Are all teachers?
Do all work mighty deeds? Do all have gifts of healing?
Do all speak in tongues? Do all interpret?

As we continue from last Sunday's reading, Paul reverses conventional standards of honor and privilege. He uses a common Greco-Roman metaphor that likens politics to a body, in which the greatest honor is given to the head and the belly (metaphors for the ruling class). Similarly, Paul compares the early church community to a body, but he flips the common metaphor to emphasize support and commonality over hierarchy. He reorients the status quo to make a shocking claim: not only are the weaker parts the most important, but

God has arranged the body paradoxically, to give greater importance to those parts that seem of lesser value. Paul's point is that the body's diverse gifts are a divine creation, so no one should desire others' gifts or create a hierarchy of certain gifts over others.

GOSPEL   LUKE 1:1-4; 4:14-21

Since many have undertaken to compile a narrative of the events
    that have been fulfilled among us,
        just as those who were eyewitnesses from the beginning
        and ministers of the word have handed them down to us,
    I too have decided,
        after investigating everything accurately anew,
        to write it down in an orderly sequence for you,
        most excellent Theophilus,
        so that you may realize the certainty of the teachings
        you have received.

Jesus returned to Galilee in the power of the Spirit,
    and news of him spread throughout the whole region.
He taught in their synagogues and was praised by all.

He came to Nazareth, where he had grown up,
    and went according to his custom
    into the synagogue on the sabbath day.
He stood up to read and was handed a scroll of the
        prophet Isaiah.
He unrolled the scroll and found the passage where it
        was written:
    The Spirit of the Lord is upon me,
        because he has anointed me
        to bring glad tidings to the poor.
    He has sent me to proclaim liberty to captives
        and recovery of sight to the blind,
        to let the oppressed go free,
        and to proclaim a year acceptable to the Lord.
Rolling up the scroll, he handed it back to the attendant and
        sat down,
    and the eyes of all in the synagogue looked intently at him.
He said to them,
    "Today this Scripture passage is fulfilled in your hearing."

This Sunday we begin our journey through the Gospel of Luke with the prologue. Theophilus (which means "friend of God") was perhaps Luke's patron. He appears again in the introduction to the book of Acts (1:1). We then skip over the infancy and childhood of Jesus (Luke 1–2) as well as the ministry of John the Baptist and the genealogy of Jesus (Luke 3) to the beginning of Jesus's ministry in Nazareth in Luke 4. Jesus is handed the scroll of Isaiah in the temple and reads from it. He declares that the prophecy has been fulfilled in him as the people watch him intently. We will find out how they respond to his declaration in next Sunday's Gospel reading. Luke has placed this incident at the beginning of Jesus's ministry, whereas the other Synoptic Gospels place it much later (see Matt 13:53-58 and Mark 6:1-6).

Ponder

Nehemiah describes the people's powerful liturgical experience upon returning to their homeland after the exile. The people weep as they hear Scripture, a powerful image to ponder on this Sunday of the Word of God. In the Gospel, perhaps hearing Jesus read from Isaiah provoked a similar feeling among the people gathered in the temple. As you pray with the readings this week, recall a time when you have experienced strong emotions when hearing or reading Scripture. Allow the memory of this experience to open you to God's presence and love.

According to Jesus's reading from Isaiah in the Gospel, divine favor is not a title of privilege but a call to transformative action. Similarly, Paul upends common ideas about privilege and power in 1 Corinthians. All of our readings remind us that we are small but important parts of something greater than ourselves. As people of faith, our reality is not one of competition and hierarchy but of mutuality and care for the common good. This week, consider how you respond to this promise and this call to be an equal and transformative member of the Body of Christ.

Fourth Sunday in Ordinary Time

FIRST READING JEREMIAH 1:4-5, 17-19

The word of the LORD came to me, saying:
Before I formed you in the womb I knew you,
before you were born I dedicated you,
a prophet to the nations I appointed you.

But do you gird your loins;
stand up and tell them
all that I command you.
Be not crushed on their account,
as though I would leave you crushed before them;
for it is I this day
who have made you a fortified city,
a pillar of iron, a wall of brass,
against the whole land:
against Judah's kings and princes,
against its priests and people.
They will fight against you but not prevail over you,
for I am with you to deliver you, says the LORD.

Jeremiah lived during Judah's downfall (sixth century BCE) and prophesied the coming exile to Babylon (586–536 BCE). Our reading comes from Jeremiah's prophetic call. In the first two verses (vv. 4-5), the divine word comes to Jeremiah, stating that God had formed Jeremiah in the womb as a potter forms clay and had set him aside (literally "dedicated" him) for service to God. We then skip to verse 17, where God commands Jeremiah to "gird [his] loins" before speaking to the people, as if in preparation for battle. Through his prophecies, Jeremiah will manifest God's strength against the "whole land" or leadership of Judah. Jeremiah's call tells us three things about Jeremiah: he is created by God and predestined to prophesy, he shares an intimate relationship with God, and this intimacy will not save him from suffering and persecution. More than any other prophet in the Hebrew Bible, we get to know Jeremiah as an individual, in particular his complicated relationship with God and his painful experiences as a prophet.

I will sing of your salvation.

SECOND READING   1 CORINTHIANS 12:31–13:13 [OR 13:4-13]

Brothers and sisters:
Strive eagerly for the greatest spiritual gifts.
But I shall show you a still more excellent way.

If I speak in human and angelic tongues,
    but do not have love,[1]
    I am a resounding gong or a clashing cymbal.
And if I have the gift of prophecy,
    and comprehend all mysteries and all knowledge;
    if I have all faith so as to move mountains,
    but do not have love, I am nothing.
If I give away everything I own,
    and if I hand my body over so that I may boast,
    but do not have love, I gain nothing.

Love is patient, love is kind.
It is not jealous, it is not pompous,
    it is not inflated, it is not rude,
    it does not seek its own interests,
    it is not quick-tempered, it does not brood over injury,
    it does not rejoice over wrongdoing
    but rejoices with the truth.
It bears all things, believes all things,
    hopes all things, endures all things.

Love never fails.
If there are prophecies, they will be brought to nothing;
    if tongues, they will cease;
    if knowledge, it will be brought to nothing.

---

1. Greek *agapē*: a love that pours itself out for others, the love with which God loves us.

For we know partially and we prophesy partially,
   but when the perfect comes, the partial will pass away.
When I was a child, I used to talk as a child,
   think as a child, reason as a child;
   when I became a man, I put aside childish things.
At present we see indistinctly, as in a mirror,
   but then face to face.
At present I know partially;
   then I shall know fully, as I am fully known.
So faith, hope, love remain, these three;
   but the greatest of these is love.

Following Paul's discussion of spiritual gifts in chapter 12, he moves to the "more excellent" way, the path that exceeds all others: love. According to Paul, all spiritual gifts have their limitations and the potential to create divisions. The Corinthian community has over-emphasized the acquisition of spiritual gifts to the detriment of love, the greatest gift of all and the one that "builds up" the community (see 1 Cor 8). Paul emphasizes the enduring and universal power of love and carefully describes its attributes. Although this passage is often used in marriage ceremonies, the love that Paul speaks of is not marriage specific but is an all-encompassing love that pours itself out selflessly for others without discrimination. Finally, Paul compares our imperfect knowledge and understanding of God with the fullness of understanding in the world to come.

GOSPEL   LUKE 4:21-30

Jesus began speaking in the synagogue, saying:
   "Today this Scripture passage is fulfilled in your hearing."
And all spoke highly of him
   and were amazed at the gracious words that came from
      his mouth.
They also asked, "Isn't this the son of Joseph?"
He said to them, "Surely you will quote me this proverb,
   'Physician, cure yourself,' and say,
   'Do here in your native place
      the things that we heard were done in Capernaum.' "

And he said, "Amen, I say to you,
  no prophet is accepted in his own native place.
Indeed, I tell you,
  there were many widows in Israel in the days of Elijah
  when the sky was closed for three and a half years
  and a severe famine spread over the entire land.
It was to none of these that Elijah was sent,
  but only to a widow in Zarephath in the land of Sidon.
Again, there were many lepers in Israel
  during the time of Elisha the prophet;
  yet not one of them was cleansed, but only Naaman
    the Syrian."
When the people in the synagogue heard this,
  they were all filled with fury.
They rose up, drove him out of the town,
  and led him to the brow of the hill
  on which their town had been built,
  to hurl him down headlong.
But Jesus passed through the midst of them and went away.

This week's Gospel begins with a repetition of the final verse from last week (4:21) in which Jesus states that he is the fulfillment of Isaiah's prophecy. Such a statement would have shocked an ancient audience (and hopefully shocks us as well!). Luke then describes the people's astonishment and admiration at Jesus's teachings. The verb tense suggests that this admiration continues for some unknown period of time, during which Jesus speaks "gracious" words that reveal and exude his prophetic authority. Suddenly, there is an abrupt change of attitude. Luke's placement of this synagogue account does not make sense, for it takes place too early in Jesus's ministry. Note that Jesus has not yet been to Capernaum (see Luke 4:31), and here he derides the people for actions (their lack of acceptance) that they have yet to take. In both Matthew's (13:54-58) and Mark's (6:1-6) versions, this account takes place after people fail to accept Jesus in his hometown. In their accounts, the people merely "[take] offense" at Jesus, and Jesus is "amazed at their lack of faith." In Luke's version, the people's response is intensified. Jesus reminds the people of stories in the books of Kings in which prophets demonstrate God's power to foreigners. These stories provoke the people but are in keeping with Luke's overall perspective throughout Luke-Acts: Jesus's mission is a universal one, for Jews and Gentiles alike. The last few verses are written in a similar style as the rejection of Stephen and Paul in Acts (7:58; 13:50), offering an example of the continuity between the ministry of Jesus and the future ministries of his apostles.

Ponder

Our readings from Jeremiah and 1 Corinthians describe the dynamic between God's love for us and our ability to love in return. Through our experience of God's unconditional love, we are called to love others with the same selfless, enduring love. In our first reading, God loves Jeremiah, creating him in the womb and consecrating him before birth to speak God's word to the people. In our second reading, Paul carefully articulates the qualities and manifestations of this love: it is not a fairytale love or a question of simple feeling but of hard work, as both Paul and Jeremiah demonstrate. As you ponder our readings this week, consider praying for a deepening understanding of and commitment to love.

In the Gospel, the people turn quickly from admiration and wonder to fury when Jesus speaks to them bluntly (perhaps too bluntly!). It is a strange scene in the Gospel, one that is out of place in the arc of Jesus's ministry. The fury of the people is unmatched in Mark's or Matthew's similar accounts. Imagine the Gospel scene—what Jesus looks and acts like, how he speaks, what he desires from the people. What might have shifted the tone so quickly and dramatically? Finally, imagine that Jesus is speaking to you. What is his message, and what kind of response does he hope to inspire in you?

Fifth Sunday in Ordinary Time

FIRST READING   ISAIAH 6:1-2a, 3-8

In the year King Uzziah died,
   I saw the Lord seated on a high and lofty throne,
   with the train of his garment filling the temple.
Seraphim were stationed above.

They cried one to the other,
   "Holy, holy, holy is the LORD of hosts!
All the earth is filled with his glory!"
At the sound of that cry, the frame of the door shook
   and the house was filled with smoke.

Then I said, "Woe is me, I am doomed!
For I am a man of unclean lips,
   living among a people of unclean lips;
   yet my eyes have seen the King, the LORD of hosts!"
Then one of the seraphim flew to me,
   holding an ember that he had taken with tongs from the altar.

He touched my mouth with it, and said,
   "See, now that this has touched your lips,
   your wickedness is removed, your sin purged."

Then I heard the voice of the Lord saying,
   "Whom shall I send? Who will go for us?"
"Here I am," I said; "send me!"

In our reading, the prophet Isaiah experiences a vision of God enthroned in the temple's holy of holies, the innermost room containing the ark of the covenant that was considered to be God's dwelling place. The seraphs (literally "fiery beings") are God's attendants, and the hymn they sing is well-known in current Catholic and Jewish liturgy. Isaiah recognizes that he is not pure enough to stand before God, so he first goes through a ritual of mouth cleansing with a hot coal. Such rituals were common among priests in ancient Mesopotamia before they could speak on behalf of their gods. When God asks Isaiah, "Who will go for us?" the plural form likely refers to the entire divine assembly (including the seraphim in attendance). Isaiah is instantly willing. This reading is therefore known as Isaiah's call narrative. He prophesied around 742–733 BCE.

RESPONSORIAL PSALM   PSALM 138:1-2, 2-3, 4-5, 7-8

In the sight of the angels I will sing your praises, Lord.

SECOND READING   1 CORINTHIANS 15:1-11 [OR 15:3-8, 11]

I am reminding you, brothers and sisters,
    of the gospel I preached to you,
    which you indeed received and in which you also stand.
Through it you are also being saved,
    if you hold fast to the word I preached to you,
    unless you believed in vain.
For I handed on to you as of first importance what I also received:
    that Christ died for our sins
    in accordance with the Scriptures;
    that he was buried;
    that he was raised on the third day
    in accordance with the Scriptures;
    that he appeared to Cephas, then to the Twelve.
After that, he appeared to more
    than five hundred brothers at once,
    most of whom are still living,
    though some have fallen asleep.
After that he appeared to James,
    then to all the apostles.
Last of all, as to one born abnormally,
    he appeared to me.
For I am the least of the apostles,
    not fit to be called an apostle,
    because I persecuted the church of God.
But by the grace of God I am what I am,
    and his grace to me has not been ineffective.
Indeed, I have toiled harder than all of them;
    not I, however, but the grace of God that is with me.
Therefore, whether it be I or they,
    so we preach and so you believed.

This week, we jump forward from 1 Corinthians 12 to 15, where Paul develops an argument for the resurrection of the dead. Following a common Greco-Roman belief that the soul separated from the body after death, some of the Corinthian community claimed there was no physical resurrection. Paul reminds them that faith in physical resurrection is essential for believers in Christ. He quotes from an early Christian creed (see Rom 4:24-25; 10:9-10) and provides a list of witnesses to Christ's resurrection that concludes with himself. The phrase "one born abnormally" (or "one untimely born"; NRSV) refers to stillborn births. Paul uses the expression to demonstrate his lowly status because of his previous hostility to Christ's message. Like Isaiah in the first reading, Paul recognizes his unworthiness as an apostle, yet he is utterly willing to be a witness through God's grace.

GOSPEL   LUKE 5:1-11

> While the crowd was pressing in on Jesus and listening to the
>   word of God,
>   he was standing by the Lake of Gennesaret.
> He saw two boats there alongside the lake;
>   the fishermen had disembarked and were washing their nets.
> Getting into one of the boats, the one belonging to Simon,
>   he asked him to put out a short distance from the shore.
> Then he sat down and taught the crowds from the boat.
> After he had finished speaking, he said to Simon,
>   "Put out into deep water and lower your nets for a catch."
> Simon said in reply,
>   "Master, we have worked hard all night and have
>   caught nothing,
>   but at your command I will lower the nets."
> When they had done this, they caught a great number of fish
>   and their nets were tearing.
> They signaled to their partners in the other boat
>   to come to help them.
> They came and filled both boats
>   so that the boats were in danger of sinking.
> When Simon Peter saw this, he fell at the knees of Jesus and said,
>   "Depart from me, Lord, for I am a sinful man."

For astonishment at the catch of fish they had made seized him
  and all those with him,
  and likewise James and John, the sons of Zebedee,
  who were partners of Simon.
Jesus said to Simon, "Do not be afraid;
  from now on you will be catching men."
When they brought their boats to the shore,
  they left everything and followed him.

After Jesus leaves the temple in Nazareth, he goes to Capernaum in Galilee to teach and heal. By the end of Luke 4, throngs of people are following Jesus throughout Galilee. It is in this context that we hear the call story of Jesus's first disciples. Luke's version of this story combines two stories from other Gospels: the call of the disciples and the miracle of the "great catch" of fish (see Matt 4:18-22; 13:1-3a; Mark 1:16-20; 4:1-2; and John 21:4-7). The Lake of Gennesaret is another name for the Sea of Galilee. The fishermen, likely exhausted after a night of unsuccessful fishing, are preparing to return home. Jesus takes Simon Peter's boat and begins teaching the people out on the lake. When Jesus tells Simon Peter to put out his nets to catch fish, Simon Peter obeys and calls Jesus "Master," indicating that he recognizes Jesus's authority. The fishermen then catch a ridiculous sum of fish, at which point Simon Peter recognizes that this authority is not merely human. Like the prophet Isaiah in our first reading, Simon Peter falls at Jesus's feet and calls himself sinful. He and the other fishermen are astonished (literally "amazed" or "in fear") at what they have witnessed. Simon Peter reacts by telling Jesus to depart from him because of his unworthiness. Jesus tells Peter not to fear, and they drop "everything" to follow him.

Ponder

Our readings are call stories. Isaiah, Paul, and Peter experience great manifestations of God's glory—Isaiah and Peter in our passages for today, and Paul elsewhere on the road to Damascus (Acts 9). Our readings reveal a connection between the experience of grace and the awareness of one's brokenness that together lead to true liberation. As he experiences God's glory, Isaiah is literally cleansed of his wrongdoings in a ritual ceremony. Paul similarly experiences the overwhelming grace of God through no merit of his own. In the Gospel, it is when Jesus tells Peter not to fear that Peter is able to follow him unreservedly. From what do you need cleansing or liberation in order to follow him more fully?

We may not experience great visions, as Isaiah or Paul did, or tangible miracles, as Peter did. Yet God does call us, often quietly, in unexpected ways and through unexpected people. Pay attention this week to the ways God may be calling you. Imagine God asking you, "Whom shall I send? Who will go for us?" Where and when do you hear that voice?

Sixth Sunday in Ordinary Time

FIRST READING   JEREMIAH 17:5-8

Thus says the LORD:
> Cursed is the one who trusts in human beings,
>> who seeks his strength in flesh,
>> whose heart turns away from the LORD.
>
> He is like a barren bush in the desert
>> that enjoys no change of season,
>
> but stands in a lava waste,
>> a salt and empty earth.
>
> Blessed is the one who trusts in the LORD,
>> whose hope is the LORD.
>
> He is like a tree planted beside the waters
>> that stretches out its roots to the stream:
>
> it fears not the heat when it comes;
>> its leaves stay green;
>
> in the year of drought it shows no distress,
>> but still bears fruit.

We last heard from the prophet Jeremiah on the Fourth Sunday in Ordinary Time. Our reading this Sunday comes from a section of divine oracles (or prophecies) issued from God through the prophet. These oracles describe the righteous and the wicked through the metaphors of drought and abundance. One who trusts in the things of the world rather than God is like the "barren bush in the desert," while one who trusts and hopes in God is like "a tree planted beside the waters." The metaphor is echoed in today's responsorial psalm, which describes the one who "delights" in God's teachings or Torah as trees planted near running water (Ps 1:3).

RESPONSORIAL PSALM   PSALM 1:1-2, 3, 4, 6

Blessed are they who hope in the Lord.

SECOND READING   1 CORINTHIANS 15:12, 16-20

Brothers and sisters:
If Christ is preached as raised from the dead,
    how can some among you say there is no resurrection of
        the dead?
If the dead are not raised, neither has Christ been raised,
    and if Christ has not been raised, your faith is vain;
    you are still in your sins.
Then those who have fallen asleep in Christ have perished.
If for this life only we have hoped in Christ,
    we are the most pitiable people of all.

But now Christ has been raised from the dead,
    the firstfruits of those who have fallen asleep.

Paul continues his long argument against members of the Corinthian community who denied the resurrection of the body (they believed only in the resurrection of the soul, in accordance with Greco-Roman beliefs; see notes for the Fifth Sunday in Ordinary Time). Throughout 1 Corinthians 15, Paul argues for the centrality of Christ's resurrection as true reality, from which everything begins and everything culminates. Without Christ's resurrection, there would be no hope for our own resurrection. Paul ends this portion of his argument with the statement that believers "are the most pitiable people of all" if hope in Christ is limited to this life. In the subsequent portion of his argument, which we skip over between this week and next, Paul describes resurrection according to a specific order: first comes Christ's resurrection, then the resurrection of all those who belong to Christ; and in the end, Christ will destroy death itself. Paul's argument will continue on the Seventh Sunday in Ordinary Time.

GOSPEL   LUKE 6:17, 20-26

Jesus came down with the Twelve
    and stood on a stretch of level ground
    with a great crowd of his disciples
    and a large number of the people

from all Judea and Jerusalem
and the coastal region of Tyre and Sidon.
And raising his eyes toward his disciples he said:
"Blessed are you who are poor,
for the kingdom of God is yours.
Blessed are you who are now hungry,
for you will be satisfied.
Blessed are you who are now weeping,
for you will laugh.
Blessed are you when people hate you,
and when they exclude and insult you,
and denounce your name as evil
on account of the Son of Man.
Rejoice and leap for joy on that day!
Behold, your reward will be great in heaven.
For their ancestors treated the prophets in the same way.
But woe to you who are rich,
for you have received your consolation.
Woe to you who are filled now,
for you will be hungry.
Woe to you who laugh now,
for you will grieve and weep.
Woe to you when all speak well of you,
for their ancestors treated the false prophets in this way."

Our Gospel reading draws from what is often referred to as Jesus's "Sermon on the Plain" in Luke 6:20-49, in comparison with the "Sermon on the Mount" in Matthew 5–7. The text describes certain "beatitudes" or blessings (compare with Matt 5:3-12) as well as their antitheses or "woes" (which have no parallel in Matthew). Luke presents Jesus's teachings as starker than Matthew does; Luke's focus is not on spiritual states (e.g., "Blessed are the poor in spirit"; Matt 5:3) but on tangible economic and social realities ("Blessed are you who are poor"; Luke 6:20). The point is that the kingdom of God flips the current world order. Those who focus on this world will find their current, ephemeral states of wealth, happiness, and satisfaction destroyed in the eternal realm. Those who suffer greatly in this world will be elevated in the next. This reversal of the world order resonates with stories about the prophets in the Hebrew Bible.

True prophets endured great suffering, but only momentarily, in this world. False prophets received acclaim in this world, which would soon be reversed in the kingdom of God. While the kingdom of God is already "among" us (Luke 17:21) and the "flipping" of the current world order has already begun, this new reality will not be fully accomplished until God's kingdom has been fully revealed.

Ponder

Jeremiah uses imagery of abundance and drought to describe two life paths: one that is oriented toward God and the other that is oriented toward this world ("flesh"). Those who choose the flesh—things like riches, honor, pride—end up like a dry, parched bush in a desert wasteland. In other words, they waste away. Those oriented toward God are "[b]lessed"; they become deeply rooted and nourished, like a constantly satiated tree. In other words, they flourish. Jeremiah urges us to take stock of our own lives and spiritual health. Which path have we chosen? Or, perhaps more realistically, in what ways do our lives reflect both drought and nourishment?

Like Jeremiah, Jesus describes two paths in Luke's Gospel. Yet the Gospel frames these paths not in terms of spiritual states like Jeremiah, but in terms of the tangible realities of life that will be reversed in the world to come. For those who succeed in this world, such success will disappear. For those who suffer and face hardships in this world, such suffering and hardships will disappear. According to Paul in our second reading, these life paths are ultimately about whether or not our lives are rooted in Christ. Our path is determined by whether we place our trust in resurrection and God's kingdom or in the fleeting realities of this world. How does a life rooted in Christ orient your daily thoughts, decisions, and actions?

Seventh Sunday in Ordinary Time

FIRST READING   1 SAMUEL 26:2, 7-9, 12-13, 22-23

In those days, Saul went down to the desert of Ziph
   with three thousand picked men of Israel,
   to search for David in the desert of Ziph.
So David and Abishai went among Saul's soldiers by night
   and found Saul lying asleep within the barricade,
   with his spear thrust into the ground at his head
   and Abner and his men sleeping around him.

Abishai whispered to David:
   "God has delivered your enemy into your grasp this day.
Let me nail him to the ground with one thrust of the spear;
   I will not need a second thrust!"
But David said to Abishai, "Do not harm him,
   for who can lay hands on the LORD's anointed and
      remain unpunished?"
So David took the spear and the water jug from their place at
      Saul's head,
   and they got away without anyone's seeing or knowing
      or awakening.
All remained asleep,
   because the LORD had put them into a deep slumber.

Going across to an opposite slope,
   David stood on a remote hilltop
   at a great distance from Abner, son of Ner, and the troops.
He said: "Here is the king's spear.
Let an attendant come over to get it.
The LORD will reward each man for his justice and faithfulness.
Today, though the LORD delivered you into my grasp,
   I would not harm the LORD's anointed."

A key focus of 1 Samuel is the complex relationship between Saul and David. Saul, Israel's first king, falls out of favor with God in 1 Samuel 13–15. Directed by God, the prophet Samuel anoints David as king while Saul is still on the throne in 1 Samuel 16. David then meets Saul, comes into Saul's court, and develops deep bonds with Saul's firstborn son, Jonathan (who takes an oath of political loyalty to David behind Saul's back), and with Saul's daughter, Michal, whom he marries in 1 Samuel 18:27. Overcome with jealousy, Saul seeks to kill David, and David flees. Saul then annuls David's marriage to Michal and gives her to another man (1 Sam 25:44). After Saul dies and David consolidates his kingship, he forcefully removes Michal from her husband (2 Sam 3). Michal comes to hate David (2 Sam 6). Neither Saul nor David is a simple character! Despite their fraught relationship, the writers of 1 Samuel emphasize David's enduring refusal to hurt Saul, whom he calls "the LORD's anointed." This refusal to kill Saul and usurp his throne echoes in two key chapters: 1 Samuel 24 and 26, the latter of which we read here.

RESPONSORIAL PSALM   PSALM 103:1-2, 3-4, 8, 10, 12-13

The Lord is kind and merciful.

SECOND READING   1 CORINTHIANS 15:45-49

Brothers and sisters:
It is written, *The first man, Adam, became a living being,*
    the last Adam a life-giving spirit.
But the spiritual was not first;
    rather the natural and then the spiritual.
The first man was from the earth, earthly;
    the second man, from heaven.
As was the earthly one, so also are the earthly,
    and as is the heavenly one, so also are the heavenly.
Just as we have borne the image of the earthly one,
    we shall also bear the image of the heavenly one.

Paul continues his defense of physical resurrection: first Christ's, then that of all believers (see notes for the Fifth and Sixth Sundays in Ordinary Time). His defense will culminate in next week's reading. Here Paul argues that we have both a physical body and a spiritual body. The first-century Jewish philosopher Philo argued for "two

Adams" (or "men") based on the two creation stories in Genesis 1 and 2. The "first Adam" was spiritual and made in God's image (Gen 1:27) and the "second Adam" was human and made of dust (Gen 2:7). Paul reorients Philo's imagery to state that the first Adam was that of Genesis 2:7, and the second Adam, made in God's image, is Christ. Some Greek manuscripts change "we shall also bear the image" to "let us bear the image," which suggests that we already bear Adam's and Christ's images simultaneously in this life (see also 2 Cor 3:18).

GOSPEL   LUKE 6:27-38

Jesus said to his disciples:
  "To you who hear I say,
  love your enemies, do good to those who hate you,
  bless those who curse you, pray for those who mistreat you.
To the person who strikes you on one cheek,
  offer the other one as well,
  and from the person who takes your cloak,
  do not withhold even your tunic.
Give to everyone who asks of you,
  and from the one who takes what is yours do not demand
      it back.
Do to others as you would have them do to you.
For if you love those who love you,
  what credit is that to you?
Even sinners love those who love them.
And if you do good to those who do good to you,
  what credit is that to you?
Even sinners do the same.
If you lend money to those from whom you expect repayment,
  what credit is that to you?
Even sinners lend to sinners,
  and get back the same amount.
But rather, love your enemies and do good to them,
  and lend expecting nothing back;
  then your reward will be great
  and you will be children of the Most High,
  for he himself is kind to the ungrateful and the wicked.
Be merciful, just as your Father is merciful.

"Stop judging and you will not be judged.
Stop condemning and you will not be condemned.
Forgive and you will be forgiven.
Give, and gifts will be given to you;
   a good measure, packed together, shaken down,
     and overflowing,
   will be poured into your lap.
For the measure with which you measure
   will in return be measured out to you."

As with the beatitudes and woes of last Sunday's Gospel, the point in this continuing excerpt from the Sermon on the Plain is that the kingdom of God reverses the expected world order. Here Jesus focuses on reputation and one's capacity to love, drawing upon teachings from the Hebrew Bible and other early Jewish teachers. He argues that it means nothing to treat others according to human standards of fairness. His disciples are to treat others like God does—with radical, impractical love and mercy, expecting nothing in return (see Exod 22:24-26 and Lev 25:36-37). Jesus's statement "Do to others as you would have them do to you" mirrors that of another first-century Jewish teacher, Rabbi Hillel, who is famously reported to have said, "What is hateful to you, do not do to anyone else." In the end, Jesus says, people will receive according to the "measure" they give to others. The Greek text shifts from "you" plural (vv. 27-28) to singular (vv. 29-30) and back to plural (vv. 32-36), suggesting that this sermon was originally a compilation of Jesus's teachings.

Ponder

Our readings invite us to a radical reorientation of perspective. In the Gospel, when Jesus calls his followers to "hear," he means not only to listen but to act. To "hear" is to act always with mercy and love, even in response to such things as hatred, violence, and judgment. This is a daily lesson and choice. Daily, we choose how we respond to those around us. Daily, we can choose to see the image of God in others, no matter who they are or how they act toward us. David sees this image in Saul in the first reading. He loved, respected, and valued Saul even when Saul wished him harm. If you examine your own life experiences, do you believe in this choice?

"[W]e shall . . . bear the image of the heavenly one," says Paul. Our readings suggest that transformation into God's image begins by imitating God. Paul promises that through faith and God's grace, we will be transformed fully into the divine image when we die. Yet Jesus pushes us further. He calls us to transformation now. Between Paul and Jesus, we see a balance of faith and action. As believers, we trust that our lives are on a path that returns us to God, no matter what. This is Paul's promise. Yet faith is also a practice, and our bodies are God's tools on earth now. That is Jesus's call. How do you balance faith in what is to come with actions in the world now?

Eighth Sunday in Ordinary Time

FIRST READING   SIRACH 27:4-7

When a sieve is shaken, the husks[1] appear;
  so do one's faults when one speaks.
As the test of what the potter molds is in the furnace,
  so in tribulation is the test of the just.[2]
The fruit of a tree shows the care it has had;
  so too does one's speech disclose the bent of one's mind.[3]
Praise no one before he speaks,
  for it is then that people are tested.

The Wisdom teachings in Sirach are a collection of simple statements regarding skillful living. One of the preferred discussion topics in Wisdom literature is right speech, which we see here (see also Sir 20:1-8, 18-20; 22:27–23:15). According to our reading, speech exposes a person's true character, specifically "the bent of one's mind" (a more literal translation is "the thoughts/reasonings of one's heart"). The writer uses metaphors of agriculture (the shaking of a sieve to separate the grain from the refuse or unwanted elements) and pottery (the firing of a clay object in the furnace to demonstrate the potter's true ability) as comparisons for how our speech reveals the truth of who we are.

RESPONSORIAL PSALM   PSALM 92:2-3, 13-14, 15-16

Lord, it is good to give thanks to you.

---

1. "Husks": literally the "refuse" or "garbage pile" (Greek *kopria*).
2. Most English translations (including the NABRE and NRSV) follow the Greek witnesses that state, "the test of a person is in conversation," rather than what we read here: "so in tribulation is the test of the just."
3. Note the connection to Matt 7:20: "So by their fruits you will know them."

SECOND READING   1 CORINTHIANS 15:54-58

Brothers and sisters:
When this which is corruptible clothes itself with incorruptibility
    and this which is mortal clothes itself with immortality,
    then the word that is written shall come about:
    Death is swallowed up in victory.
        Where, O death, is your victory?
        Where, O death, is your sting?
The sting of death is sin,
    and the power of sin is the law.
But thanks be to God who gives us the victory
    through our Lord Jesus Christ.

Therefore, my beloved brothers and sisters,
    be firm, steadfast, always fully devoted to the work of the Lord,
    knowing that in the Lord your labor is not in vain.

In our final reading from 1 Corinthians this season, we reach the culmination of Paul's argument regarding resurrection (see notes for the Fifth through Seventh Sundays in Ordinary Time). Paul promises the Corinthian community that all believers will be resurrected, or literally will "clothe" themselves with "immortality," because of Christ's resurrection. According to Paul, the "word that is written" (Scripture) predicts Christ's eventual defeat of death itself. The Scripture passage Paul references here is Hosea 13:14, which he interprets and applies in a distinct way (in the actual context of the book of Hosea, the reference is not about defeating death but rather about God calling upon "death" and the underworld to punish Israel for its sins). In Paul's explanation, death is like a scorpion, and its sting injects the "poison," which is sin. Jesus Christ defeats the scorpion. Paul therefore exhorts the community to be unwavering in their commitment to Christ, trusting in the promise of resurrection.

GOSPEL   LUKE 6:39-45

Jesus told his disciples a parable,
    "Can a blind person guide a blind person?
    Will not both fall into a pit?

No disciple is superior to the teacher;
　　but when fully trained,
　　every disciple will be like his teacher.
Why do you notice the splinter in your brother's eye,
　　but do not perceive the wooden beam in your own?
How can you say to your brother,
　　'Brother, let me remove that splinter in your eye,'
　　when you do not even notice the wooden beam in your
　　　　own eye?
You hypocrite! Remove the wooden beam from your eye first;
　　then you will see clearly
　　to remove the splinter in your brother's eye.

"A good tree does not bear rotten fruit,
　　nor does a rotten tree bear good fruit.
For every tree is known by its own fruit.
For people do not pick figs from thornbushes,
　　nor do they gather grapes from brambles.
A good person out of the store of goodness in his heart
　　　　produces good,
　　but an evil person out of a store of evil produces evil;
　　for from the fullness of the heart the mouth speaks."

Last Sunday's reading from the Sermon on the Plain set a high standard for Christian living. How do we live up to this standard, becoming the people Jesus calls us to be? This week, Jesus's teachings answer that question through a dual focus on (1) the need for good spiritual guides, and (2) the importance of self-awareness and self-examination. Today's reading contains more practical lessons about right living than last week's Gospel. These lessons are modeled after Israelite Wisdom literature, including our first reading from Sirach. Jesus begins with discipleship: every disciple should look for a teacher or guide who is more spiritually mature. If well-trained, the disciple will eventually become equal to the teacher (compare with Matt 10:24-25 and John 13:16; 15:20). This message contains a subtle underlying warning to choose one's guides well, for on the path of faith, a bad teacher can poison the disciple. And of course, the ultimate guide and teacher is Jesus himself. Jesus then continues with a lesson on hypocrisy: do not judge the other, he says, while failing to examine one's own faults. Then, using agricultural imagery, Jesus compares one's actions to rotten versus good fruit, sayings that connect to Sirach and Psalm 92 (our responsorial psalm). Our hearts are like storehouses; what they produce—good or bad—demonstrates what is in the heart. We miss the final four verses of the sermon (Luke 6:46-49), where Jesus exhorts the people not simply to listen but to act upon his words. This final exhortation returns us to Jesus's call in 6:27 ("But to you who hear I say . . ."), which assumes listening that results in action.

Ponder

In our readings from Sirach and Luke, speech is described as a form of action that reveals the fruits of who we are. Throughout the Bible, speech is a powerful force. That which is spoken, whether a curse or a blessing, takes on a life of its own that cannot be reversed (see, for example, Isaac's blessing of Jacob rather than Esau in Gen 27). Speech has the power to hurt or heal, to unite or divide. Jesus reiterates the power of speech in his teachings. This week, pay attention to what you say and how it reveals what you think and what is in your heart. As you do, invite Christ into your mind and heart, to penetrate the inner depths and cleanse what is there.

This Sunday we conclude Paul's case for resurrection, which begins with Christ and extends to all of us. As we leave 1 Corinthians, consider Paul's final exhortations to his community to "be firm, steadfast, always fully devoted to the work of the Lord, knowing that in the Lord your labor is not in vain." The point, as Paul tells us, is to be confident in the reality and promise of resurrection and to allow that confidence to infuse and animate everything we do. As you pray with Paul's letter, consider what practices help you to be "firm" and "steadfast" in faith. How aware are you that your labor, your work, ultimately has a purpose that extends beyond what you can see?

Ninth Sunday in Ordinary Time

FIRST READING   1 KINGS 8:41-43

In those days, Solomon prayed in the temple, saying,
   "To the foreigner, who is not of your people Israel,
   but comes from a distant land to honor you
   —since they will learn of your great name
   and your mighty hand and your outstretched arm—,
   when he comes and prays toward this temple,
   listen from your heavenly dwelling.
Do all that foreigner asks of you,
   that all the peoples of the earth may know your name,
   may fear you as do your people Israel,
   and may acknowledge that this temple which I have built
   is dedicated to your honor."

Our reading draws from King Solomon's prayer of dedication to the newly constructed Jerusalem temple in 1 Kings 8. The construction of the so-called "First Temple" in Jerusalem marked an important turning point for Judah's centralization of religion and politics. The temple's importance is underscored by the long and detailed description of its construction and dedication in 1 Kings 5–8. It was understood to be the particular locus of divine presence in Judah because it housed the ark of the covenant (or the ark of God), a gold-covered chest containing the stone tablets of the commandments (see Exod 25 and Deut 10). The ark draws comparisons to the eucharistic tabernacles in Roman Catholic sanctuaries, except that only the Jerusalem sanctuary housed the ark. It was therefore the most sacred religious site in Judah, a place for regular pilgrimage, worship, and sacrifice. The temple was destroyed by the Babylonians around 586 BCE and rebuilt in the postexilic period under the Persians (ca. 516 BCE). The period of the "Second Temple" lasted until its destruction around 70 CE and makes a consistent appearance in the Gospel stories about Jesus.

RESPONSORIAL PSALM   PSALM 117:1, 2

Go out to all the world and tell the good news.
or: Alleluia.

SECOND READING   GALATIANS 1:1-2, 6-10

Paul, an apostle not from human beings nor through a human
    being
    but through Jesus Christ and God the Father
    who raised him from the dead,
    and all the brothers who are with me,
    to the churches of Galatia.

I am amazed that you are so quickly forsaking
    the one who called you by the grace of Christ
    for a different gospel—not that there is another.
But there are some who are disturbing you
    and wish to pervert the gospel of Christ.
But even if we or an angel from heaven
    should preach to you a gospel
    other than the one that we preached to you,
    let that one be accursed!
As we have said before, and now I say again,
    if anyone preaches to you a gospel
    other than what you have received, let that one be accursed!

Am I now currying favor with humans or with God?
Or am I seeking to please people?
If I were still trying to please people,
    I would not be a slave of Christ.

This Sunday we begin a semi-continuous reading of Galatians, which
we will continue through the Fourteenth Sunday in Ordinary Time.
Likely written in the mid-50s CE, the letter reveals a critical moment
in the early Christian movement in relation to its identity and mission. In this historical period, the movement was still very much
connected to Judaism, yet an increasing number of its members were
Gentiles (thanks in large part to Paul). As a result, the question arose

regarding the extent to which converts should be made to adhere to Jewish law and tradition. In the book of Acts, Paul's position is that the demands of the Jewish law place an unnecessary burden upon Gentile Christians. In Galatians, he pushes his point further to argue that "righteousness," a covenant relationship with God through faith in Christ, sets one free of observance to Jewish law. To require Gentile believers to adhere to the law would render Christ's death meaningless. In this opening salutation, Paul introduces key themes of his letter: his apostolic authority, Christ's death as an act of liberation, and the "different gospel" being preached by Jewish-Christians who believed Gentiles should convert fully to Judaism. While most of Paul's letters begin with a message of thanksgiving, these opening verses contain only rebuke.

GOSPEL   LUKE 7:1-10

When Jesus had finished all his words to the people,
    he entered Capernaum.
A centurion there had a slave who was ill and about to die,
    and he was valuable to him.
When he heard about Jesus, he sent elders of the Jews to him,
    asking him to come and save the life of his slave.
They approached Jesus and strongly urged him to come, saying,
    "He deserves to have you do this for him,
    for he loves our nation and built the synagogue for us."
And Jesus went with them,
    but when he was only a short distance from the house,
    the centurion sent friends to tell him,
    "Lord, do not trouble yourself,
    for I am not worthy to have you enter under my roof.
Therefore, I did not consider myself worthy to come to you;
    but say the word and let my servant be healed.
For I too am a person subject to authority,
    with soldiers subject to me.
And I say to one, 'Go,' and he goes;
    and to another, 'Come here,' and he comes;
    and to my slave, 'Do this,' and he does it."

When Jesus heard this he was amazed at him
  and, turning, said to the crowd following him,
    "I tell you, not even in Israel have I found such faith."
When the messengers returned to the house,
  they found the slave in good health.

After he concludes the Sermon on the Plain ("all his words to the people"), Jesus enters Capernaum, a city in Galilee (see also Luke 4:31). This story of the healing of a Gentile's slave echoes the story of Elisha's healing of the Aramean army commander Naaman in 2 Kings 5:1-14 (see the reference to this prophetic account in Luke 4:27). A Roman centurion commanded one hundred soldiers in the army. It is therefore striking that such a man would care so deeply about one of his slaves (the slave is not merely "valuable" but is "highly-valued," "precious," or even "dear," according to the nuances of the Greek term *entimos*). As demonstrated by the story of Cornelius, a centurion and the first Gentile convert to faith in Christ in Acts 10, a Roman officer could be a friend of the Jews and even "fear" God (Acts 10:2, 22). The unnamed centurion in today's reading is a benefactor of the Jerusalem synagogue, and the Jewish elders or leaders view him as "deserv[ing]" or "worthy" of Jesus's help, out of gratitude for his patronage. Yet the centurion declares himself "not worthy" that Jesus enter his home, knowing that Jesus could incur ritual impurity by entering the home of a Gentile. His reverence for Judaism, his understanding of Jesus's authority, and his belief that Jesus's word alone (even at a distance!) would have the power to heal demonstrate remarkable respect and belief in Jesus. Even Jesus is "amazed" and marvels at "such faith."

Ponder

Our readings reveal a tension between two realities: buildings and other spaces (including our bodies) can be loci of divine presence, yet the Divine transcends all physical constraints and limitations. Solomon recognizes this tension in his prayer of dedication to the temple. He states that not even the "highest heavens" can contain God (1 Kgs 8:27), even as he honors the temple as a sacred space where "all the peoples of the earth" will come to know the God of Israel. Solomon's prayer that all people revere God is realized in the centurion; he deems himself (and his home) unworthy of Jesus's presence, yet Jesus honors the man's faith and heals his servant without physically entering his home. Our readings prompt us to consider the tension between sacred space and the Sacred that transcends space. In what places or through which people do you experience God most fully, and in what places (or through whom) is God's presence more difficult to experience?

While we partake of the Eucharist in our own particular parishes and communities, the sacrament "transcends us and stretches out to embrace all of humanity."[1] The words that we recite before receiving the Eucharist, based on the centurion's statements in Luke, invite us to meditate on this paradox ("Lord, I am not worthy that you should enter under my roof, but only say the word and my soul shall be healed"). Notably, Jesus never came into physical contact with the centurion. We are at a much greater distance from Jesus in time and place, yet we believe that the presence of the risen Christ extends far beyond any temporal boundaries. When we pray these words, we are drawn into this great Mystery that connects us across every divide and that calls us to break down the false walls that we construct around Jesus and around our communities.

---

1. Timothy Radcliffe, O.P., "Preaching to the Perplexed," *Priests and People* (December 2002), 442.

Tenth Sunday in Ordinary Time

FIRST READING   1 KINGS 17:17-24

Elijah went to Zarephath of Sidon to the house of a widow.
The son of the mistress of the house fell sick,
    and his sickness grew more severe until he stopped breathing.
So she said to Elijah,
    "Why have you done this to me, O man of God?
Have you come to me to call attention to my guilt
    and to kill my son?"
Elijah said to her, "Give me your son."
Taking him from her lap, he carried the son to the upper room
    where he was staying, and put him on his bed.
Elijah called out to the LORD:
    "O LORD, my God,
    will you afflict even the widow with whom I am staying
    by killing her son?"
Then he stretched himself out upon the child three times
    and called out to the LORD:
    "O LORD, my God,
    let the life breath return to the body of this child."
The LORD heard the prayer of Elijah;
    the life breath returned to the child's body and he revived.
Taking the child, Elijah brought him down into the house
    from the upper room and gave him to his mother.
Elijah said to her, "See! Your son is alive."
The woman replied to Elijah,
    "Now indeed I know that you are a man of God.
The word of the LORD comes truly from your mouth."

Elijah was one of Israel's great prophets. He lived during the reign of King Ahab, who encouraged worship of the storm god Baal alongside worship of the God of Israel. In 1 Kings 17, to demonstrate the impotence of this "storm" god, God issues a drought across the entire land. The drought extends up to the heart of Baal-worshiping territory: Sidon in Phoenicia. When Elijah travels to Sidon, an unnamed widow and son are on the verge of death because of the drought.

The woman offers Elijah hospitality, and he performs a miracle, multiplying her last remaining flour and oil, thus saving the woman and her son. For this reason, the woman blames Elijah when her son suddenly falls ill; having already shown that he works miracles, she believes that Elijah has caused the boy's death. Demonstrating great compassion for the widow, Elijah cries out to God and goes through an elaborate, full-body process to revive the boy. He "stretche[s] himself out" across the body of the boy in a strange ritual process that is later repeated by the prophet Elisha (see 2 Kgs 4:32-35). The word for "life breath" (Hebrew *nepeš*) is connected to the throat area where one can feel the movement of the breath. After Elijah brings the boy back to life, the woman acknowledges that Elijah is a "man of God" and believes in the God of Israel.

RESPONSORIAL PSALM   PSALM 30:2, 4, 5-6, 11, 12, 13

I will praise you, Lord, for you have rescued me.

SECOND READING   GALATIANS 1:11-19

I want you to know, brothers and sisters,
    that the gospel preached by me is not of human origin.
For I did not receive it from a human being, nor was I taught it,
    but it came through a revelation of Jesus Christ.

For you heard of my former way of life in Judaism,
    how I persecuted the church of God beyond measure
    and tried to destroy it, and progressed in Judaism
    beyond many of my contemporaries among my race,
    since I was even more a zealot for my ancestral traditions.
But when God, who from my mother's womb had set me apart
    and called me through his grace,
    was pleased to reveal his Son to me,
    so that I might proclaim him to the Gentiles,
    I did not immediately consult flesh and blood,
    nor did I go up to Jerusalem
    to those who were apostles before me;
    rather, I went into Arabia and then returned to Damascus.

Then after three years I went up to Jerusalem
 to confer with Cephas and remained with him for fifteen days.
But I did not see any other of the apostles,
 only James the brother of the Lord.

After Paul's introductory greetings in last Sunday's reading, he describes his conversion experience from being a persecutor of the church to becoming God's instrument of revelation to the Gentiles. He emphasizes God's initiative in calling him and revealing Christ to him, using language that echoes prophetic call narratives (e.g., Jer 1:5: "Before I formed you in the womb I knew you, / before you were born I dedicated you"). Paul's zeal for his "ancestral traditions" recalls important figures in the Hebrew Bible, including Elijah (see 1 Kgs 19:10), who used violence in order to defend the purity of monotheistic belief in the God of Israel. In referring to himself as having "progressed" in Judaism, Paul incorporates a term from Stoic philosophy, which refers to one's progress in cultivating virtues. Paul's description of the events subsequent to his conversion is difficult to reconcile with the account in Acts 9, where he meets with all the disciples in Jerusalem, not merely with Peter and James. He refers to Peter as "Cephas," the Aramaic word for "rock."

GOSPEL   LUKE 7:11-17

Jesus journeyed to a city called Nain,
 and his disciples and a large crowd accompanied him.
As he drew near to the gate of the city,
 a man who had died was being carried out,
 the only son of his mother, and she was a widow.
A large crowd from the city was with her.
When the Lord saw her,
 he was moved with pity for her and said to her,
 "Do not weep."
He stepped forward and touched the coffin;
 at this the bearers halted,
 and he said, "Young man, I tell you, arise!"
The dead man sat up and began to speak,
 and Jesus gave him to his mother.

Fear seized them all, and they glorified God, exclaiming,
 "A great prophet has arisen in our midst,"
 and "God has visited his people."
This report about him spread through the whole of Judea
 and in all the surrounding region.

From Capernaum, Jesus journeys twenty-three miles southwest to Nain, where he encounters a funeral procession. The story mirrors Elijah's encounter with the widow and her son in the first reading. In both accounts, the death of a widow's only son leaves her utterly destitute (in the ancient world, a woman's husband and sons were her social and financial security net). The funeral procession here is therefore a metaphoric burial for two. When Jesus sees the widow mourning, he is "moved with pity for her." The Greek term *splanchnizomai* connotes a deep, visceral response of compassion. Jesus suffers with her as Elijah suffered with the widow in 1 Kings 17, and his reaction reflects God's care and compassion for those on the margins of society. In the Sermon on the Plain (Luke 6:20-49), Jesus says, "Blessed are you who are now weeping," but here, he tells the widow not to weep. Unlike Elijah in the first reading, Jesus does very little physically to revive the boy, though touching the funeral coffin violated Jewish purity laws. The phrase "gave him to his mother" is an exact quote from 1 Kings 17:23 (see also Luke 9:42). The word "fear" is akin to wonder and awe; the people recognize the divine presence through Jesus. Like the first reading, the miracle elicits the reaction of the people, and they call him a great prophet akin to Elijah.

Ponder

Our readings recount obvious miracles: Elijah's and Jesus's acts of raising the dead and Paul's conversion experience. Yet underlying these miracles are less "showy" miracles that are equally the work of divine agency. The widow offers Elijah hospitality when she has nothing left to give; Paul lives out his calling with great devotion; Elijah and Jesus reveal God's compassion to someone on the margins of society. These understated, even ordinary, miracles happen constantly in and around us. They are signs of hope, of God's grace working insistently in our world with our help. When was the last time you noticed or experienced such a miracle?

"Hear, O LORD, and have pity on me." We might imagine both women in our readings crying out this verse from our responsorial psalm (30:11). The Hebrew verb for "pity" is *ḥānan*, which means to "show favor," "be merciful," or even "yearn toward." Such remarkable mercy is a key divine trait: *God yearning toward us*. Connected to this yearning is love and the desire for the full thriving and dignity of all creation. We see such love manifest through Elijah's and Jesus's miracles when they save motherless widows from destitution. Yet underlying their actions is also social critique—an insistence upon the dignity of every human being in every situation. May we also be conduits of mercy, working with steadfast love for the dignity and thriving of all of God's creation.

Eleventh Sunday in Ordinary Time

FIRST READING   2 SAMUEL 12:7-10, 13

Nathan said to David:
"Thus says the LORD God of Israel:
'I anointed you king of Israel.
I rescued you from the hand of Saul.
I gave you your lord's house and your lord's wives for your own.
I gave you the house of Israel and of Judah.
And if this were not enough, I could count up for you still more.
Why have you spurned the LORD and done evil in his sight?
You have cut down Uriah the Hittite with the sword;
    you took his wife as your own,
    and him you killed with the sword of the Ammonites.
Now, therefore, the sword shall never depart from your house,
    because you have despised me
    and have taken the wife of Uriah to be your wife.' "
Then David said to Nathan,
    "I have sinned against the LORD."
Nathan answered David:
    "The LORD on his part has forgiven your sin:
    you shall not die."

The above reading is a small slice from a detailed narrative of David's moral unraveling that begins in 2 Samuel 11: David stays at home when he should be off to war with his troops, spies Bathsheba (Uriah's wife) bathing, sends for her, sleeps with her, impregnates her, has Uriah killed on the battlefield, and takes Bathsheba as his own wife. As a result, and in keeping with Nathan's prophecies, their first child dies. Their second child, however, is Solomon, who becomes king after David. In 1–2 Chronicles, books that retell the history of Israel found in the books of Samuel and Kings, the entire story of David and Bathsheba is sanitized of anything that would make David seem less than perfect. Yet the Gospel of Matthew revels in this kind of messy past that leads up to Jesus, and Bathsheba ("the wife of Uriah") is one of only four women mentioned in Matthew's genealogy of Jesus.

For people of faith, David is an essential figure: he reminds us of the power of sin, the reality of human frailty, and the mercy of God that works with and through us despite our lesser tendencies.

RESPONSORIAL PSALM   PSALM 32:1-2, 5, 7, 11

Lord, forgive the wrong I have done.

SECOND READING   GALATIANS 2:16, 19-21

Brothers and sisters:
We who know that a person is not justified by works of the law
    but through faith in Jesus Christ,
    even we have believed in Christ Jesus
    that we may be justified by faith in Christ
    and not by works of the law,
    because by works of the law no one will be justified.
For through the law I died to the law,
    that I might live for God.
I have been crucified with Christ;
    yet I live, no longer I, but Christ lives in me;
    insofar as I now live in the flesh,
    I live by faith in the Son of God
    who has loved me and given himself up for me.
I do not nullify the grace of God;
    for if justification comes through the law,
    then Christ died for nothing.

In this section of Galatians (2:11-21, an excerpt of which we read here), Paul describes an earlier dispute with Peter ("Cephas") to underscore similar issues now facing the Galatian community. In Antioch, where Gentiles had been accepted into the life of the early Christian community, Peter participated in the communal meals. At these meals, Gentile and Jewish believers ate together without regard for Jewish food laws (note: according to these laws, nothing prohibited Jews from eating *with* Gentiles, only from eating certain foods). Later, other Jewish emissaries of the early church arrived, whom Paul calls "false brothers" (2:4), because they believed that Gentiles needed to convert fully to Judaism in order to participate in the Jesus movement. Apparently, Peter then withdrew from these communal meals out of concern that he would be judged by his Jewish peers. To Paul, Peter's actions were hypocritical and contrary to the truth of the gospel. In our reading, Paul addresses his fellow Jews ("we"), first by stating that "we" are Jews by nature and not Gentile sinners, that is, those who do not have the law (2:15). Yet "we" Jewish believers know that a person is not brought into right relationship with God by "works of the law" but by faith in Christ. From the works of the law, Paul writes, no one will be justified or declared righteous (he quotes loosely from Ps 143:2). He then switches to "I" to state that he has "died to the law" through unity in Christ, a unity signified by baptism. Through faith, Paul shares in the crucifixion and resurrection so that Christ, crucified and living, is present in him. To claim that righteousness comes through the law therefore renders Christ's death unnecessary.

GOSPEL   LUKE 7:36–8:3 [OR 7:36-50]

A Pharisee invited Jesus to dine with him,
    and he entered the Pharisee's house and reclined at table.
Now there was a sinful woman in the city
    who learned that he was at table in the house of the Pharisee.
Bringing an alabaster flask of ointment,
    she stood behind him at his feet weeping
    and began to bathe his feet with her tears.
Then she wiped them with her hair,
    kissed them, and anointed them with the ointment.
When the Pharisee who had invited him saw this he said
        to himself,
    "If this man were a prophet,
    he would know who and what sort of woman this is who is
        touching him,
    that she is a sinner."
Jesus said to him in reply,
    "Simon, I have something to say to you."
"Tell me, teacher," he said.
    "Two people were in debt to a certain creditor;
    one owed five hundred days' wages and the other owed fifty.

Since they were unable to repay the debt, he forgave it for both.
Which of them will love him more?"
Simon said in reply,
   "The one, I suppose, whose larger debt was forgiven."
He said to him, "You have judged rightly."

Then he turned to the woman and said to Simon,
   "Do you see this woman?
When I entered your house, you did not give me water for
      my feet,
   but she has bathed them with her tears
   and wiped them with her hair.
You did not give me a kiss,
   but she has not ceased kissing my feet since the time I entered.
You did not anoint my head with oil,
   but she anointed my feet with ointment.
So I tell you, her many sins have been forgiven
   because she has shown great love.
But the one to whom little is forgiven, loves little."
He said to her, "Your sins are forgiven."
The others at table said to themselves,
   "Who is this who even forgives sins?"
But he said to the woman,
   "Your faith has saved you; go in peace."

Afterward he journeyed from one town and village to another,
   preaching and proclaiming the good news of the kingdom
      of God.
Accompanying him were the Twelve
   and some women who had been cured of evil spirits
      and infirmities,
   Mary, called Magdalene, from whom seven demons had
      gone out,
   Joanna, the wife of Herod's steward Chuza,
   Susanna, and many others who provided for them out of
      their resources.

We move from Jesus's raising of a widow's son (7:11-17) to a story
of forgiveness and extravagant love (see parallel but quite different
accounts of a woman anointing Jesus in Matt 26:6-13; Mark 14:3-9;

and John 12:1-8). The scene takes place in the home of a Pharisee named Simon. Jesus has a relationship with Simon (who calls him "teacher"), and it seems quite normal to share meals with him; Simon's hospitality was not part of a plot to trap Jesus. Yet there is some lack of warmth toward Jesus, for Simon does not extend common courtesies to his guest, such as washing his feet. Simon then judges both the unnamed woman and Jesus. He reasons that Jesus must not be a prophet, for a prophet would have known that this woman was a sinner and stayed away from her. Jesus then proves himself to be a prophet and more, not only by his acceptance and love of the woman, but by knowing Simon's thoughts. The subsequent parable points out the differences between the woman and Simon in their behaviors. The praiseworthy quality of the woman, it seems, is not her faith so much as her extravagant care for Jesus, who tells her that she has already been forgiven (the Greek *apheōntai* points to a past action that is ongoing in the present). The woman's extravagant care is then mirrored in our final verses: women who have experienced Jesus's compassion provide for him from their own resources.

Ponder

The second reading and the Gospel are mirrors, pointing out the ease with which we judge others. As we listen to the readings, we may notice that we subconsciously begin to judge those whom the narrators accuse of judging others. The readings therefore target us and become mirrors to reflect on our own tendencies. Simon's quick judgment of the woman in the Gospel prevented him from looking deeper into the truth of who this woman was. Yet, as Pope Francis has said, "Jesus urges each of us never to stop at the surface of things, especially when we have a person before us. We are called to look beyond, to focus on the heart. . . . No one can be excluded from the mercy of God."[1] As you pray with the Gospel, how do Jesus's words to Simon speak to you?

Our readings are also medicine. "[T]he one to whom little is forgiven, loves little," says Jesus to Simon. Given that God is mercy, there is no such thing as being forgiven just a "little." We are all forgiven everything. These readings urge us to become David, the psalmist, Paul, the unnamed woman in the Gospel, and even Simon, all of whom experience God's compassionate gaze upon them. Allow yourself to be open and vulnerable, to feel God's loving gaze upon you. It is this experience of extravagant love that gives us the grace to love and forgive in return.

1. Pope Francis, Homily, St. Peter's Basilica, Celebration of Penance: Communal Reconciliation Service with Individual Confession and Absolution, March 13, 2015.

Twelfth Sunday in Ordinary Time

FIRST READING   ZECHARIAH 12:10-11; 13:1

Thus says the LORD:
I will pour out on the house of David
and on the inhabitants of Jerusalem
a spirit of grace and petition;
and they shall look on him[1] whom they have pierced,
and they shall mourn for him as one mourns for an only son,
and they shall grieve over him as one grieves over a firstborn.

On that day the mourning in Jerusalem shall be as great
as the mourning of Hadadrimmon in the plain of Megiddo.

On that day there shall be open to the house of David
and to the inhabitants of Jerusalem,
a fountain to purify from sin and uncleanness.

The postexilic book of Zechariah appears only twice in our three-year Sunday cycle. The final three chapters (Zech 12–14) are eschatological and reflect a traditional Jewish understanding of the coming or "day" of the Lord as coinciding with the return of the Davidic monarchy to Jerusalem. The broader context of the above text is a vision of Judah's great victory in battle against all the nations. The terms "grace" and "petition" indicate God's mercy and renewal. The one who is "pierced" is a martyr of some sort, perhaps one who dies in battle or the writer of the text (the latter option is suggested by the first-person voice in the phrase "they shall look on me whom they have pierced," which our translation changes to "him"). The Greek version of the Hebrew Bible (known as the Septuagint) translates the same phrase as "they shall look on him whom they have insulted." Christians commonly interpret this anonymous person as prefiguring Jesus. Hadadrimmon is either the Canaanite storm god Hadad, or the highest god of Damascus, Rimmon, whose death was mourned each year at the return of the dry season. The final verse (which skips

---

1. "On him" translates literally as "on me" in the Hebrew.

over 12:12-14 to the beginning of chapter 13) shifts from mourning to cleansing. This future messianic kingdom will lead to purification and, eventually, to rejoicing.

RESPONSORIAL PSALM   PSALM 63:2, 3-4, 5-6, 8-9

My soul is thirsting for you, O Lord my God.

SECOND READING   GALATIANS 3:26-29

Brothers and sisters:
Through faith you are all children of God in Christ Jesus.
For all of you who were baptized into Christ
    have clothed yourselves with Christ.
There is neither Jew nor Greek,
    there is neither slave nor free person,
    there is not male and female;
    for you are all one in Christ Jesus.
And if you belong to Christ,
    then you are Abraham's descendant,
    heirs according to the promise.

Paul continues his discussion in Galatians on faith as the core of Christian identity. Here he is likely quoting from an old baptismal formula. Through faith resulting in baptism, social and religious distinctions are dissolved and believers become united with Christ as God's adopted children. (We find similar Pauline erasures of distinctions in 1 Cor 12:13 and Col 3:11.) United with Christ and as God's adopted children, believers also become heirs to the promise once given to Abraham. Earlier in the chapter, Paul interprets Christ alone as Abraham's true "offspring" or "seed" (v. 16). Therefore, when believers are united with Christ, they too become Abraham's true offspring.

GOSPEL   LUKE 9:18-24

Once when Jesus was praying in solitude,
    and the disciples were with him,
    he asked them, "Who do the crowds say that I am?"
They said in reply, "John the Baptist;
    others, Elijah;
    still others, 'One of the ancient prophets has arisen.' "
Then he said to them, "But who do you say that I am?"
Peter said in reply, "The Christ of God."
He rebuked them
    and directed them not to tell this to anyone.

He said, "The Son of Man must suffer greatly
    and be rejected by the elders, the chief priests, and the scribes,
    and be killed and on the third day be raised."

Then he said to all,
    "If anyone wishes to come after me, he must deny himself
    and take up his cross daily and follow me.
For whoever wishes to save his life will lose it,
    but whoever loses his life for my sake will save it."

Similar accounts of Jesus's first prediction of his passion are in Matthew 16:13-25 and Mark 8:27-35. Unlike the other Synoptics, Luke grounds his account within Jesus's inner world and the powerful image of Jesus "praying in solitude." Some scholars suggest that Jesus continues praying with the disciples through this entire text, for we never hear that he stops praying before entering into discussion with them. When Jesus asks the disciples who the crowds say he is, their differing responses reflect different Jewish messianic expectations during the first century CE. In Hebrew, "Christ of God" translates as "Messiah of God," or more literally, "God's anointed one." To be God's "anointed" originally referred to anointed kings. According to Jewish apocalyptic ideas, in the end times God would reinstate the Davidic line and the political glory of Jerusalem (see the first reading). Jesus's scolding of his disciples may reflect his attempt to prevent confusion, for he would not fulfill Jewish expectations of the return of a triumphant king in a literal way. Jesus reminds his disciples that following him means walking in his footsteps, which means walking a path of suffering, dying, and rising. To die, according to Jesus, is to "deny" oneself or "lose" one's life. In other words, Jesus calls his disciples to die to selfish, self-oriented tendencies, instead dedicating themselves to service, to pouring themselves out as Christ pours himself out for others (see also the language of God "pour[ing] out" in the reading from Zechariah).

Ponder

"But who do you say that I am?" The disciples have just been on their first mission—exorcising, healing, and witnessing Jesus's miraculous feeding of the crowds. He has been their model of a life of service and love for others. But when Peter answers Jesus's question correctly, that Jesus is the Christ, the anointed one, the one who saves, he does not yet fully understand his own response. Peter is in a process of growth. So are we. To be a disciple is more of a verb than a noun. It is a persistent, daily choice and an active process of learning to follow Christ's self-sacrificial footsteps. This is what it means to take up our cross daily. Each day, Jesus asks us to respond to who he is with our lives. Imagine Jesus turning to you and asking, "Who do you say that I am?" How do you choose to respond today?

To be a disciple is to be in relationship with God, a relationship that is rooted in and fed by a life of prayer. Our readings contain vivid imagery of what an active prayer life might feel like. In Psalm 63, prayer is the soul "thirsting" for God, desiring God and revering God. It is to be a "divine-absorbed" rather than a self-absorbed person. To pray is to open oneself to the experience of divine grace and mercy poured out on us, as described in Zechariah. When we pray, we are in Christ and are "clothed" with Christ, to use Paul's imagery. Allow our readings to draw you into prayer and open you to the mercy and love of God around and within you.

Thirteenth Sunday in Ordinary Time

FIRST READING   1 KINGS 19:16b, 19-21

The LORD said to Elijah:
   "You shall anoint Elisha, son of Shaphat of Abel-meholah,
   as prophet to succeed you."

Elijah set out and came upon Elisha, son of Shaphat,
   as he was plowing with twelve yoke of oxen;
   he was following the twelfth.
Elijah went over to him and threw his cloak over him.
Elisha left the oxen, ran after Elijah, and said,
   "Please, let me kiss my father and mother goodbye,
   and I will follow you."
Elijah answered, "Go back!
Have I done anything to you?"
Elisha left him and, taking the yoke of oxen, slaughtered them;
   he used the plowing equipment for fuel to boil their flesh,
   and gave it to his people to eat.
Then Elisha left and followed Elijah as his attendant.

Elisha was Elijah's successor and a prophet to the northern kingdom of Israel during the time of the divided monarchy (around the ninth century BCE). Normally, prophets anointed kings, so this is a unique depiction of God instructing Elijah to anoint another prophet. A "yoke" was a wooden crossbeam that fastened over the necks of two oxen and attached to a plow, so twelve yoke of oxen likely equates to twenty-four animals. The number twelve alludes to the tribes of Israel and indicates that Elisha comes from a wealthy family. When Elijah throws the mantle over Elisha, it is both a sign of ownership and a symbolic act that signals the transference of prophetic power. Like Jesus in our Gospel reading, Elijah asks Elisha to leave behind his former life without hesitation in order to follow him. It is unclear, however, why Elisha cannot simply say goodbye; his request to give his parents a parting kiss would be quite common. Elijah's response to Elisha's request is also enigmatic. Some scholars propose that it is not admonishment but consent, meaning something like "Go ahead.

Am I stopping you?" The burning of the yoke symbolizes Elisha's break with his former life.

RESPONSORIAL PSALM   PSALM 16:1-2, 5, 7-8, 9-10, 11

You are my inheritance, O Lord.

SECOND READING   GALATIANS 5:1, 13-18

Brothers and sisters:
For freedom Christ set us free;
    so stand firm and do not submit again to the yoke of slavery.

For you were called for freedom, brothers and sisters.
But do not use this freedom
    as an opportunity for the flesh;
    rather, serve one another through love.
For the whole law is fulfilled in one statement,
    namely, *You shall love your neighbor as yourself.*
But if you go on biting and devouring one another,
    beware that you are not consumed by one another.

I say, then: live by the Spirit
    and you will certainly not gratify the desire of the flesh.
For the flesh has desires against the Spirit,
    and the Spirit against the flesh;
    these are opposed to each other,
    so that you may not do what you want.
But if you are guided by the Spirit, you are not under the law.

Nearing the end of his letter to the Galatians, Paul encourages the Gentile believers to stand firm against those who believe they must convert fully to Judaism to be true members of the believing community. As described in the notes for the Ninth Sunday in Ordinary Time, Paul's primary argument is that, for Gentile converts in particular, to seek righteousness through the law was incompatible with their new faith or "righteousness" in Christ. We skip verses 2-12 in this reading, which are all about circumcision—Paul tells the community that "Christ will be of no benefit" to them if they allow themselves to be circumcised. Returning to our reading, Paul reminds the community that they have been freed from "the flesh" (that is, self-indulgence and selfish impulses) and are now guided by the Spirit. It is important to remember that for Paul, it is not the law that is bad but rather humans who are incapable of following it (see Rom 7:14, in which Paul states that "the law is spiritual; but I am of the flesh, sold into slavery under sin"; NRSV). Following our reading, Paul describes the "works of the flesh" (fornication, impurity, licentiousness, idolatry, sorcery, enmities, strife, jealousy, anger, quarrels, dissensions, factions, envy, drunkenness, and carousing) and the "fruit of the Spirit" (love, joy, peace, patience, kindness, generosity, faithfulness, gentleness, and self-control; vv. 19-23; NRSV).

GOSPEL   LUKE 9:51-62

When the days for Jesus' being taken up were fulfilled,
    he resolutely determined[1] to journey to Jerusalem,
    and he sent messengers ahead of him.
On the way they entered a Samaritan village
    to prepare for his reception there,
    but they would not welcome him
    because the destination of his journey was Jerusalem.
When the disciples James and John saw this they asked,
    "Lord, do you want us to call down fire from heaven
    to consume them?"
Jesus turned and rebuked them, and they journeyed to
        another village.

As they were proceeding on their journey someone said to him,
    "I will follow you wherever you go."
Jesus answered him,
    "Foxes have dens and birds of the sky have nests,
    but the Son of Man has nowhere to rest his head."

And to another he said, "Follow me."
But he replied, "Lord, let me go first and bury my father."
But he answered him, "Let the dead bury their dead.

---

1. "Resolutely determined": the Greek reads literally, "made firm his face."

But you, go and proclaim the kingdom of God."
And another said, "I will follow you, Lord,
  but first let me say farewell to my family at home."
To him Jesus said, "No one who sets a hand to the plow
  and looks to what was left behind is fit for the kingdom of God."

The fact that Jesus "resolutely determine[s]" to go to Jerusalem suggests that he knew the task ahead and did not want to die. The Samaritans of a particular village then reject him, which anticipates what is to come in Jerusalem. Samaria is a geographical designation for what was once the northern kingdom of Israel, which fell to the Assyrians in 722 BCE. Judeans developed different cultural and religious traditions from the people of Samaria; after the exile, there was serious tension between the two groups that continued until Jesus's day (and even to this day). Judean Jews did not acknowledge Samaritans as legitimate heirs of Israel, and Samaritans did not believe the Jerusalem temple was the legitimate sanctuary. (For further details on the Samaritans, see Gospel notes for the Twenty-Eighth Sunday in Ordinary Time Gospel notes.) In this reading, James and John play into these stereotypes by asking Jesus if they should "call down fire from heaven to consume them," which is what Elijah the prophet did with the prophets of Baal in 1 Kings 18. Jesus rightly rebukes them for their ignorance (one chapter later, in Luke 10, we read the parable of the Good Samaritan). Jesus then continues on the road, meeting people and discussing the demands of discipleship. In the second meeting he states that the "dead" (spiritually dead) should bury the "dead" (physically dead), while those who are alive should proclaim the kingdom of God. In the third meeting, Jesus refers to the first reading and Elisha's burning of the plow as a metaphor for burning the old life.

Ponder

Freedom does not necessarily mean ease. The gift of choice can be difficult. In the context of discipleship, our readings reflect the freedom of choice as well as the difficulty and cost of our choices. Our Gospel reading begins with Jesus "resolutely determin[ing]" to follow the path to crucifixion. He meets three potential disciples on the road and warns them of the cost of following him. Maybe he is also speaking to himself. In his statements we hear echoes of Elisha, who may or may not have said goodbye to his parents before breaking from his old life. In the narrative gaps and silences of our texts, we are invited to listen to our own inner reaction when we are called. How do we respond?

Cultural and religious conflicts are the historical backdrop to today's readings. Luke's Gospel reveals the deeply-rooted conflict between those who lived in the north (Samaritans) versus the south (Judeans) of Israel. Galatians reflects the first-century struggle among converts to early Christianity, which at that time was an inner-Jewish movement of Jesus followers. We, too, live in a world of conflict and division. The human tendency to create boundaries and walls is strong, but Paul reminds us that true freedom lies in letting go of selfish, individualistic tendencies in order to live in love, which is what leads to true unity. Who do you view as "other"? How does Paul's call to unity both challenge and comfort you today?

Fourteenth Sunday in Ordinary Time

FIRST READING   ISAIAH 66:10-14c

Thus says the LORD:
Rejoice with Jerusalem and be glad because of her,
   all you who love her;
exult, exult with her,
   all you who were mourning over her!
Oh, that you may suck fully
   of the milk of her comfort,
that you may nurse with delight
   at her abundant breasts!
   For thus says the LORD:
Lo, I will spread prosperity over Jerusalem like a river,
   and the wealth of the nations like an overflowing torrent.
As nurslings, you shall be carried in her arms,
   and fondled in her lap;
as a mother comforts her child,
   so will I comfort you;
   in Jerusalem you shall find your comfort.

When you see this, your heart shall rejoice
   and your bodies flourish like the grass;
the LORD's power shall be known to his servants.

Our reading comes from the closing chapter in Isaiah, which focuses on God's vindication of Israel and the restoration of Jerusalem after the Babylonian exile. The text opens and closes with joy. Different Hebrew terms for "rejoice" saturate the first verse, which translates literally as, "Rejoice with Jerusalem and rejoice in her, all you who love her; rejoice rejoicing with her . . . !" Jerusalem and other cities are commonly depicted as women in the Bible, often in texts of lamentation or judgment. Here, Jerusalem is depicted as a nursing mother who provides nourishment for her children, the returned Judeans. This imagery then transfers to God, who will act similarly as a loving, comforting mother to Israel. Though excluded from our reading, the final verses in the chapter describe how God will create "new heavens" and a "new earth," and all people will see God's glory manifested through Jerusalem (v. 22).

RESPONSORIAL PSALM   PSALM 66:1-3, 4-5, 6-7, 16, 20

Let all the earth cry out to God with joy.

SECOND READING   GALATIANS 6:14-18

Brothers and sisters:
May I never boast except in the cross of our Lord Jesus Christ,
    through which the world has been crucified to me,
    and I to the world.
For neither does circumcision mean anything, nor
        does uncircumcision,
    but only a new creation.
Peace and mercy be to all who follow this rule
    and to the Israel of God.

From now on, let no one make troubles for me;
    for I bear the marks of Jesus on my body.

The grace of our Lord Jesus Christ be with your spirit,
    brothers and sisters. Amen.

We conclude our semi-continuous reading of Galatians with this postscript, Paul's last words to the community. In these final, powerful statements, Paul contrasts the vanity of those who boast in their own self-reliance to his boasting in utter dependence on God's grace. The world (Greek *kosmos*) denotes all that is against God—pleasures and ambitions related to the "flesh" or selfish living. Paul has died to this way of life, not through some mystical experience but through the transforming power of Jesus's death. The concept of becoming a "new creation" draws from Judaism (see notes on our Isaiah reading) and is of ultimate importance to early Christianity. To become a "new creation" is to be transformed into Christ; it means an entire reshaping of the meaning of one's existence, not through external signs such as circumcision, but through one's own participation in the death—and ultimately the resurrection—of Christ (Rom 6:8;

Phil 3:10-11). Paul applies the model of Jewish blessings ("peace and mercy") to those who follow "this rule" (i.e., that circumcision does not "mean anything"). When he speaks of the "marks" of Jesus (*stigmata* in Greek), he is perhaps referring to his own sufferings as brands that mark him as a slave of Christ. The final sentence begins with the classic format found at the conclusion of Paul's letters. He calls the Galatians "brothers and sisters," meaning that he is reconciled to them through Christ.

GOSPEL   LUKE 10:1-12, 17-20 [OR 10:1-9]

At that time the Lord appointed seventy-two others
    whom he sent ahead of him in pairs
    to every town and place he intended to visit.
He said to them,
    "The harvest is abundant but the laborers are few;
    so ask the master of the harvest
    to send out laborers for his harvest.
Go on your way;
    behold, I am sending you like lambs among wolves.
Carry no money bag, no sack, no sandals;
    and greet no one along the way.
Into whatever house you enter, first say,
    'Peace to this household.'
If a peaceful person lives there,
    your peace will rest on him;
    but if not, it will return to you.
Stay in the same house and eat and drink what is offered to you,
    for the laborer deserves his payment.
Do not move about from one house to another.
Whatever town you enter and they welcome you,
    eat what is set before you,
    cure the sick in it and say to them,
    'The kingdom of God is at hand for you.'
Whatever town you enter and they do not receive you,
    go out into the streets and say,
    'The dust of your town that clings to our feet,
    even that we shake off against you.'
Yet know this: the kingdom of God is at hand.

I tell you,
> it will be more tolerable for Sodom on that day than for that
> > town."

The seventy-two returned rejoicing, and said,
> "Lord, even the demons are subject to us because of your name."
Jesus said, "I have observed Satan fall like lightning from the sky.
Behold, I have given you the power to 'tread upon serpents' and
> scorpions
and upon the full force of the enemy and nothing will harm you.
Nevertheless, do not rejoice because the spirits are subject to you,
> but rejoice because your names are written in heaven."

Our Gospel text parallels the call of the twelve disciples (see Mark 6:7-13; Luke 9:1-6). The number seventy-two (or seventy, according to other manuscripts) recalls the seventy elders chosen by Moses (Exod 24:1; Num 11:16). The image of "lambs among wolves" signifies how the disciples should act—gentle and vulnerable—despite unavoidable hostility (wolves eat lambs). The mission is urgent, as implied by how quickly the disciples are to move, without the burden of extra things, even forgoing customary greetings on the road. Once they arrive at a place, they are to settle into one house and accept with hospitality what they are offered. The "peace" upon households connects with Christ's salvation, which has the power to extend to others through the disciples. The kingdom of God "is at hand" in Jesus's coming, and it is embodied in the disciples' work. The "dust" that the disciples shake off is a gesture of abandonment and is paralleled in Luke 9:5 as well as in Acts 13:51. Those who reject the disciples will be rejected themselves, and they will be worse off than the people of Sodom in Genesis 19, who never had the opportunity for repentance. In the Hebrew Bible, the *śāṭān* (which means "the adversary" in Hebrew) is part of the heavenly court and argues with God like a prosecuting attorney (hence the phrase "the devil's advocate"; see Job 1). Only later does this figure transform into "Satan," or the devil. His "fall . . . . from the sky" represents the powerful results of the disciples' mission. Jesus has already conquered Satan, and the effects of this will be felt in the church and through the disciples. Elsewhere, God protects against "serpents and scorpions" (see Deut 8:15). Luke then reminds the disciples of the dangers of overemphasizing external wonders or miracles; they are, instead, to rejoice in their salvation.

Ponder

Our readings are steeped in joy. They imagine, yearn for, and promise new heavens and a new earth, the coming of the kingdom of God. This is a transformed, unified world of peace, justice, and love. For Isaiah, Jerusalem becomes the center of this new creation, a space of healing and renewal, where God will comfort and care for Israel as a loving mother tenderly cares for her children. The psalmist envisions this newness manifesting throughout nature and "all the earth." For Paul, our own bodies become the locus of this new creation, united with Christ through the cross. How do you imagine new heavens and a new earth, the kingdom of God in this world or the next? What would it look like to become a new creation now—in yourself, your family, your community?

"The harvest is abundant but the laborers are few." We are the laborers. Jesus calls us to set out with courage and sincerity as lambs among the "wolves," meaning all the elements in our society, our institutions, and even in ourselves that threaten to devour those who spread the gospel. We are called to be people of hope in a fractured world, to be active reminders that all people are called to life and joy even in the midst of chaos, division, and suffering. As Dorothy Day said, "Our faith is stronger than death, our philosophy is firmer than flesh, and the spread of the Kingdom of God upon the earth is more sublime and more compelling."[1] May God give us the grace to live this day as "new creations," manifesting the compelling beauty of God's kingdom through our relationships, our work, and our actions.

---

1. Dorothy Day, "Liturgy and Sociology," *The Catholic Worker* (December 1935), 4.

Fifteenth Sunday in Ordinary Time

FIRST READING   DEUTERONOMY 30:10-14

Moses said to the people:
"If only you would heed the voice of the Lord, your God,
and keep his commandments and statutes
that are written in this book of the law,
when you return to the Lord, your God,
with all your heart and all your soul.

"For this command that I enjoin on you today
is not too mysterious and remote for you.
It is not up in the sky, that you should say,
'Who will go up in the sky to get it for us
and tell us of it, that we may carry it out?'
Nor is it across the sea, that you should say,
'Who will cross the sea to get it for us
and tell us of it, that we may carry it out?'
No, it is something very near to you,
already in your mouths and in your hearts;
you have only to carry it out."

Our reading comes from Moses's farewell speech to the people, as they stand poised to enter the Promised Land (Moses knows he will not enter with them). As part of their physical return to Israel, Moses calls them to interior conversion (literally "return" to God). A few verses earlier, Moses tells the people that God will "circumcise your hearts" in order to "love the Lord, your God, with your whole heart and your whole being" (v. 6). This statement and the verses that follow emphasize the necessity for a new covenant that is written on the heart (see also Jer 31:33), which interiorizes the ancient tradition of covenant-making and radically deepens the notion of one's personal relationship with God and Torah ("teaching" or "law"). Our reading illustrates how God's word, law, or commandment is rooted within the human person; it is not lofty or for the few and far between. Neither is it external, rigid, or exclusive. Rather, the commandment to love and to follow God is the most intimate part of the person—it is "very near" and needs only to be carried out. This understanding of God's law later develops into mystical understandings of Torah in the Wisdom tradition (see Prov 8; Sir 24). Subsequent to our reading, Moses exhorts the people to follow God's commandments and "[c]hoose life, then, that you and your descendants may live" (v. 19).

RESPONSORIAL PSALM PSALM 19:8, 9, 10, 11
(ALT. 69:14, 17, 30-31, 33-34, 36, 37)

Your words, Lord, are Spirit and life.

SECOND READING COLOSSIANS 1:15-20

Christ Jesus is the image of the invisible God,
    the firstborn of all creation.
For in him were created all things in heaven and on earth,
    the visible and the invisible,
    whether thrones or dominions or principalities or powers;
    all things were created through him and for him.
He is before all things,
    and in him all things hold together.
He is the head of the body, the church.
He is the beginning, the firstborn from the dead,
    that in all things he himself might be preeminent.
For in him all the fullness was pleased to dwell,
    and through him to reconcile all things for him,
    making peace by the blood of his cross
    through him, whether those on earth or those in heaven.

We begin a semi-continuous reading of Colossians that will take us through the Eighteenth Sunday in Ordinary Time (see also notes for Easter Sunday). The city of Colossae was located in Asia Minor (contemporary Turkey), about 110 miles east of Ephesus. Paul (or one of his followers) wrote this letter to this early Christian community—composed of Gentiles and Jewish believers—while he was in prison. He was pleased with the community's growth and progress, but he was also concerned with certain teachings that emphasized observance of Jewish practices and rituals, including esoteric, mystical experiences. Paul's letter reflects the close, interconnected relationship between Judaism and Christianity in the first century, yet its polemical tone also reveals a growing tension between the traditions. These introductory verses (which likely draw from an early Christian hymn) describe Christ's relationship to the world and to all creation in a manner that resonates with Jewish Wisdom or Sophia (see Prov 8; Sir 24; also John 1:1-18). Jesus is the "image" of God, meaning the perfect, visible expression of the divine. As "firstborn," he has supremacy over the universe. "[T]hrones" and "powers" are terms that represent spiritual forces or even angels. The "body" and "church" describe the unity of the Christian community. Christ is the first to be resurrected ("firstborn from the dead"), and the "fullness" of God's power is present in and through him.

GOSPEL   LUKE 10:25-37

There was a scholar of the law who stood up to test Jesus and
    said,
    "Teacher, what must I do to inherit eternal life?"
Jesus said to him, "What is written in the law?
How do you read it?"
He said in reply,
    "You shall love the Lord, your God,
    with all your heart,
    with all your being,
    with all your strength,
    and with all your mind,
    and your neighbor as yourself."
He replied to him, "You have answered correctly;
    do this and you will live."

But because he wished to justify himself, he said to Jesus,
    "And who is my neighbor?"
Jesus replied,
    "A man fell victim to robbers
    as he went down from Jerusalem to Jericho.
They stripped and beat him and went off leaving him half-dead.
A priest happened to be going down that road,
    but when he saw him, he passed by on the opposite side.

Likewise a Levite came to the place,
  and when he saw him, he passed by on the opposite side.
But a Samaritan traveler who came upon him
  was moved with compassion at the sight.
He approached the victim,
  poured oil and wine over his wounds and bandaged them.[1]
Then he lifted him up on his own animal,
  took him to an inn, and cared for him.
The next day he took out two silver coins
  and gave them to the innkeeper with the instruction,
  'Take care of him.
If you spend more than what I have given you,
  I shall repay you on my way back.'
Which of these three, in your opinion,
  was neighbor to the robbers' victim?"
He answered, "The one who treated him with mercy."
Jesus said to him, "Go and do likewise."

A lawyer or scholar of Jewish law comes to "test" Jesus ("test" can also translate as "tempt"). His question is foolish, for eternal life is ultimately a gift from God to God's people, not something to be gained through actions. When Jesus asks him to interpret the law, the scholar brings together the two great commandments of the Torah: love of God and love of neighbor (Deut 6:5; Lev 19:18). Wishing to show himself righteous (or "justify himself"), he then asks Jesus who his neighbor is. In Hebrew, the words for "neighbor" (*rēaʿ*) and "evil one" or enemy (*raʿ*) are strikingly similar, so one could argue that the commandment to love one's "neighbor" includes even the one perceived to be bad or evil (in other words, the commandment extends to everyone). More importantly, the stranger or resident alien is included in this commandment, for within the context of Leviticus 19, the command to love one's neighbor "as yourself" (19:18) is paralleled with the command to "love the alien as yourself" (19:34). In terms of the story's setting, the distance between Jerusalem and Jericho is eighteen miles, including a steep drop, and the road was dangerous. The priest and Levite do not ignore the injured man because of ritual

---

1. Wine was used as an antiseptic.

laws, as illustrated by the following points: (1) ritual impurity laws are limited to touching corpses, not helping the injured; (2) if the man had been dead, Jewish law would have required that the corpse be treated with the utmost respect (e.g., see Tobit 1:16-18); and (3) they are going away from the Jerusalem temple, not toward it, and ritual purity would only be a concern if they were on their way to worship in the temple. The story is not about purity laws but about community. Jews fit into three groups: priests, Levites, and Israelites. The story shocks because we are to assume that the third person Jesus mentions will be an Israelite and not a Samaritan, a perceived enemy of the Jews.[2] In Jesus's final question, he reframes the scholar's question. It is not "who is *my* neighbor" (a question that sets the scholar up to do the minimum that is required) but rather "to whom am *I* a neighbor?" (a question that sets hearers up to proactively seek out those who need them). By reminding the lawyer that the Samaritan acts as a true neighbor, Jesus also pushes us to think about our own stereotypes and how a perceived enemy might be our true neighbor.

---

2. The story recalls 2 Chronicles 28:8-15, in which Samaritans care for Jewish victims.

Ponder

In our Gospel reading, Jesus does not answer the scholar's question directly. Instead, he returns the question, asking, "How do you read it?" In other words, what does the scholar think he must do to "inherit" or choose life? He clearly knows that choosing life means following the Torah's call to love God and neighbor, yet there is dissonance between his head-knowledge and his heart-knowledge. As you pray with the Gospel, imagine the interaction between Jesus and the scholar. Put yourself in the scholar's shoes. Now turn the question on yourself: what does it mean to you to inherit or choose life now? How does this choice manifest in your actions?

We are called to love and mercy. As Dorothy Day wrote, "There is nothing that we can do but love, and dear God—please enlarge our hearts to love each other, to love our neighbor, to love our enemy as well as our friend."[3] This commandment to love is rooted within our very selves, as Deuteronomy describes. We need only listen and "carry it out," as Moses says, or "[g]o and do," as Jesus tells the scholar. "Love" is a simple teaching. Yet simple does not mean easy, and the ability to act with love and mercy is tied to our humility, introspective prayer, and repentance. With grace, at times we succeed in acting with love from our deepest and truest selves. At times we fail. And yet the beauty of our faith is that there is no limit to how often we can return and humble ourselves before God and begin again. How might you begin again today?

3. Dorothy Day, "Love Is the Measure," *The Catholic Worker* (June 1946), 2.

Sixteenth Sunday in Ordinary Time

The LORD appeared to Abraham by the terebinth of Mamre,
  as he sat in the entrance of his tent,
  while the day was growing hot.
Looking up, Abraham saw three men standing nearby.
When he saw them, he ran from the entrance of the tent to
    greet them;
  and bowing to the ground, he said:
  "Sir, if I may ask you this favor,
  please do not go on past your servant.
Let some water be brought, that you may bathe your feet,
  and then rest yourselves under the tree.
Now that you have come this close to your servant,
  let me bring you a little food, that you may refresh yourselves;
  and afterward you may go on your way."
The men replied, "Very well, do as you have said."

Abraham hastened into the tent and told Sarah,
  "Quick, three measures of fine flour! Knead it and make rolls."
He ran to the herd, picked out a tender, choice steer,
  and gave it to a servant, who quickly prepared it.
Then Abraham got some curds and milk,
  as well as the steer that had been prepared,
  and set these before the three men;
  and he waited on them under the tree while they ate.

They asked Abraham, "Where is your wife Sarah?"
He replied, "There in the tent."
One of them said, "I will surely return to you about this time
    next year,
  and Sarah will then have a son."

The above story depicts ancient Middle Eastern ideals of hospitality and generosity, in contrast to the shocking inhospitality displayed by Sodom and Gomorrah in the chapter that follows (Gen 19). In our story, Abraham and Sarah entertain the Divine, who manifests mysteriously as three men. In return, they are promised that Sarah will have a child. When Abraham sees "three men," he recognizes they are special guests, greeting them formally and deferentially. Whether he knows they are divine beings, however, is unclear. He first greets them as a single person ("sir" and "you"), but the pronouns soon shift to the plural "you" in Hebrew. Throughout the story, words that express rapid motion underscore Abraham and Sarah's single-minded desire to provide for their guests. They do so extravagantly, offering their finest animal (as if it were an offering to God) as well as more common offerings of milk and curd. When Sarah overhears one of the men telling Abraham that she will have a son, she laughs, as she and Abraham are both over 100 years old. Although Abraham has heard this promise many times (see Gen 12:2; 13:15-16; 15:4-5; 17:4-21), this is perhaps the first time Sarah hears of it. Abraham had also laughed at the idea in Genesis 17:17. The verb "to laugh" (*ṣāḥaq*) prefigures the name Isaac ("he laughs").

RESPONSORIAL PSALM   PSALM 15:2-3, 3-4, 5

He who does justice will live in the presence of the Lord.

SECOND READING   COLOSSIANS 1:24-28

Brothers and sisters:
Now I rejoice in my sufferings for your sake,
    and in my flesh I am filling up
    what is lacking in the afflictions of Christ
    on behalf of his body, which is the church,
    of which I am a minister
    in accordance with God's stewardship given to me
    to bring to completion for you the word of God,
    the mystery hidden from ages and from generations past.
But now it has been manifested to his holy ones,
    to whom God chose to make known the riches of the glory
    of this mystery among the Gentiles;
    it is Christ in you, the hope for glory.

It is he whom we proclaim,
     admonishing everyone and teaching everyone with all wisdom,
     that we may present everyone perfect[1] in Christ.

We move from last week's description of Christ's supremacy to Paul's description of his own sufferings as an apostle of Christ. Among other things, he has been physically and verbally abused, ostracized, and imprisoned (the letter is written from jail). When he writes that he is "filling up" what is lacking in Christ's afflictions and that he is "bring[ing] to completion" the word of God, Paul is referring both to his role as an apostle and to the fact that followers of Christ will suffer in this world. Paul's vocation is to complete Christ's teachings by bringing the message to places where Christ has not preached. The "afflictions of Christ" are the sufferings endured by the apostles in spreading such a message. Paul states that the "mystery" of Christ is not for the few but for the whole world. His goal is "perfect[ion]" or maturity through the wisdom of Christ; that is, perfect understanding of and participation in the crucified and risen Christ.

GOSPEL   LUKE 10:38-42

Jesus entered a village
     where a woman whose name was Martha welcomed him.
She had a sister named Mary
     who sat beside the Lord at his feet listening to him speak.[2]
Martha, burdened[3] with much serving,[4] came to him and said,
     "Lord, do you not care
     that my sister has left me by myself to do the serving?
Tell her to help me."
The Lord said to her in reply,
     "Martha, Martha, you are anxious and worried about
          many things.
There is need of only one thing.

---

1. "Perfect" can also mean "complete" or "mature."
2. The phrase translates literally as "listening to his word (*logos*)."
3. "Burdened": Greek *perispaō* also translates as "distracted."
4. "Serving": Greek *diakonia*, meaning service or ministry.

Mary has chosen the better part[5]
and it will not be taken from her."

Our reading directly follows last Sunday's parable of the Good Samaritan. Again, Jesus acts in a surprising way. In last week's reading, he unexpectedly pointed to the Samaritan as the one acting as a true neighbor. This week, he interacts with two women in their home. Both passages exemplify Luke's focus on Jesus's relationship with those on the margins: non-Jews, women, and all people deemed "other." We know from John's Gospel that Jesus "loved Martha and her sister [Mary] and Lazarus" (11:5). If anything, John's Gospel places even greater emphasis on Jesus's love for Martha than Mary. Some commentators propose that the purpose of this passage within its cultural context was to make a claim about women's roles in apostolic ministry (they were to be silent rather than actively engaged). As contemporary readers, we may be tempted to identify with just one of the women. Yet Mary and Martha represent different aspects of the human person. Notice the details: it is Martha, not Mary, who welcomes Jesus and provides hospitality. It may seem unfair or confusing that she does not have the "better part" (hospitality was of great import to the ancient world), yet perhaps the "better part," according to Jesus, is about interior disposition. Hospitality itself is not the problem, but rather the problem arises from the fact that Martha is "burdened" or distracted by it. Mary's singular focus is listening to the Word. It is this constant attention to Jesus that is the better part, no matter the setting or activity.

5. "Better part" translates literally as "good portion."

Ponder

Genesis 18 is an example of extravagant hospitality and single-minded care for the other. In their generosity, Abraham and Sarah unknowingly entertain angels (see Gen 19:1; Heb 13:2). It is one thing to focus our attention on those we consider to be important in some way. It is quite another to focus our attention on strangers, on those with whom we have no connection or from whom we receive nothing tangible in return. And yet, recalling the parable of the Good Samaritan, our ability to act as "neighbor" to others should be not only consistent but extravagant, no matter the guest. Consider the relationships in your life and in your community. Is there someone you are being called to reach out to, someone overlooked, perhaps even someone you consider difficult? How might you reach out, not because you "should," but out of love and with pure intentions?

The Gospel states that Martha was "burdened with much serving." In his discussion about the "better part," Jesus may be demonstrating the importance of a healthy balance between the internal and the external life, between contemplation and action. He may also be juxtaposing a life of distraction with a life of attention. If we compare the Gospel to Genesis, we see that Abraham and Sarah are engaged in hospitality like Martha, yet they are not burdened, distracted, or anxious. Today, we live in a fast-paced, overscheduled, technology-saturated world. Distraction is our daily bread. Our readings invite us to stop, pay attention, and examine our interior lives and motivations. How might we practice paying attention so we, too, might choose the better part?

Seventeenth Sunday in Ordinary Time

FIRST READING   GENESIS 18:20-32

In those days, the LORD said: "The outcry against Sodom and
    Gomorrah is so great,
and their sin so grave,
that I must go down and see whether or not their actions
fully correspond to the cry against them that comes to me.
I mean to find out."

While Abraham's visitors walked on farther toward Sodom,
    the LORD remained standing before Abraham.
Then Abraham drew nearer and said:
    "Will you sweep away the innocent with the guilty?
Suppose there were fifty innocent people in the city;
    would you wipe out the place, rather than spare it
    for the sake of the fifty innocent people within it?
Far be it from you to do such a thing,
    to make the innocent die with the guilty
    so that the innocent and the guilty would be treated alike!
Should not the judge of all the world act with justice?"
The LORD replied,
    "If I find fifty innocent people in the city of Sodom,
I will spare the whole place for their sake."
Abraham spoke up again:
    "See how I am presuming to speak to my Lord,
    though I am but dust and ashes!
What if there are five less than fifty innocent people?
Will you destroy the whole city because of those five?"
He answered, "I will not destroy it, if I find forty-five there."
But Abraham persisted, saying, "What if only forty are found
    there?"
He replied, "I will forbear doing it for the sake of the forty."
Then Abraham said, "Let not my Lord grow impatient if I go on.
What if only thirty are found there?"
He replied, "I will forbear doing it if I can find but thirty there."

Still Abraham went on,
  "Since I have thus dared to speak to my Lord,
  what if there are no more than twenty?"
The LORD answered, "I will not destroy it, for the sake of
  the twenty."
But he still persisted:
  "Please, let not my Lord grow angry if I speak up this last time.
  What if there are at least ten there?"
He replied, "For the sake of those ten, I will not destroy it."

After God visits Abraham and Sarah (see last Sunday's reading), Abraham accompanies God (or "the men," according to 18:16) on the journey toward Sodom. As they walk, God decides to discuss with Abraham the possible destruction of Sodom, for God has a special relationship with Abraham; his descendants have been chosen to model God's justice and righteousness (v. 19). Abraham then poses questions about God's own justice that lead God to reconsider the fate of the city (similar to Moses's negotiations with God in Exod 32:9-14). Our passage invites readers to grapple with the concepts of divine retribution and collective responsibility. Abraham poses the question of whether the justice of a few can gain mercy for the whole. His primary desire is to know by what standard God will give a guilty or not-guilty verdict on the city. Over and over, God's response is "I will not destroy," underscoring God's mercy. The text does not give a final or precise standard, and in the end, the momentary reprieve will not save Sodom. Later in Genesis 19, Abraham and Sarah's earlier hospitality (Gen 18) will present a contrast with Sodom's extreme lack of hospitality, when visitors enter Sodom and are almost raped by the men of the city. In this case, the sin is the violation of the sacred duty of hospitality. God then destroys Sodom and Gomorrah, which become the prototypical sinful cities in the Bible.

RESPONSORIAL PSALM   PSALM 138:1-2, 2-3, 6-7, 7-8

Lord, on the day I called for help, you answered me.

SECOND READING   COLOSSIANS 2:12-14

Brothers and sisters:
You were buried with him in baptism,
    in which you were also raised with him
    through faith in the power of God,
    who raised him from the dead.
And even when you were dead
    in transgressions and the uncircumcision of your flesh,
    he brought you to life along with him,
    having forgiven us all our transgressions;
obliterating the bond against us, with its legal claims,
    which was opposed to us,
    he also removed it from our midst, nailing it to the cross.

Paul's letter continues with an excerpt from a longer theological argument (2:6-23) about death and new life in Christ, describing it as a "circumcision" not of flesh but of spirit. These verses offer a metaphor against the Jewish law; God nails the legal system to the cross, and the community is "buried" and "raised" with Christ through baptism and faith.

GOSPEL   LUKE 11:1-13

Jesus was praying in a certain place, and when he had finished,
    one of his disciples said to him,
    "Lord, teach us to pray just as John taught his disciples."
He said to them, "When you pray, say:
    Father, hallowed be your name,
        your kingdom come.
        Give us each day our daily bread
        and forgive us our sins
        for we ourselves forgive everyone in debt to us,
        and do not subject us to the final test."

And he said to them, "Suppose one of you has a friend
    to whom he goes at midnight and says,
    'Friend, lend me three loaves of bread,
    for a friend of mine has arrived at my house from a journey

and I have nothing to offer him,'
and he says in reply from within,
'Do not bother me; the door has already been locked
and my children and I are already in bed.
I cannot get up to give you anything.'
I tell you,
    if he does not get up to give the visitor the loaves
    because of their friendship,
    he will get up to give him whatever he needs
    because of his persistence.[1]

"And I tell you, ask and you will receive;
    seek and you will find;
    knock and the door will be opened to you.
For everyone who asks, receives;
    and the one who seeks, finds;
    and to the one who knocks, the door will be opened.
What father among you would hand his son a snake
    when he asks for a fish?
Or hand him a scorpion when he asks for an egg?
If you then, who are wicked,
    know how to give good gifts to your children,
    how much more will the Father in heaven
    give the Holy Spirit to those who ask him?"

Matthew's longer version of the "Our Father" (which contains seven petitions in contrast to Luke's five) takes place in the context of the Sermon on the Mount (Matt 6:9-15). Luke's shorter version occurs while Jesus is praying, and his disciples ask him to teach them to pray as John the Baptist taught his disciples. Luke's version is different enough from Matthew's to suggest that it may stem from a separate liturgical tradition in the early church. Both versions are communal prayers that contain both a view of the eschatological (end times) and a concrete focus on daily life. God is the one from whom disciples receive daily nourishment and forgiveness as well as deliverance from the final trial. Jesus then shifts from *what* to pray

---

1. "Persistence" (Greek *anaideia*) translates more literally as "shamelessness" or "impudence." The focus is on bold requests.

to *how* to pray, using metaphors of friendship and family. In the end, Jesus does not state that people will get exactly what they request; rather, he invites them to trust that God's love is assurance that they will receive what they need.

Ponder

Our Genesis story begins with the great "outcry" against Sodom and Gomorrah. In seeking to destroy Sodom, God's primary concern is the victims, those who are "crying out" for help in their suffering. The story then wrestles with what it means for God to act justly toward all people, balancing mercy for the sinful and justice for the suffering. The conversation between God and Abraham depicts God's astonishing openness to listening to and even learning from human intercession and prayer. It also depicts the radical quality of God's mercy toward those we might view as irredeemable. Finally, our story demonstrates the reality of judgment. How do you make sense of the relationship between divine mercy and judgment in our world today?

Saint Teresa of Avila is said to have written, "Much more is accomplished by a single word of the Our Father said, now and then, from our heart, than by the whole prayer repeated many times in haste and without attention." The theme of deep intimacy with God, or prayer "from our heart," runs through our readings. Abraham demonstrates persistence and trust that he may speak openly and honestly before God. The psalmist represents the victims, those who trust that God is on the side of the lowly and the oppressed. And Jesus explains both what to pray and how to pray, inviting the disciples to trust that God will respond out of love and goodness. As you pray with this week's readings, practice bringing yourself fully and honestly to God—even if you are angry, upset, or doubting—trusting that God will respond in love and justice.

Eighteenth Sunday in Ordinary Time

Vanity of vanities, says Qoheleth,
vanity of vanities![1] All things are vanity!

Here is one who has labored with wisdom and knowledge
and skill,
and yet to another who has not labored over it,
he must leave property.
This also is vanity and a great misfortune.
For what profit comes to man from all the toil and anxiety
of heart
with which he has labored under the sun?
All his days sorrow and grief are his occupation;
even at night his mind is not at rest.
This also is vanity.

"Ecclesiastes" is the Greek translation of the Hebrew *Qoheleth*, which means "Teacher" or "Gatherer." The author is a philosopher/theologian and a teacher in the Wisdom tradition of ancient Israel who likely wrote this text between the fifth and third centuries BCE. Living under Persian rule, this was a time of economic uncertainty that allowed for great upward mobility as well as severe debt. Within this context, the author struggles with human attempts to be in control and get ahead in a world that is not only contradictory but ultimately absurd. He repeats certain phrases, including "vanity of vanities" (or "futility of futilities," "breath of breath") and "under the sun" throughout the book. While much of the book seems pessimistic, the author was a devout man whose foundational teaching is the importance of remaining oriented toward God and detached from the fleeting things of this world (e.g., 5:1-7). Our reading deals with the leveling effect of death, which takes away any advantage one might have had

---

1. "Vanity": Hebrew *hebel*, which translates alternatively as "futility" or "breath." This is also the term that underlies the name "Abel" in the story of Cain and Abel (Gen 4).

in life. There is no advantage to toiling in life, for people cannot take the fruit of their toil with them when they die and are discontent by worrying about it when they live.

RESPONSORIAL PSALM   PSALM 90:3-4, 5-6, 12-13

If today you hear his voice, harden not your hearts.

SECOND READING   COLOSSIANS 3:1-5, 9-11

Brothers and sisters:
If you were raised with Christ, seek what is above,
    where Christ is seated at the right hand of God.
Think of what is above, not of what is on earth.
For you have died,
    and your life is hidden with Christ in God.
When Christ your life appears,
    then you too will appear with him in glory.

Put to death, then, the parts of you that are earthly:
    immorality, impurity, passion, evil desire,
    and the greed that is idolatry.
Stop lying to one another,
    since you have taken off the old self with its practices
    and have put on the new self,
    which is being renewed, for knowledge,
    in the image of its creator.
Here there is not Greek and Jew,
    circumcision and uncircumcision,
    barbarian, Scythian, slave, free;
    but Christ is all and in all.

Our final reading from Colossians describes the ethical implications of faith in Christ. To be crucified with Christ through baptism means a shift in orientation toward Christ's supremacy or what is "above." This ultimate reality is "hidden" to nonbelievers but has been revealed to believers. Paul tells the community to reject the sins or parts of their previous life that were oriented toward the things of this world as they live into the "new self" brought about through baptism. This new self realizes the profound union of "all" in Christ. The final verse is a rejection of privileges based on ethnicity, gender, and socioeconomic status (see also Gal 3:28).

GOSPEL   LUKE 12:13-21

Someone in the crowd said to Jesus,
    "Teacher, tell my brother to share the inheritance with me."
He replied to him,
    "Friend, who appointed me as your judge and arbitrator?"
Then he said to the crowd,
    "Take care to guard against all greed,
    for though one may be rich,
    one's life does not consist of possessions."

Then he told them a parable.
"There was a rich man whose land produced a bountiful harvest.
He asked himself, 'What shall I do,
    for I do not have space to store my harvest?'
And he said, 'This is what I shall do:
    I shall tear down my barns and build larger ones.
There I shall store all my grain and other goods
    and I shall say to myself, "Now as for you,
    you have so many good things stored up for many years,
    rest, eat, drink, be merry!" '
But God said to him,
    'You fool, this night your life will be demanded of you;
    and the things you have prepared, to whom will they belong?'
Thus will it be for all who store up treasure for themselves
    but are not rich in what matters to God."

Like our Ecclesiastes reading, the Gospel passage describes the "vanity" of greed and the "toil" that comes from an orientation toward the accrual of things in this life. In Luke 12, a large crowd flocks to Jesus, who proceeds to issue a series of teachings and parables. In this passage, someone in the crowd tells Jesus to make his (older) brother share his inheritance. According to Torah stipulations, the oldest son receives double the inheritance of the younger son. In his response, Jesus shows no interest in ensuring equitable division. Instead, he warns against greed and material satisfaction. He then tells a parable that suggests awareness of Ecclesiastes or similar Wisdom teachings in the Hebrew Bible. Like our reading from Ecclesiastes, Jesus's point is that death is the great equalizer. In life, to focus on or to be claimed by material gain causes impoverishment in what truly matters to God. And what is it that truly matters? It is, first and foremost, to seek God's kingdom (12:31).

Ponder

Unlike our contemporary capitalist culture, the ancient world was necessarily communal. People needed each other in order to survive, and it was much easier to see how one person's hoarding led to another's starvation. The Gospel parable plays on this context to describe a man who erroneously views his contentment as rooted in personal gain. God calls the man a "fool" and demands his life back using transactional language (see also Luke 6:30). The man has wasted his life, committing his energies to personal accumulation rather than communal care. This week, our readings invite us to ponder how we commit our own energies. Which of our actions are self-focused in a way that can cause anxiety and division? What actions are rooted in a desire for communion with God and others?

"Teach us to number our days aright, / that we may gain wisdom of heart" (Ps 90:12). According to our readings, what truly gives us perspective is knowledge of how fleeting life is. How will we orient ourselves during our precious time on earth? We can easily become attached to the "wealth" of this world, a path that Ecclesiastes describes as "vanity" and Paul as "greed that is idolatry." Or we can orient ourselves toward what is "above" (Colossians) or "what matters to God" (Luke). Allow yourself time to examine your motivations this week. In what ways are your actions, thoughts, and interests rooted in a desire to build up the kingdom of God versus a desire for your own self-gain? According to our readings, only one path leads to true wealth.

Nineteenth Sunday in Ordinary Time

FIRST READING   WISDOM 18:6-9

The night of the passover was known beforehand to our fathers,
   that, with sure knowledge of the oaths in which they put
      their faith,
   they might have courage.
Your people awaited the salvation of the just
   and the destruction of their foes.
For when you punished our adversaries,
   in this you glorified us whom you had summoned.
For in secret the holy children of the good were offering sacrifice
   and putting into effect with one accord the divine institution.

The book of Wisdom is a Jewish text from the early first century CE. It was likely written in Alexandria, Egypt, or another major center in the Hellenistic (Greek) world. Because of its late dating, its place of composition, and the fact that it was written in Greek (not Hebrew), the book was ultimately preserved in early Christian, not Jewish, circles. The text blends Hellenistic philosophy and Jewish understanding to convince its hearers to follow the path of the righteous (the path to God and life) versus the path of the unrighteous (the path to death). Our reading falls within an elaborate set of chapters that compares the exodus and the Israelites/Egyptians to the righteous/unrighteous. Here the author collapses the past and present to describe the killing of the firstborn in Egypt alongside the giving of the laws at Sinai (Exod 24:7) and the institution of Passover. According to the author, the Israelites in Egypt were already offering sacrifices and singing songs associated with the conclusion of the Passover meal (see the conclusion of v. 9, missing from the above text, in which they sing "ancestral hymns of praise"). The "divine institution" also translates as "divine law" and could refer either to the Passover celebration or to the Torah.

RESPONSORIAL PSALM   PSALM 33:1, 12, 18-19, 20-22

Blessed the people the Lord has chosen to be his own.

SECOND READING   HEBREWS 11:1-2, 8-19 [OR 11:1-2, 8-12]

Brothers and sisters:
Faith is the realization of what is hoped for
    and evidence of things not seen.
Because of it the ancients were well attested.

By faith Abraham obeyed when he was called to go out to a place
    that he was to receive as an inheritance;
    he went out, not knowing where he was to go.
By faith he sojourned in the promised land as in a foreign country,
    dwelling in tents with Isaac and Jacob, heirs of the
        same promise;
    for he was looking forward to the city with foundations,
    whose architect and maker is God.
By faith he received power to generate,
    even though he was past the normal age
    —and Sarah herself was sterile—
    for he thought that the one who had made the promise
        was trustworthy.
So it was that there came forth from one man,
    himself as good as dead,
    descendants as numerous as the stars in the sky
    and as countless as the sands on the seashore.

All these died in faith.
They did not receive what had been promised
    but saw it and greeted it from afar
    and acknowledged themselves to be strangers and aliens
        on earth,
    for those who speak thus show that they are seeking
        a homeland.
If they had been thinking of the land from which they had come,
    they would have had opportunity to return.
But now they desire a better homeland, a heavenly one.
Therefore, God is not ashamed to be called their God,
    for he has prepared a city for them.

By faith Abraham, when put to the test, offered up Isaac,
    and he who had received the promises was ready to offer his
        only son,
    of whom it was said,
    "Through Isaac descendants shall bear your name."
He reasoned that God was able to raise even from the dead,
    and he received Isaac back as a symbol.

We will be reading from Hebrews (written ca. 60–90 CE) through the Twenty-Second Sunday in Ordinary Time. Hebrews reads as an early Christian sermon. It is an extraordinary theological piece with both a high Christology (emphasis on the divinity of Christ) and a clear recognition of Jesus's humanity. Speaking to Jewish-Christians who may be falling away from the early Christian movement, the letter argues for belief in Jesus Christ to an audience steeped in the Jewish Scriptures (the Hebrew Bible) and rituals. Today's text draws from a long section that describes the Hebrew Bible's great cloud of witnesses to faith, a list of people who "did not receive what had been promised" (a "better covenant" in Christ; 8:6), yet who understood the promise through faith. Eventually, all of these witnesses will be "made perfect" through Christ's death and resurrection (11:40).

GOSPEL   LUKE 12:32-48 [OR 12:35-40]

Jesus said to his disciples:
    "Do not be afraid any longer, little flock,
    for your Father is pleased to give you the kingdom.
Sell your belongings and give alms.
Provide money bags for yourselves that do not wear out,
    an inexhaustible treasure in heaven
    that no thief can reach nor moth destroy.
For where your treasure is, there also will your heart be.

"Gird your loins and light your lamps
    and be like servants who await their master's return from a
        wedding,
    ready to open immediately when he comes and knocks.

Blessed are those servants
  whom the master finds vigilant on his arrival.
Amen, I say to you, he will gird himself,
  have them recline at table, and proceed to wait on them.
And should he come in the second or third watch
  and find them prepared in this way,
  blessed are those servants.
Be sure of this:
  if the master of the house had known the hour
  when the thief was coming,
  he would not have let his house be broken into.
You also must be prepared, for at an hour you do not expect,
  the Son of Man will come."

Then Peter said,
  "Lord, is this parable meant for us or for everyone?"
And the Lord replied,
  "Who, then, is the faithful and prudent steward
  whom the master will put in charge of his servants
  to distribute the food allowance at the proper time?
Blessed is that servant whom his master on arrival finds doing so.
Truly, I say to you, the master will put the servant
  in charge of all his property.
But if that servant says to himself,
  'My master is delayed in coming,'
  and begins to beat the menservants and the maidservants,
  to eat and drink and get drunk,
  then that servant's master will come
  on an unexpected day and at an unknown hour
  and will punish the servant severely
  and assign him a place with the unfaithful.
That servant who knew his master's will
  but did not make preparations nor act in accord with his will
  shall be beaten severely;
  and the servant who was ignorant of his master's will
  but acted in a way deserving of a severe beating
  shall be beaten only lightly.
Much will be required of the person entrusted with much,
  and still more will be demanded of the person entrusted
    with more."

The first portion of our reading (vv. 32-34) offers a conclusion to Jesus's famous discourse on worry (see 12:22-34) in which Jesus tells the crowd not to worry about what they will eat, drink, or wear, but instead to seek the kingdom of God. The remaining teachings are about vigilance, responsiveness, and faith. The first (vv. 35-40) uses the metaphor of a master and servants to describe vigilance and readiness for the end times or eschaton. To "gird one's loins" means to draw up one's long robes and tuck them into the belt at the waist to facilitate easy movement. Jewish practice divided the night into three watches; those who are vigilant in waiting for Christ through-out the night will be served in the banquet of heaven. The point is that Christians must always be ready, for nobody knows the exact time that Christ will return. Christ, the master, ultimately desires to wait on the servants. The final teaching (vv. 41-48) is a parable that describes the correlation between those who are given great responsibility and are thus called to great faithfulness.

Ponder

Passover is a Jewish holiday that commemorates liberation from slavery into a new reality as God's chosen people. It is an occasion for hope and celebration. It is also a challenge to consider the continued existence of slavery in our world (physical, emotional, and spiritual) and to work for the freedom of all people. Both Passover for Jews and Easter for Christians are occasions for remembering and continually making present the promise of what is "already" and "not yet": freedom from all forms of slavery, resurrection into new life. In what concrete ways do Passover and Easter inspire you to work for freedom?

St. Basil the Great once wrote, "What is the mark of a Christian? It is to watch daily and hourly and to stand prepared in that state of total responsiveness pleasing to God, knowing that the Lord will come at an hour that [one] does not expect."[1] Our Gospel reading challenges us in a different way than it did a first-century-CE audience. Early Christians believed that Christ's Parousia (or return) would happen at any moment. To be ready, one needed to be courageous and liberated from all attachments. Two thousand years later, we still await that return, which may no longer seem so imminent. What does the Gospel mean for us today? As you pray with the Gospel, explore what it means for you to maintain a stance of readiness and responsiveness to God.

---

1. St. Basil the Great, *The Morals* 22 (FC 9:205), *Saint Basil: Ascetical Works*, trans. Sister M. Monica Wagner (Washington, DC: Catholic University of America Press, 1999), 203.

Twentieth Sunday in Ordinary Time

FIRST READING   JEREMIAH 38:4-6, 8-10

In those days, the princes said to the king:
"Jeremiah ought to be put to death;
he is demoralizing the soldiers who are left in this city,
and all the people, by speaking such things to them;
he is not interested in the welfare of our people,
but in their ruin."
King Zedekiah answered: "He is in your power";
for the king could do nothing with them.
And so they took Jeremiah
and threw him into the cistern of Prince Malchiah,
which was in the quarters of the guard,
letting him down with ropes.
There was no water in the cistern, only mud,
and Jeremiah sank into the mud.

Ebed-melech, a court official,
went there from the palace and said to him:
"My lord king,
these men have been at fault
in all they have done to the prophet Jeremiah,
casting him into the cistern.
He will die of famine on the spot,
for there is no more food in the city."
Then the king ordered Ebed-melech the Cushite
to take three men along with him,
and draw the prophet Jeremiah out of the cistern before he
should die.

For more information on Jeremiah, see notes for the First Sunday
of Advent and the Fourth Sunday in Ordinary Time. According to
traditional understanding, Jeremiah's ministry began around 627
BCE during the "golden age" of King Josiah of Judah (640–609 BCE)
and continued at least until the Babylonian deportation in 586 BCE.
Jeremiah himself was deported to Egypt. Jeremiah was a fierce advo-

cate for the religious reforms that had been instituted under Josiah, especially the removal of syncretic worship (meaning the worship of other gods alongside the God of Israel). Jeremiah believed that Judah's continued worship of foreign gods angered God and would inevitably lead to the Babylonian conquest and the fall of Judah. His prophecies of impending doom and surrender to the Babylonians angered many people, who sought his death. In the verses preceding our passage, Jeremiah tells the people that those who surrender to the Babylonians will live, whereas those who fight against them will die by "the sword, starvation, and disease" (38:2-3). The officials (translated "princes" above) held political power over the king, and they sought to get rid of Jeremiah because he was discouraging or "demoralizing" the soldiers and the people. The cistern's dryness indicates that this incident occurred in the summer, before the Babylonian king Nebuchadnezzar's final assault of Judah in August of 586 BCE. The man who saves Jeremiah and recognizes his innocence is Ebed-melech (whose name translates as "servant of the king"). He is a eunuch (see v. 7) and an Ethiopian ("Cushite") and is therefore a foreigner to Judah.

RESPONSORIAL PSALM   PSALM 40:2, 3, 4, 18

Lord, come to my aid!

SECOND READING   HEBREWS 12:1-4

Brothers and sisters:
Since we are surrounded by so great a cloud of witnesses,
    let us rid ourselves of every burden and sin that clings to us
    and persevere in running the race that lies before us
    while keeping our eyes fixed on Jesus,
    the leader and perfecter of faith.
For the sake of the joy that lay before him
    he endured the cross, despising its shame,
    and has taken his seat at the right of the throne of God.
Consider how he endured such opposition from sinners,
    in order that you may not grow weary and lose heart.
In your struggle against sin
    you have not yet resisted to the point of shedding blood.

After the letter's lengthy catalog of faithful witnesses from the Hebrew Bible, we come to this magnificent exhortation to perseverance. This great "cloud of witnesses" culminates with Jesus, the ultimate model. We find the same description of Jesus as the "leader" and "perfecter of faith" in Hebrews 2:10. The letter often repeats the notion of "perfection" or being "made perfect" in faith, in relation to both Christ and his followers (e.g., 11:40 and 12:23). The Greek word for "leader" (*archēgos*; see also Acts 5:31) also translates as "author" (Acts 3:15) or "pioneer." The expression "despising its shame" means that Jesus disregarded or looked down upon the shame that he would have to endure.

GOSPEL   LUKE 12:49-53

Jesus said to his disciples:
"I have come to set the earth on fire,
   and how I wish it were already blazing!
There is a baptism with which I must be baptized,
   and how great is my anguish until it is accomplished!
Do you think that I have come to establish peace on the earth?
No, I tell you, but rather division.
From now on a household of five will be divided,
   three against two and two against three;
   a father will be divided against his son
   and a son against his father,
   a mother against her daughter
   and a daughter against her mother,
   a mother-in-law against her daughter-in-law
   and a daughter-in-law against her mother-in-law."

Our reading immediately follows last week's parable regarding those from whom much "will be demanded" (12:42-48). Here Jesus discusses the controversial nature of his mission (see also Matt 10:34-36). Fire is a symbol of divinity and of purification in the Bible (see, for example, Exod 3:2; Luke 3:16; Acts 2:3), and "baptism" here signifies Jesus's death. In other words, Jesus has come to cleanse and engulf the earth with the flames of his Spirit, which he will accomplish through his death. Jesus acknowledges his own pain and anguish in the meantime as he awaits this stage in his journey. The last verse regarding the inevitable fracturing of relationships that his mission will cause draws from Micah 7:6. The choice of discipleship is not lukewarm but is like the flames of a fire. It is the decision to place loyalty to Jesus even above family loyalty, a decision that can naturally lead to divisions and misunderstandings in relationships.

Ponder

Jeremiah is one of the most relatable prophets in the Hebrew Bible because he is so real. Compelled to be God's mouthpiece, he is shunned and persecuted. Like Jesus, he does not hide his anguish and suffering. Jeremiah cries out that he experiences God's message "as if fire is burning in my heart, / imprisoned in my bones . . . !" (20:9). Yet, like Jesus, he perseveres, and ultimately hope lies at the center of his prophecies. For Jeremiah, the suffering of his people is the fire of purification that leads to new life. Jeremiah is a universal figure for all those who endure and have endured difficulty, pain, misunderstanding, and even death as they witness to God. As you pray with our readings, who among the great cloud of human witnesses—past and present—are your models for hope, courage, and perseverance on your faith journey?

On this path of discipleship, we are far from perfect. To mess up is to be human, and we try to hold our mistakes lightly. Yet as Hebrews states, we persevere, shedding ourselves of our sins as athletes shed themselves of encumbering clothing. In doing so, we look toward Jesus as our ultimate guide toward "perfection" or complete maturity in our faith. How does his example inspire you to persevere?

Twenty-First Sunday in Ordinary Time

FIRST READING   ISAIAH 66:18-21

Thus says the LORD:
I know their works and their thoughts,
and I come to gather nations of every language;
   they shall come and see my glory.
I will set a sign among them;
   from them I will send fugitives to the nations:
   to Tarshish, Put and Lud, Mosoch, Tubal and Javan,
   to the distant coastlands
   that have never heard of my fame, or seen my glory;
   and they shall proclaim my glory among the nations.
They shall bring all your brothers and sisters from all the nations
   as an offering to the LORD,
   on horses and in chariots, in carts, upon mules and
      dromedaries,
   to Jerusalem, my holy mountain, says the LORD,
   just as the Israelites bring their offering
   to the house of the LORD in clean vessels.
Some of these I will take as priests and Levites, says the LORD.

Our reading draws from the final chapter in Isaiah, which focuses on God's restoration and ingathering of all righteous people to the new Jerusalem, both Israel and the Gentiles ("the nations") (vv. 14-16). The survivors ("fugitives") from among the nations will then go out to the ends of the earth to "proclaim [the] glory" of God and gather the Israelites in exile, their "brothers and sisters," who will return as a vast offering to God. They will come from the following places: Tarshish (either Tarsus in southern Turkey or Tartessus in Spain), Put (in Libya), Lud (Lydia in Asia Minor or modern-day Turkey), Tubal (also in Asia Minor), and Javan (in Greece or Ionia). As in the beginning of Isaiah (2:2-4), all people will gather in the holy city of Jerusalem to see God's "glory" or divinity made manifest. Those who are taken to be priests and Levites are from Israel, not the nations. The concluding verses of the chapter describe God's permanent "new

heavens and . . . new earth" (vv. 22-23) and the fate of the wicked
(v. 24).

RESPONSORIAL PSALM   PSALM 117:1, 2

Go out to all the world and tell the Good News.
or: Alleluia.

SECOND READING   HEBREWS 12:5-7, 11-13

Brothers and sisters,
You have forgotten the exhortation addressed to you as children:
   "My son, do not disdain the discipline of the Lord
   or lose heart when reproved by him;
   for whom the Lord loves, he disciplines;
   he scourges every son he acknowledges."
Endure your trials as "discipline";
   God treats you as sons.
For what "son" is there whom his father does not discipline?
At the time,
   all discipline seems a cause not for joy but for pain,
   yet later it brings the peaceful fruit of righteousness
   to those who are trained by it.

So strengthen your drooping hands and your weak knees.
Make straight paths for your feet,
   that what is lame may not be disjointed but healed.

According to the author of Hebrews, the early Christian community
has forgotten the call to treat suffering as divine "discipline" or instruction (Greek *paideia*). This word repeats consistently throughout
our reading to stress its importance. The author quotes from Proverbs
3:11-12, a Wisdom text in the Hebrew Bible that frames the acquisition of wisdom through the lens of a parent giving instructions
to a son. We skip verses 8-10, which compare human parenting to
divine parenting: if we respect and trust our human parents, how
much more should we be willing to respect God's instruction? Such
wise and loving instruction can be painful in the short term, yet

its ultimate purpose is to lead to healing and righteousness. The final verses quote from Isaiah 35:3 ("drooping hands and . . . weak knees") and Proverbs 4:26 ("straight paths") and connect to the imagery of athletes from verses 1-3 (see last Sunday's reading).

GOSPEL   LUKE 13:22-30

Jesus passed through towns and villages,
    teaching as he went and making his way to Jerusalem.
Someone asked him,
    "Lord, will only a few people be saved?"
He answered them,
    "Strive to enter through the narrow gate,
    for many, I tell you, will attempt to enter
    but will not be strong enough.
After the master of the house has arisen and locked the door,
    then will you stand outside knocking and saying,
    'Lord, open the door for us.'
He will say to you in reply,
    'I do not know where you are from.'
And you will say,
    'We ate and drank in your company and you taught in
        our streets.'
Then he will say to you,
    'I do not know where you are from.
Depart from me, all you evildoers!'
And there will be wailing and grinding of teeth
    when you see Abraham, Isaac, and Jacob
    and all the prophets in the kingdom of God
    and you yourselves cast out.
And people will come from the east and the west
    and from the north and the south
    and will recline at table in the kingdom of God.
For behold, some are last who will be first,
    and some are first who will be last."

Skipping over teachings, parables, and a story of healing (Luke 12:54–13:21), we begin today's Gospel reading with the reminder that Jesus is heading toward his death in Jerusalem. This next phase of his journey (13:22–17:19) is characterized by the urgency of his mission and its demands, and it includes teachings on rejection and salvation. In this passage, Luke compiles a number of statements that can also be found in Matthew 7:13-14, 22-23; 8:11-12; and 19:30 (see also Mark 10:31). Luke describes salvation both as physical work (to "strive" denotes athletic training; Greek *agōnizomai*) and as passive (one does not save oneself but is "saved" by God). In the parable of the "master of the house" (God), people are invited to enter but fail to respond until it is too late. They used to eat and drink in communion with the master, but now they are thrown out of his company. They will watch their great ancestors—patriarchs Abraham, Isaac, and Jacob alongside the prophets—all eating together without them. Instead, they will be replaced by those coming from all directions, who could be both Jews living in the diaspora (away from Judah) and Gentiles. Jesus's challenge to his hearers is that on the road to salvation, there is no such thing as complacency; the first become last, and vice versa.

Ponder

Our reading from Isaiah concludes a long book that spans multiple centuries (700s–500s BCE). It is filled with suffering, loss, punishment, and the promise of redemption and return to Jerusalem. At the conclusion of the book, the author imagines creatively and vividly what this return will look like and who will be included in the new Jerusalem. Surprisingly, the very nations who have been a source of suspicion and pain will be the ones to proclaim the glory of God and bring the exiled Israelites home to Jerusalem tenderly and as treasured possessions. Both Isaiah and the Gospel stress the inclusion of those who are least expected in God's plan of salvation. For those of us who imagine ourselves on the outside and undeserving, this is a great consolation. For those of us on the "inside," who would we least expect and perhaps be shocked to find included?

"Lord, will only a few people be saved?" This is an age-old question: who is "in" and who is "out"? It is also the wrong question. Jesus's answer in Luke is to focus on our own salvation. Our readings depict a tension between our striving, as athletes strive, and God's promise to lead us into righteousness. To be a person of faith is a call to lifelong discipline and perseverance in order to enter this "narrow gate," and yet it is a gate that God can graciously open for all people. Our readings call us to lean into the hard work of discipleship while simultaneously trusting wholeheartedly in God's love, faithfulness, and desire for our well-being and that of every person.

Twenty-Second Sunday in Ordinary Time

FIRST READING   SIRACH 3:17-18, 20, 28-29

My child, conduct your affairs with humility,
and you will be loved more than a giver of gifts.
Humble yourself the more, the greater you are,
and you will find favor with God.
What is too sublime for you, seek not,
into things beyond your strength search not.
The mind of a sage appreciates proverbs,
and an attentive ear is the joy of the wise.
Water quenches a flaming fire,
and alms atone for sins.

For background notes on the book of Sirach, see notes for the Eighth Sunday in Ordinary Time. A theme of this section of the book is humility before God (3:17-29). Humility points away from oneself to glorify God, and a truly humble person is esteemed by God and respected by others. According to the author, two main sources of wisdom are an "attentive" or listening ear toward what is taught (in other words, the Torah), and proverbs or teachings that come from the wise sages of Israel. The author espouses intellectual modesty and eschews thinking that speculates beyond the range of human experience (vv. 21-24). The author (a teacher of younger pupils) may also be writing to keep students from being overly inquisitive and questioning the teacher. This focus on accepting a wise teacher's instruction at face value was common in the Wisdom teachings of the ancient world.

RESPONSORIAL PSALM   PSALM 68:4-5, 6-7, 10-11

God, in your goodness, you have made a home for the poor.

SECOND READING   HEBREWS 12:18-19, 22-24a

Brothers and sisters:
You have not approached that which could be touched
    and a blazing fire and gloomy darkness
    and storm and a trumpet blast
    and a voice speaking words such that those who heard
    begged that no message be further addressed to them.
No, you have approached Mount Zion
    and the city of the living God, the heavenly Jerusalem,
    and countless angels in festal gathering,
    and the assembly of the firstborn enrolled in heaven,
    and God the judge of all,
    and the spirits of the just made perfect,
    and Jesus, the mediator of a new covenant,
    and the sprinkled blood that speaks more eloquently than that
        of Abel.

This is our final reading from Hebrews this season. The author contrasts Mount Sinai, the site of the covenant made between God and Israel, and Mount Zion (the new Jerusalem), the site of the new covenant established by the "sprinkled blood" of Jesus. The author draws heavily from imagery in the Hebrew Bible to make his comparisons, especially Exodus and Deuteronomy. The phrase "that which could be touched" refers to the deep, palpable darkness over Egypt in Exodus 10:21, as well as to the mountain of God that should not be touched (Exod 19:22; Deut 4:11-12). Images of a "blazing fire," "darkness," a "storm," a "trumpet blast," and a "voice" all point to the theophany at Mount Sinai (Exod 19:16-19; Deut 4:11-12). In Exodus 20:19 and Deuteronomy 5:25, the people beg not to hear the divine message directly. The contrasting imagery of Mount Zion, the angels, and the firstborn enrolled in heaven reflect an apocalyptic perspective (see also Dan 7:10; 11:8; Rev. 21:2-7). Jesus's sacrifice is contrasted with Abel's murder in Genesis 4, after which Abel's blood cries out to God from the ground (Gen 4:10).

GOSPEL   LUKE 14:1, 7-14

On a sabbath Jesus went to dine
   at the home of one of the leading Pharisees,
   and the people there were observing him carefully.

He told a parable to those who had been invited,
   noticing how they were choosing the places of honor at
      the table.
"When you are invited by someone to a wedding banquet,
   do not recline at table in the place of honor.
A more distinguished guest than you may have been invited
     by him,
   and the host who invited both of you may approach you
     and say,
   'Give your place to this man,'
   and then you would proceed with embarrassment
   to take the lowest place.
Rather, when you are invited,
   go and take the lowest place
   so that when the host comes to you he may say,
   'My friend, move up to a higher position.'
Then you will enjoy the esteem of your companions at the table.
For everyone who exalts himself will be humbled,
   but the one who humbles himself will be exalted."
Then he said to the host who invited him,
   "When you hold a lunch or a dinner,
   do not invite your friends or your brothers
   or your relatives or your wealthy neighbors,
   in case they may invite you back and you have repayment.
Rather, when you hold a banquet,
   invite the poor, the crippled, the lame, the blind;
   blessed indeed will you be because of their inability to
     repay you.
For you will be repaid at the resurrection of the righteous."

Earlier in Luke, Jesus dines in the home of another Pharisee and
is intensely critical of the people gathered (11:37-53). Here, Jesus
is again critical, though in a far less severe manner. The people are

"observing him carefully" with interest yet without hostility (see, in contrast, Luke 6:7 and 11:53). Jesus begins his parable by quoting from Proverbs 25:6-7, a book in the Wisdom tradition of ancient Israel (like the book of Sirach, from which our first reading draws). We find similar teachings about the reversal of fortunes in God's kingdom for those who exalt themselves or are "first" in this world in Luke 13:30 and 18:14. Sabbath meals are supposed to anticipate the kingdom of God, yet Jesus points out how this meal fails: it reflects pride rather than humility and exclusivity rather than a welcoming openness. Our parable leads into another parable—the parable of the great dinner in Luke 14:15-24, in which Jesus makes a further point about "insiders" and "outsiders"; those who are first invited to eat in the kingdom of God fail to arrive, and in their place all those on the margins ("the poor, the crippled, the lame, the blind") are welcomed to the meal.

Ponder

Our readings are an invitation "to remember where we stand."[1] Where we stand is always before God. When we remember this, everything that places the self at the center—including privilege, knowledge, fame—becomes meaningless. What is meaningful is a life that places God at the center. Our readings invite us to a reorientation of perspective from being self-centered to God-centered. Sirach describes this reorientation as humility—or literally "groundedness"—in God ("humility" comes from the Latin *humilis*, "on the ground," connected to *humus*, or "earth"). This week, how might you practice "groundedness" in God, remembering where and before whom you stand?

"[B]lessed indeed will you be because of their inability to repay you." A paradoxical promise runs through our readings. In one sense, the promise is focused on the individual—each of us will be "blessed" for doing good deeds. Yet the ultimate goal of being kind and generous is not to receive a personal blessing or fulfill a commandment. Instead, it is to build God's kingdom by helping others—those who are marginalized, forgotten, and underprivileged. It is to work toward a reversal of the social system so that those on the top and those on the bottom meet in the middle, gathered around the same metaphoric table. Then we will all be blessed and righteous, not only as individuals but as the kingdom of God and the Body of Christ.

---

1. Monika K. Hellwig, *Gladness Their Escort: Homiletic Reflections for Sundays and Feastdays, Years A, B and C* (Collegeville: Liturgical Press, 1987), 369.

Twenty-Third Sunday
in Ordinary Time

FIRST READING   WISDOM 9:13-18b

Who can know God's counsel,
   or who can conceive what the LORD intends?
For the deliberations of mortals are timid,
   and unsure are our plans.
For the corruptible body burdens the soul
   and the earthen shelter weighs down the mind that has
      many concerns.
And scarce do we guess the things on earth,
   and what is within our grasp we find with difficulty;
      but when things are in heaven, who can search them out?
Or who ever knew your counsel, except you had given wisdom
   and sent your holy spirit from on high?
And thus were the paths of those on earth made straight.

For background notes on the book of Wisdom, see the Nineteenth
Sunday in Ordinary Time. The book was written in the Hellenistic
period (late first century BCE to first century CE), yet the author
claims to be King Solomon, who ruled in the tenth century BCE.
Our reading draws from a longer petition for wisdom (9:1-18) that
is based on Solomon's prayer in 1 Kings 3:6-9. The above verses
ponder the insignificance of humans while expressing faith that God
can grant wisdom and understanding. The opening question ("Who
can know God's counsel?") echoes Isaiah 40:13-14 (also Sir 1:2-6). A
common philosophical belief in the Greco-Roman period was that
the body burdened or weighed down the soul. According to our text,
what unburdens and leads to true understanding is divine Wisdom
as a manifestation of God. Our reading skips the final, key phrase in
verse 18: "and people learned what pleases you, / and were saved by
Wisdom." One of the book's key themes is that "Wisdom" has saving
powers that elsewhere only God possesses.

RESPONSORIAL PSALM   PSALM 90:3-4, 5-6, 12-13, 14 and 17

In every age, O Lord, you have been our refuge.

SECOND READING   PHILEMON 9-10, 12-17

I, Paul, an old man,
   and now also a prisoner for Christ Jesus,
   urge you on behalf of my child Onesimus,
   whose father I have become in my imprisonment;
   I am sending him, that is, my own heart, back to you.
I should have liked to retain him for myself,
   so that he might serve me on your behalf
   in my imprisonment for the gospel,
   but I did not want to do anything without your consent,
   so that the good you do might not be forced but voluntary.
Perhaps this is why he was away from you for a while,
   that you might have him back forever,
   no longer as a slave
   but more than a slave, a brother,
   beloved especially to me, but even more so to you,
   as a man and in the Lord.
So if you regard me as a partner, welcome him as you would me.

During one of Paul's periods of incarceration, he wrote this correspondence to Philemon and the church that was in his house. The letter is only twenty-five verses long, and this is the only time we read from it in our Sunday lectionary cycle. Onesimus (whose name means "useful" or "beneficial") was enslaved by Philemon; at some point he either ran away or was sent to care for Paul in prison. During that time, Onesimus became a convert to the gospel. Slavery in the Greco-Roman world was legal and often the result of bankruptcy or need. For an enslaved person to be freed, the "owner" would first expect recompense. This letter is Paul's appeal to Philemon for one of three possible outcomes (it is unclear which one Paul ultimately seeks): (1) forgive Onesimus's transgressions and accept him back as a slave, (2) allow Onesimus to be sent back to Paul to care for him in prison, or (3) accept Onesimus back not only as a free person without debt but as a brother in Christ. Although our reading implies that the third option was Paul's desired outcome, the letter as a whole supports all three possibilities. Regardless of what Paul is requesting, he is strongly exhorting Philemon to do what is "good." Paul inundates the letter with wordplay in Greek. For example, he refers to Onesimus intimately as "my child" and "my own heart" (the word for "heart," *splagchna*, is a synonym for the Greek word "child," *pais*). Paul also says that he has become a "father" to (literally "begotten") Onesimus.

GOSPEL   LUKE 14:25-33

Great crowds were traveling with Jesus,
  and he turned and addressed them,
  "If anyone comes to me without hating his father and mother,
  wife and children, brothers and sisters,
  and even his own life,
  he cannot be my disciple.
Whoever does not carry his own cross and come after me
  cannot be my disciple.
Which of you wishing to construct a tower
  does not first sit down and calculate the cost
  to see if there is enough for its completion?
Otherwise, after laying the foundation
  and finding himself unable to finish the work
  the onlookers should laugh at him and say,
  'This one began to build but did not have the resources
    to finish.'
Or what king marching into battle would not first sit down
  and decide whether with ten thousand troops
  he can successfully oppose another king
  advancing upon him with twenty thousand troops?
But if not, while he is still far away,
  he will send a delegation to ask for peace terms.
In the same way,
  anyone of you who does not renounce all his possessions
  cannot be my disciple."

We move from Jesus at table (last week) to Jesus on the road to Jerusalem, accompanied by a large crowd. Alluding to the moment when he will literally take up his own cross, Jesus describes what it means figuratively for his disciples to take up their own. Ultimately, discipleship is a response to grace, but it also makes great demands and can come at a high cost. The point of our Gospel is that followers of Jesus must be devoted to him to the point of giving up everything (and paradoxically gaining everything; see Luke 12:33). To underscore his meaning, Luke employs severe and shocking imagery of "hating" one's family and even oneself (compare with gentler language in Matt 10:37-38), which is best understood as hyperbole. Indeed, in the ancient world, much more than our own, people did not conceive of themselves so much as individuals but as inextricable parts of a community or extended family. The language of "hating" one's family would therefore have been even more shocking than it is to us today. The parables about building and going out to battle warn Jesus's disciples that following him requires careful assessment of resources (a metaphor for one's commitment) beforehand. Discipleship requires a total surrender of one's resources or renunciation of "all . . . possessions," another strong statement that Luke employs to make his point.

Ponder

Our first reading and responsorial psalm contrast our transience and fragility with God's eternity. To be human is to be "weigh[ed] down" by our lives and our concerns. We are like dust and fleeting, "changing grass." Yet the remarkable promise is that God loves us and works within our fragility. Manifesting as divine Wisdom, God's "holy spirit" leads us slowly into freedom and truth. Our task is to be open and ready to respond, handing over our burdens and all that enslaves us in order to accept God's invitation. What weighs you down or enslaves you today? As you name these things, allow God entry into your burdens to carry them for you, to carry you, and to help set you free.

Sadly, to be Christian today is often synonymous with being "normal" or acceptable. It is not viewed as something that requires great effort or comes at a steep price. According to Paul and Luke, this is not true discipleship. Discipleship means the willingness to purge ourselves of everything—material possessions that clutter our lives as well as interior possessions that clutter our minds—in order to give ourselves freely to God and serve all who need us. In the Gospel, Jesus asks the crowds to calculate the cost of discipleship and to weigh it against that which they hold most dear. What is it that you hold most dear? What does discipleship cost in your own life?

Twenty-Fourth Sunday
in Ordinary Time

FIRST READING   EXODUS 32:7-11, 13-14

The LORD said to Moses,
  "Go down at once to your people,
  whom you brought out of the land of Egypt,
  for they have become depraved.
They have soon turned aside from the way I pointed out to them,
  making for themselves a molten calf and worshiping it,
  sacrificing to it and crying out,
  'This is your God, O Israel,
  who brought you out of the land of Egypt!'
I see how stiff-necked this people is," continued the LORD
      to Moses.
"Let me alone, then,
  that my wrath may blaze up against them to consume them.
Then I will make of you a great nation."

But Moses implored the LORD, his God, saying,
  "Why, O LORD, should your wrath blaze up against your
      own people,
  whom you brought out of the land of Egypt
  with such great power and with so strong a hand?
Remember your servants Abraham, Isaac, and Israel,
  and how you swore to them by your own self, saying,
  'I will make your descendants as numerous as the stars in
      the sky;
  and all this land that I promised,
  I will give your descendants as their perpetual heritage.' "
So the LORD relented in the punishment
  he had threatened to inflict on his people.

The setting is Mount Sinai. While Moses is conversing with God, the Israelites grow desperate as they wait for him (he is their prophet, the sole mediator of God's word to them). They create a figurine of a golden calf through which to worship the God who "brought [them]

249

out of the land of Egypt." (Note that in earlier Israelite and Canaanite traditions, calves and bulls were common images of the divine.) This episode is mirrored in 1 Kings 12:25-33, when the first king of the northern kingdom of Israel (Jeroboam) erects two golden calves as images of God. In our reading, God threatens to consume the people in justified anger. Yet Moses persuades God to renounce this plan by inquiring as to what the Egyptians would say and by reminding God that the covenant with the people of Israel is eternal and everlasting. God listens to Moses and relents. The Hebrew term "relent" (*niham*) also means "to comfort" or "to have compassion." In other words, God both relents and has compassion on the people. The episode recalls Genesis 18, in which Abraham persuades God to relent from punishment against Sodom (at least momentarily); it suggests that God can be persuaded by human intercessors. The text is also a reminder that Moses is the true servant and defender of Israel.

RESPONSORIAL PSALM   PSALM 51:3-4, 12-13, 17, 19 (LUKE 15:18)

I will rise and go to my father.

SECOND READING   1 TIMOTHY 1:12-17

Beloved:
I am grateful to him who has strengthened me, Christ Jesus
     our Lord,
   because he considered me trustworthy
   in appointing me to the ministry.
I was once a blasphemer and a persecutor and arrogant,
   but I have been mercifully treated
   because I acted out of ignorance in my unbelief.
Indeed, the grace of our Lord has been abundant,
   along with the faith and love that are in Christ Jesus.
This saying is trustworthy and deserves full acceptance:
   Christ Jesus came into the world to save sinners.
Of these I am the foremost.
But for that reason I was mercifully treated,
   so that in me, as the foremost,

Christ Jesus might display all his patience as an example
for those who would come to believe in him for everlasting life.
To the king of ages, incorruptible, invisible, the only God,
honor and glory forever and ever. Amen.

For the next seven weeks, we will be reading from 1–2 Timothy. Though we refer to the writer as "Paul," Pauline authorship is doubtful. The letters are named for Paul's "true child" (1 Tim 1:2) and disciple, whom Paul designates to continue his legacy and pass down his teachings faithfully. The letters envision the church as a "household of God" (1 Tim 3:15) rooted in specific roles for its members (bishops, deacons, elders, widows, etc.). Today's reading describes Christ's mercy, which Paul has received in the most profound way, transforming him into a true teacher and witness to Christ. Paul becomes the model of conversion or full transformation that can be dramatic and instantaneous, but more often is a slow, subtle, ongoing life process.

GOSPEL   LUKE 15:1-32 [OR 15:1-10]

Tax collectors and sinners were all drawing near to listen to Jesus,
    but the Pharisees and scribes began to complain, saying,
    "This man welcomes sinners and eats with them."
So to them he addressed this parable.
"What man among you having a hundred sheep and losing one
        of them
    would not leave the ninety-nine in the desert
    and go after the lost one until he finds it?
And when he does find it,
    he sets it on his shoulders with great joy
    and, upon his arrival home,
    he calls together his friends and neighbors and says to them,
    'Rejoice with me because I have found my lost sheep.'
I tell you, in just the same way
    there will be more joy in heaven over one sinner who repents
    than over ninety-nine righteous people
    who have no need of repentance.

"Or what woman having ten coins and losing one
    would not light a lamp and sweep the house,
    searching carefully until she finds it?

And when she does find it,
  she calls together her friends and neighbors
  and says to them,
  'Rejoice with me because I have found the coin that I lost.'
In just the same way, I tell you,
  there will be rejoicing among the angels of God
  over one sinner who repents."

Then he said,
  "A man had two sons, and the younger son said to his father,
  'Father give me the share of your estate that should come
      to me.'
So the father divided the property between them.
After a few days, the younger son collected all his belongings
  and set off to a distant country
  where he squandered his inheritance on a life of dissipation.
When he had freely spent everything,
  a severe famine struck that country,
  and he found himself in dire need.
So he hired himself out to one of the local citizens
  who sent him to his farm to tend the swine.
And he longed to eat his fill of the pods on which the swine fed,
  but nobody gave him any.
Coming to his senses he thought,
  'How many of my father's hired workers
  have more than enough food to eat,
  but here am I, dying from hunger.
I shall get up and go to my father and I shall say to him,
  "Father, I have sinned against heaven and against you.
I no longer deserve to be called your son;
  treat me as you would treat one of your hired workers." '
So he got up and went back to his father.
While he was still a long way off,
  his father caught sight of him,
  and was filled with compassion.
He ran to his son, embraced him and kissed him.
His son said to him,
  'Father, I have sinned against heaven and against you;
  I no longer deserve to be called your son.'
But his father ordered his servants,

'Quickly bring the finest robe and put it on him;
     put a ring on his finger and sandals on his feet.
Take the fattened calf and slaughter it.
Then let us celebrate with a feast,
     because this son of mine was dead, and has come to life again;
     he was lost, and has been found.'
Then the celebration began.
Now the older son had been out in the field
     and, on his way back, as he neared the house,
     he heard the sound of music and dancing.
He called one of the servants and asked what this might mean.
The servant said to him,
     'Your brother has returned
     and your father has slaughtered the fattened calf
     because he has him back safe and sound.'
He became angry,
     and when he refused to enter the house,
     his father came out and pleaded with him.
He said to his father in reply,
     'Look, all these years I served you
     and not once did I disobey your orders;
     yet you never gave me even a young goat to feast on with my
          friends. But when your son returns,
     who swallowed up your property with prostitutes,
     for him you slaughter the fattened calf.'
He said to him,
     'My son, you are here with me always;
     everything I have is yours.
But now we must celebrate and rejoice,
     because your brother was dead and has come to life again;
     he was lost and has been found.' "

Lurking behind Luke 15 is the question of whether anyone is beyond the limits of God's mercy. The answer is no, as depicted in three parables that underscore a divine mercy that breaks all human rationale. God's mercy is like the shepherd who abandons ninety-nine sheep in the desert to search for a single one (not to worry—other shepherds would be left to guard the rest!), or like a woman who turns her house upside down in order to recover a "coin" (literally a *drachma* in Greek; no paltry sum, it could feed a whole family for a day). And in the parable of the Prodigal Son, God is a Jewish father who joyfully welcomes home a wayward son with no strings attached (for more on this parable, see notes for the Fourth Sunday of Lent). The purpose of these parables is to push the limits of how we imagine divine mercy. It is extravagant, limitless, and marked by unbridled joy at human conversion. Because Jesus's disciples have such a merciful God (whose mercy exceeds that of any human), they (and we) can embark trustingly and joyfully with Jesus on the way to God.

Ponder

In the broader context of Exodus, divine anger and punishment are entirely justified against a people who continually turn their backs on God. Yet God's primary character trait in our reading and throughout the Bible is not anger but mercy. In Exodus, this mercy occurs even before human repentance and helps guide the people to authentic remorse. Similarly, Paul describes God's mercy breaking through and forcefully transforming him so that he could repent. The Gospel parables underscore God's relentless search for us that precedes and invites our conversion. How do you experience God's relentless search for you?

Our readings call us to participate in God's joyful, unbridled acts of mercy. 1 Timothy reminds us that Christ's primary task is to "save sinners." As Christ's Body on earth, this is also our task—to reach out, to help others grow and transform, to practice mercy and love. Exodus is a powerful story of human mercy, as Moses intercedes on behalf of his people and successfully changes God's mind. And in the Gospel, human characters as God's agents work tirelessly for the one lost sheep, coin, or son. Our readings encourage us to ponder the interplay of mercy, repentance, and forgiveness in our own lives: in what we have received, in what we need or desire from God and others, and in our ability to extend mercy and love to all we encounter—joyfully, tirelessly, and generously.

Twenty-Fifth Sunday
in Ordinary Time

FIRST READING   AMOS 8:4-7

Hear this, you who trample upon the needy
and destroy the poor of the land!
"When will the new moon be over," you ask,
"that we may sell our grain,
and the sabbath, that we may display the wheat?
We will diminish the ephah,
add to the shekel,
and fix our scales for cheating!
We will buy the lowly for silver,
and the poor for a pair of sandals;
even the refuse of the wheat we will sell!"
The LORD has sworn by the pride of Jacob:
Never will I forget a thing they have done!

Amos is one of two prophetic books (along with Hosea) that focuses on the northern kingdom of Israel. The book is attributed to a humble farmer and herder and a native of the southern kingdom of Judah. He traveled to Israel during its most prosperous era (ca. 760–750 BCE), prior to its demise and fall to Assyria in 720 BCE. This was a time of social and religious corruption, and Amos's primary focus was "justice" and "righteousness" (see, for example, his well-known call to "let justice surge like waters, / and righteousness like an unfailing stream" in 5:24). He prophesied specifically against those on top who abused positions of privilege and wealth for further profit. The "new moon" was a time during which no work was permitted; here Amos condemns those who observe holy days while practicing injustice against their neighbors. To "diminish the ephah" was to sell less than its apparent volume (the ephah was a unit of dry measure for grain), and to "add to the shekel" was to overcharge. We will read Amos again next week.

RESPONSORIAL PSALM   PSALM 113:1-2, 4-6, 7-8

Praise the Lord who lifts up the poor.
or: Alleluia.

SECOND READING   1 TIMOTHY 2:1-8

Beloved:
First of all, I ask that supplications, prayers,
    petitions, and thanksgivings be offered for everyone,
    for kings and for all in authority,
    that we may lead a quiet and tranquil life
    in all devotion and dignity.
This is good and pleasing to God our savior,
    who wills everyone to be saved
    and to come to knowledge of the truth.
        For there is one God.
        There is also one mediator between God and men,
        the man Christ Jesus,
        who gave himself as ransom for all.
This was the testimony at the proper time.
For this I was appointed preacher and apostle
    —I am speaking the truth, I am not lying—,
    teacher of the Gentiles in faith and truth.

It is my wish, then, that in every place the men should pray,
    lifting up holy hands, without anger or argument.

Our reading from 1 Timothy outlines specific instructions on prayer, which Paul describes as "supplications, prayers, petitions, and thanksgivings." These various forms of prayer should be offered for everyone, not only members of the Christian community. In the reading, Paul is not urging favoritism for kings and authority figures; instead, he prays for those in positions of power so that the Christian community can live in peace and harmony with its neighbors, devoting themselves to worship and to living dignified, quiet lives. The Greek word translated as "devotion" (*eusebeia*) also translates as "godliness" or "piety." The letter contains a strong emphasis on God as the single, universal savior and on Christ as the single mediator between God and human beings.

GOSPEL   LUKE 16:1-13 [OR 16:10-13]

Jesus said to his disciples,
  "A rich man had a steward
  who was reported to him for squandering his property.
He summoned him and said,
  'What is this I hear about you?
Prepare a full account of your stewardship,
  because you can no longer be my steward.'
The steward said to himself, 'What shall I do,
  now that my master is taking the position of steward away
    from me?
I am not strong enough to dig and I am ashamed to beg.
I know what I shall do so that,
  when I am removed from the stewardship,
  they may welcome me into their homes.'
He called in his master's debtors one by one.
To the first he said,
  'How much do you owe my master?'
He replied, 'One hundred measures of olive oil.'
He said to him, 'Here is your promissory note.
Sit down and quickly write one for fifty.'
Then to another the steward said, 'And you, how much do
    you owe?'
He replied, 'One hundred kors of wheat.'
The steward said to him, 'Here is your promissory note;
  write one for eighty.'
And the master commended that dishonest[1] steward for
  acting prudently.

"For the children of this world
  are more prudent in dealing with their own generation
  than are the children of light.
I tell you, make friends for yourselves with dishonest wealth,[2]
  so that when it fails, you will be welcomed into
    eternal dwellings.

---

1. "Dishonest": more literally, "unrighteous" (Greek *adikia*).
2. "Dishonest wealth": the Greek phrase translates literally as "mammon of unrighteousness." Mammon is a Greek transliteration of the Aramaic term for "wealth"
or "money."

> The person who is trustworthy in very small matters
>   is also trustworthy in great ones;
> and the person who is dishonest in very small matters
>   is also dishonest in great ones.
> If, therefore, you are not trustworthy with dishonest wealth,
>   who will trust you with true wealth?
> If you are not trustworthy with what belongs to another,
>   who will give you what is yours?
> No servant can serve two masters.
> He will either hate one and love the other,
>   or be devoted to one and despise the other.
> You cannot serve both God and mammon."

Luke 16 offers a series of parables about wealth and material goods, or what Luke refers to as "dishonest wealth" (or literally "mammon of unrighteousness"; see footnote). Today's reading leads to the parable of the rich man and Lazarus (next Sunday). Unlike many Gospel parables with clear messages, the parable in the first half of our reading is rather opaque. The rich man has a steward who is accused of squandering his master's property. The language of "rich man" suggests that the man is not to be liked or admired (as in the rich man and Lazarus). The text may also allude to the rich man's practice of usury (i.e., lending money at very high rates of interest). Once fired, the steward acts decisively and creatively for his own survival by reducing people's debts to his master. Strangely, the steward is not beaten or punished for his actions. Instead, the master commends him for acting "prudently" (Greek *phronimōs*), a word that refers to practical action taken to accomplish a particular goal. This seems to be the point of the parable in the context of Jesus's subsequent explanation: the steward himself is an unrighteous child "of this world" rather than a child "of light," yet his ingenuity and resolve are what disciples of Jesus should have regarding what matters to them ("eternal dwellings"). While the steward serves mammon (wealth), they serve God. To "make friends . . . with dishonest wealth" (i.e., the wealth of *this* world or material wealth) is not to serve it but to be trustworthy with it in order to be entrusted with "true wealth" (the wealth of God's kingdom). Disciples have no choice but to deal with material wealth, yet they are to do so prudently (as if it were a "friend" or equal but not a "master"), not allowing it to seduce them away from God.

Ponder

Our readings make a distinction between single- and split-minded orientations. Amos describes the split-minded religiosity of the wealthy, while Luke's parable describes the single-minded focus of the dishonest steward. The parable is meant to discomfort, for we are not supposed to like the steward, yet his resolve and focused determination are to be admired. Unlike the steward, however, our resolve should be oriented toward God, not toward short-term gain. Ultimately, both Amos and Luke condemn those who are self-serving and warn us of the insidious attraction of material goods. As you pray with these texts, examine the role money and other material things play in your own life. What do you do that helps you purify your intentions and focus on what truly matters?

The parable of the dishonest steward is notoriously difficult to interpret, but it tells us something important about cultivating relationships that are forward-looking. The steward does so with his master's "debtors," relieving them of the stress and burden of debt. Of course, the motivations for his actions are selfish; he seeks his own short-term survival. In contrast, true relationships are cultivated not toward one's self-gain but toward a vision of the kingdom of God. First Timothy describes this vision in terms of unity and God's desire that all may be saved and come to "knowledge of the truth" (2:4). Explore the motivations behind your relationships. To what extent are they self-oriented, and to what extent are they oriented toward this vision of the kingdom of God?

Twenty-Sixth Sunday in Ordinary Time

FIRST READING   AMOS 6:1a, 4-7

Thus says the LORD the God of hosts:
Woe to the complacent in Zion!
Lying upon beds of ivory,
    stretched comfortably on their couches,
they eat lambs taken from the flock,
    and calves from the stall!
Improvising to the music of the harp,
    like David, they devise their own accompaniment.
They drink wine from bowls
    and anoint themselves with the best oils;
    yet they are not made ill by the collapse of Joseph!
Therefore, now they shall be the first to go into exile,
    and their wanton revelry shall be done away with.

Our reading is an indictment against complacency, apathy, and gluttony. The prophet speaks to the "complacent" or elite of both Judah ("Zion") in the south and Israel ("Joseph") in the north, those whose lives involve excessive consumption and luxury similar to the "rich man" in today's Gospel. They make use of elaborate furniture with ivory panels, eat the choicest meat (calves from the stall subsist only on milk, so their meat is very tender), and have musical entertainment at meals. The reference to David may be ironic as a subtle reference to pride, for David was remembered as a great musician. These elites drink wine from ceremonial "bowls" (Hebrew *mizraq*) reserved for the altar, and they anoint themselves with the "best" (or more literally "first") oils that also have ceremonial use. Meanwhile, they are apathetic to the decline of their own people. Amos correctly prophesies that the elites of Israel (Joseph) will be the first to be taken into exile by the Assyrian invaders (Israel falls to Assyria about 150 years before Judah falls to Babylon).

RESPONSORIAL PSALM   PSALM 146:7, 8-9, 9-10

Praise the Lord, my soul!
or: Alleluia.

SECOND READING   1 TIMOTHY 6:11-16

But you, man of God, pursue righteousness,
    devotion, faith, love, patience, and gentleness.
Compete well for the faith.
Lay hold of eternal life, to which you were called
    when you made the noble confession in the presence of
        many witnesses.
I charge you before God, who gives life to all things,
    and before Christ Jesus,
    who gave testimony under Pontius Pilate for the
        noble confession,
    to keep the commandment without stain or reproach
    until the appearance of our Lord Jesus Christ
    that the blessed and only ruler
    will make manifest at the proper time,
    the King of kings and Lord of lords,
    who alone has immortality, who dwells in
        unapproachable light,
    and whom no human being has seen or can see.
To him be honor and eternal power. Amen.

In the conclusion of his letter, Paul urges Timothy to hold fast to his profession of faith or "noble confession" in Christ. The phrase "man of God" is used for Moses and other great prophets in the Hebrew Bible (see Deut 33:1). "Compete well" translates more literally as "fight the good fight" and symbolizes physical competition and endurance (see 1 Tim 1:18 and 2 Tim 4:7). The "commandment" (Greek *entolē*) is something a person undertakes and promises to see through, in this case Timothy's "noble confession." The notion that God dwells as light and cannot be approached directly is a common metaphor in the Hebrew Bible (see, for example, Exod 33:20).

GOSPEL   LUKE 16:19-31

Jesus said to the Pharisees:
"There was a rich man who dressed in purple garments and
    fine linen
and dined sumptuously each day.
And lying at his door was a poor man named Lazarus, covered
    with sores,
    who would gladly have eaten his fill of the scraps
    that fell from the rich man's table.
Dogs even used to come and lick his sores.
When the poor man died,
    he was carried away by angels to the bosom of Abraham.
The rich man also died and was buried,
    and from the netherworld, where he was in torment,
    he raised his eyes and saw Abraham far off
    and Lazarus at his side.
And he cried out, 'Father Abraham, have pity on me.
Send Lazarus to dip the tip of his finger in water and cool
        my tongue,
    for I am suffering torment in these flames.'
Abraham replied,
    'My child, remember that you received
    what was good during your lifetime
    while Lazarus likewise received what was bad;
    but now he is comforted here, whereas you are tormented.
Moreover, between us and you a great chasm is established
    to prevent anyone from crossing who might wish to go
    from our side to yours or from your side to ours.'
He said, 'Then I beg you, father,
    send him to my father's house, for I have five brothers,
    so that he may warn them,
    lest they too come to this place of torment.'
But Abraham replied, 'They have Moses and the prophets.
Let them listen to them.'
He said, 'Oh no, father Abraham,
    but if someone from the dead goes to them, they will repent.'

Then Abraham said, 'If they will not listen to Moses and
the prophets,
neither will they be persuaded if someone should rise from
the dead.' "

Our recent parables on stewardship and the right use of wealth culminate in this parable of the rich man and Lazarus. Like last week's parable of the dishonest steward, this parable begins with "a rich man." The text describes the rich man in terms of his luxuries: purple garments (expensive, dyed cloth), fine linen, and good food. Lazarus, "a poor man," comes to us in similarly vivid terms ("lying at his door" and "covered with sores"), yet he represents the opposite extreme. The rich man's apparent cruelty contrasts with the natural compassion of dogs, who relieve suffering and pain with their tongues and have greater sympathy for Lazarus than the rich man does. To be with Abraham is synonymous with being in paradise, and to be at "the bosom of Abraham" is to be in the choicest position in paradise. Notice that the parable makes no comment on Lazarus's moral character; the focus is only on his extreme destitution. When Lazarus goes to Abraham, he finally receives the comfort and compassion denied him in this world. When the rich man calls out to Abraham, he views Lazarus as his servant, calling for him to be sent to cool his tongue. Abraham responds to the rich man gently, calling him "[m]y child." When the rich man again begs Abraham to "send" Lazarus to his father's house to warn his brothers, he demonstrates that he does not understand, nor has he truly repented. Abraham states that the Scriptures (the Hebrew Scriptures) provide all the guidance needed for right living; he also evokes Jesus's resurrection in the final comment: "neither will they be persuaded if someone should rise from the dead." The parable therefore connects the ability to hear and respond to the laws and teachings in the Hebrew Bible to the ability to believe in the resurrection of Christ (or vice versa).

Ponder

There is a great chasm in our world between the "haves" and the "have-nots," and God is on the side of the latter. Our readings from Amos and Luke are both a salve and a sword. They are a sword for those of us with privilege, and they are a comforting salve for those who suffer now. The Gospel's metaphor of a "great chasm" in the next life might also be viewed as a door separating two realities in this life. On one side, people with plenty are feasting, while on the other side, people without are starving. In this life, the door can be opened; the "haves" can join the "have-nots," sharing their plenty. Yet the unopened door now will lead to a chasm in the next life, and the scenario of feasting and starving will be flipped. As you pray with the readings, on what side of the door do you find yourself?

Our reading from 1 Timothy follows a warning to avoid love of money, which causes people to stray from the faith (6:10). Instead, Paul exhorts Timothy to "pursue" and "[c]ompete well for the faith" in order to "[l]ay hold of eternal life." Over the past few weeks, our readings have challenged us to think about our priorities, about how we orient ourselves and what we ultimately desire to "lay hold of." In some sense, the overall teaching is simple: if we pursue God with single-minded focus, all the right priorities will naturally follow. How does our reading from 1 Timothy inspire or challenge you? How might you use these words as a guide this week?

Twenty-Seventh Sunday
in Ordinary Time

FIRST READING   HABAKKUK 1:2-3; 2:2-4

How long, O LORD? I cry for help
  but you do not listen!
I cry out to you, "Violence!"
  but you do not intervene.
Why do you let me see ruin;
  why must I look at misery?
Destruction and violence are before me;
  there is strife, and clamorous discord.
Then the LORD answered me and said:
  Write down the vision clearly upon the tablets,
  so that one can read it readily.
For the vision still has its time,
  presses on to fulfillment, and will not disappoint;
if it delays, wait for it,
  it will surely come, it will not be late.
The rash one has no integrity;[1]
  but the just one, because of his faith, shall live.

We know very little about the prophet Habakkuk. He lived through a time of oppression in Judah, likely at the hands of Babylon (seventh–sixth centuries BCE), though his expressions of pain and suffering speak across historical periods. Habakkuk is preoccupied with the problem of evil and injustice in the world. He speaks in the first person on behalf of the entire community, modeling healthy human expressions of grief and protest before God. He simultaneously demonstrates trust in God's promise that those who promote evil will pass away, while those who act justly and faithfully will live. Paul will work this "heart of Habakkuk" into his own teachings on faith (Rom 1:17; Gal 3:11; see also Heb 10:38). Our reading opens with

---

1. "The rash one has no integrity": literally "the one swelled up, his spirit is not right in him."

Habakkuk's dialogue with God, in which he expresses the anguish of the people in the midst of oppression. Habakkuk finds God's toleration of the wicked and seeming unwillingness to help Judah very difficult to understand. When God answers, it is to tell Habakkuk to write down the vision so that others in the future will be able to read it. The final verse summarizes the whole prophecy: the just one will live because of faith. In Hebrew, "faith" means faithfulness, loyalty, and steadfastness. Paul also says that the just one lives by, or is "justified by," faith (Rom 3:28; Gal 2:16).

RESPONSORIAL PSALM   PSALM 95:1-2, 6-7, 8-9

If today you hear his voice, harden not your hearts.

SECOND READING   2 TIMOTHY 1:6-8, 13-14

Beloved:
I remind you to stir into flame
    the gift of God that you have through the imposition of
        my hands.
For God did not give us a spirit of cowardice
    but rather of power and love and self-control.
So do not be ashamed of your testimony to our Lord,
    nor of me, a prisoner for his sake;
    but bear your share of hardship for the gospel
    with the strength that comes from God.

Take as your norm the sound words that you heard from me,
    in the faith and love that are in Christ Jesus.
Guard this rich trust with the help of the Holy Spirit
    that dwells within us.

In the beginning of his second letter to Timothy, Paul reminds Timothy of the key role of memory in continuing to live by and make present the faith within him. According to the letter, Paul ordained Timothy personally ("the imposition of my hands"). Paul therefore calls Timothy to continue to live according to the grace bestowed on him. It seems that Timothy was inclined toward being timid ("spirit of cowardice"), and Paul reminds him that his testimony will involve both preaching and suffering. In his preaching and his personal conduct, Paul exhorts Timothy to adhere to the truths he has learned. The "rich trust" is the entire content of Christian teaching that Timothy has "heard from" Paul.

GOSPEL   LUKE 17:5-10

The apostles said to the Lord, "Increase our faith."
The Lord replied,
    "If you have faith the size of a mustard seed,
    you would say to this mulberry tree,
    'Be uprooted and planted in the sea,' and it would obey you.

"Who among you would say to your servant
    who has just come in from plowing or tending sheep in
        the field,
    'Come here immediately and take your place at table'?
Would he not rather say to him,
    'Prepare something for me to eat.
Put on your apron and wait on me while I eat and drink.
You may eat and drink when I am finished'?
Is he grateful to that servant because he did what
        was commanded?
So should it be with you.
When you have done all you have been commanded,
    say, 'We are unprofitable servants;
    we have done what we were obliged to do.' "

After the parable of the rich man and Lazarus, and additional warnings about being on guard against things "that cause sin" (17:1), the disciples say to Jesus, "Increase our faith." Jesus responds that what they have is enough; it is the quality rather than the quantity that is key. As with many of his parables, Jesus utilizes agricultural imagery. A mulberry bush can grow up to seventy feet high, and its root system is incredibly invasive. A mustard seed is small, yet it spreads like a weed and is very difficult to eliminate. Jesus states daringly that faith as tenacious as a mustard seed has the power not only to uproot the mulberry tree but to plant it in the sea! The point of the next parable, found only in Luke, is that when one has faith, or lives faithfully, there is no such thing as doing "enough" work for the gospel. Faith means complete and unceasing dedication. Echoing the mustard seed analogy, the parable also demonstrates that the faithful person will never stop "spreading" or acting in accordance with that faith. In this case, faith precedes action (works), yet true faith will always live itself out in action. In the final verse, the word translated as "unprofitable" (Greek *achreios*) literally means "worthless" or "useless." In other words, faith manifests externally as faithfulness or faithful service that is its own reward and that fulfills every desire.

Ponder

Habakkuk struggles with the problem of evil. Our reading balances his cries of anguish with God's promise of a future reality in which the "just one" will live because of his faithfulness. Today Habakkuk's vision is still moving with an inward dynamism toward its future realization, waiting to be fulfilled at the moment determined by God. As you pray with Habakkuk this week, listen to his cry: "How long, O Lord?" Allow this cry to resonate with you today, in the midst of whatever evils you are struggling with in your life, community, or society. When you hear God's response to Habakkuk, do you trust it? How does this promise comfort you, strengthen you, or change the way you live in this world today?

Faith is an inner attitude that begins with God and expresses itself through faithful service. Jesus reminds us that God implants this faith within us, which grows like a mustard seed, spreading ferociously and tenaciously. Paul exhorts Timothy to remember and "stir into flame" the gift of faith, to guard it and to be fearless in witnessing to it. Like Timothy, Paul, and Habakkuk, God calls each of us into partnership as we work to live into the promise of the coming of God's kingdom. Our readings invite us to ponder the quality of our faith right now and the actions we might take to remember and live into the gift of faith that we have been given.

Twenty-Eighth Sunday
in Ordinary Time

FIRST READING   2 KINGS 5:14-17

Naaman went down and plunged into the Jordan seven times
at the word of Elisha, the man of God.
His flesh became again like the flesh of a little child,
and he was clean of his leprosy.

Naaman returned with his whole retinue to the man of God.
On his arrival he stood before Elisha and said,
"Now I know that there is no God in all the earth,
except in Israel.
Please accept a gift from your servant."

Elisha replied, "As the Lord lives whom I serve, I will not take it";
and despite Naaman's urging, he still refused.
Naaman said: "If you will not accept,
please let me, your servant, have two mule-loads of earth,
for I will no longer offer holocaust or sacrifice
to any other god except to the LORD."

In the stories of the prophet Elisha, Israel is often consumed with
fighting against Aram or the Arameans, people who lived north of
Israel in modern-day Syria. In this story, the Aramean army commander Naaman suffers from some skin affliction ("leprosy" in the
ancient world covered a wide range of skin conditions), and he is
told by a young Israelite girl whom he has taken captive that Elisha,
the prophet of Israel, can cure him of his disease. Naaman listens
to her, which is striking, considering that the God of Israel is not
his God and that the one advising him is a young, foreign slave girl
(in other words, a "nobody" to this important man). Naaman then
travels to visit Elisha. From far off, Elisha sends him to wash in the
Jordan River seven times, which Naaman does (after first grumbling
that Elisha will not simply cure him on the spot!). When Naaman
returns to Elisha, he does so cleansed and as a convert. Elisha re-
fuses to accept a gift as it was not he but God who healed Naaman.

Naaman then wishes to take earth from the land of Israel with him in order to worship the God of Israel in Aram. In those times, it was believed that particular gods were limited to particular places and people; therefore, Naaman had to take the actual soil of Israel with him in order to worship the God of Israel.

RESPONSORIAL PSALM   PSALM 98:1, 2-3, 3-4

The Lord has revealed to the nations his saving power.

SECOND READING   2 TIMOTHY 2:8-13

Beloved:
Remember Jesus Christ, raised from the dead, a descendant
    of David:
    such is my gospel, for which I am suffering,
    even to the point of chains, like a criminal.
But the word of God is not chained.
Therefore, I bear with everything for the sake of those who
    are chosen,
    so that they too may obtain the salvation that is in Christ Jesus,
    together with eternal glory.
This saying is trustworthy:
    If we have died with him
    we shall also live with him;
    if we persevere
    we shall also reign with him.
    But if we deny him
    he will deny us.
    If we are unfaithful
    he remains faithful,
    for he cannot deny himself.

Paul continues to speak of faith, focusing here on the importance of staying faithful to the gospel message even in times of suffering. The first statement ("Remember Jesus Christ, raised from the dead, a descendant of David") is a concise expression of Paul's entire message. Though Paul is in chains (in prison), the word of God is not, both because of other disciples and because of Paul himself, who is spreading the gospel despite imprisonment. His sufferings are "for the sake of" all believers—the "chosen" or "elect" (NRSV)—so they may one day share in Christ's "eternal glory." When Paul speaks of dying and rising with Christ, he speaks not only of baptism and the promise of life after death but also of how this process unfolds in this life, particularly in the process of persevering through physical suffering and hardship. In the final verse, Paul reminds Timothy that, regardless of whether human beings stay faithful to Christ, Christ remains faithful to God's purposes.

GOSPEL   LUKE 17:11-19

As Jesus continued his journey to Jerusalem,
  he traveled through Samaria and Galilee.
As he was entering a village, ten lepers met him.
They stood at a distance from him and raised their voices, saying,
  "Jesus, Master! Have pity on us!"
And when he saw them, he said,
  "Go show yourselves to the priests."
As they were going they were cleansed.
And one of them, realizing he had been healed,
  returned, glorifying God in a loud voice;
  and he fell at the feet of Jesus and thanked him.
He was a Samaritan.
Jesus said in reply,
  "Ten were cleansed, were they not?
Where are the other nine?
Has none but this foreigner returned to give thanks to God?"
Then he said to him, "Stand up and go;
  your faith has saved you."

Today's Gospel story is unique to Luke. The first verse does not make geographical sense—Samaria and Galilee in the north are far afield from Jerusalem. But geography is not the point. Similar to the story of a foreigner's healing and conversion in 2 Kings, here the "foreigner" (literally "another race") who is healed and saved is a Samaritan from northern Israel. The Samaritans had a long and storied past with Judeans—later Jews—in the south. Beginning in the preexilic period (ca. ninth century BCE), they worshiped in different ways; those from Judah emphasized a single sanctuary in Jerusalem, while those from the north—Israel or Samaria—had many local sanctuaries. Then the two kingdoms fell to foreign empires: Israel to Assyria (ca. 722 BCE) and Judah to Babylon (ca. 586 BCE). Judaism emerged from the Babylonian exile, and when Judeans returned from exile they were very different from their northern neighbors, whom they referred to first as "Samarians" and then as "Samaritans." To Judeans, the Samaritans were non-Jews. As Jesus journeys through Samaria, the ten lepers (those suffering from skin ailments) did not call out "unclean," which was the prescribed response to warn and thus protect others from contracting highly contagious skin diseases (see Lev 13:45). Instead, they cry out for mercy. Jesus instructs them to show themselves to their priests as required by law (when a person was healed of a skin infliction, they had to be inspected before rejoining the community; see Lev 14:2-3). Yet Jesus tells them to do so *before* they are healed. When they are healed on the way, only one—the Samaritan—returns to glorify God. This one is then truly "saved" (Greek *sōzō* connotes both salvation and healing).

Ponder

Suffering or illness (whether physical, mental, or spiritual) elicits different reactions. It can lead to isolation and separation (self-imposed or otherwise) from families, communities, and even faith. Or, suffering can lead to deeper connections with God and others. In 2 Kings, Naaman's disease opened him to deeper connections, pushing him to reach out and listen to foreigners. As a result, he was healed. The lepers in the Gospel had been forcefully separated from their communities, and they cried out to Jesus for healing and reintegration. Take time to ponder your own response to suffering. To whom do you turn in times of difficulty, pain, and brokenness? How do you hear and respond to the suffering of others?

"[T]he word of God is not chained," writes Paul. Our readings challenge us to consider how open we are to the liberating and inclusive word of God in our communities today. We are called to join the responsorial psalm in genuine joy over the gospel's inclusive message and to help facilitate the free and open movement of the Spirit. After all, Paul reminds us, the liberating and liberated word of God will not be chained by human fear, selfishness, or lack of imagination. As we pray with the readings this week, how is God calling us to break down barriers and work to heal fractures in our families, our communities, and our church?

Twenty-Ninth Sunday
in Ordinary Time

In those days, Amalek came and waged war against Israel.
Moses, therefore, said to Joshua,
  "Pick out certain men,
  and tomorrow go out and engage Amalek in battle.
I will be standing on top of the hill
  with the staff of God in my hand."
So Joshua did as Moses told him:
  he engaged Amalek in battle
  after Moses had climbed to the top of the hill with Aaron
      and Hur.
As long as Moses kept his hands raised up,
  Israel had the better of the fight,
  but when he let his hands rest,
  Amalek had the better of the fight.
Moses' hands, however, grew tired;
  so they put a rock in place for him to sit on.
Meanwhile Aaron and Hur supported his hands,
  one on one side and one on the other,
  so that his hands remained steady till sunset.
And Joshua mowed down Amalek and his people
  with the edge of the sword.

As the Israelites move through the desert from Egypt to Canaan, they encounter a number of difficulties. One is the military threat of Amalek, a semi-nomadic group based in the Sinai Peninsula. In the story, God works through Moses's rod or staff to secure Israel's victory. This is the same rod through which God defeated Pharaoh and through which God (through Moses) either produces water or renders it undrinkable (Exod 7:15-19; 17:5-6). The reading demonstrates Moses's tenacity, his humility, and his remarkable intimacy with God. Moses is oriented fully toward God, open to God's power working through him. When tired, he allows others to help him. This is the first time the Bible mentions Moses's successor, Joshua, who will eventually lead Israel into the Promised Land.

RESPONSORIAL PSALM   PSALM 121:1-2, 3-4, 5-6, 7-8

Our help is from the Lord, who made heaven and earth.

SECOND READING   2 TIMOTHY 3:14–4:2

Beloved:
Remain faithful to what you have learned and believed,[1]
   because you know from whom you learned it,
   and that from infancy you have known the sacred Scriptures,
   which are capable of giving you wisdom for salvation
   through faith in Christ Jesus.
All Scripture is inspired by God
   and is useful for teaching, for refutation, for correction,
   and for training in righteousness,
   so that one who belongs to God may be competent,
   equipped for every good work.

I charge you in the presence of God and of Christ Jesus,
   who will judge the living and the dead,
   and by his appearing and his kingly power:
   proclaim the word;
   be persistent whether it is convenient or inconvenient;[2]
   convince, reprimand, encourage through all patience
      and teaching.

We enter into 2 Timothy midthought this week, as Paul is instructing Timothy to avoid those of corrupt mind and "counterfeit faith" (3:8), those who love only themselves (3:2) and never come to understand "truth" (3:7). Instead, Timothy is to remain firm in his ministry and remember what he has learned from Paul and other teachers. The

1. The verb "believed" (Greek *pistoō*) translates literally as "to firmly believe," in the sense of being faithful to or trustworthy in something.
2. The phrase "whether it is convenient or inconvenient" translates literally as "whether the time is favorable or unfavorable."

"sacred Scriptures" are the Jewish Scriptures (the Hebrew Bible), which offer true instruction when read in the context of faith in Christ. These verses about Scripture are commonly cited in discussions of biblical inspiration and the continued relevance of "all" Scripture today. The final verse on persistence in speech, whether it is convenient or not, is unusual advice, for other ancient texts counsel more judicious and careful use of speech. Apparently when it comes to "proclaim[ing] the word," Paul has no use for caution or convenience.

GOSPEL   LUKE 18:1-8

Jesus told his disciples a parable
  about the necessity for them to pray always without
    becoming weary.
He said, "There was a judge in a certain town
  who neither feared God nor respected any human being.
And a widow in that town used to come to him and say,
  'Render a just decision for me against my adversary.'
For a long time the judge was unwilling, but eventually
  he thought,
  'While it is true that I neither fear God nor respect any
    human being,
  because this widow keeps bothering me
  I shall deliver a just decision for her
  lest she finally come and strike me.' "[3]
The Lord said, "Pay attention to what the dishonest judge says.
Will not God then secure the rights of his chosen ones
  who call out to him day and night?
Will he be slow to answer them?
I tell you, he will see to it that justice is done for them speedily.
But when the Son of Man comes, will he find faith on earth?"

This is the first of two parables on prayer found only in Luke (we will read the second next week). Luke is writing for a community that is struggling to understand when and how Christ will return. They

---

3. "Strike me" is a boxing metaphor that translates literally as "hit me under the eye."

had expected his return to happen very soon after his resurrection. Now, with the passage of time, they must reenvision how to remain faithful in a difficult world and for an unknown period of time. Luke insists on perseverance, humility, and prayer, reminding the community that God will not abandon them. Prayer, as we find out in the last verse, must be grounded in fidelity to God. In the parable, the widow is the epitome of powerlessness; she lives in a patriarchal society and has lost her advocate (her husband). Her "adversary" is likely a rich, influential man. Jesus ("[t]he Lord") explains the parable by saying that while it may appear that God delays in responding to our petitions, in actuality, God responds "speedily." The parable has at least two core messages: (1) *Persistence.* In the parable, the woman could symbolize either the community of believers praying persistently and with faith, or God working ceaselessly for justice. In the Hebrew Bible, there are myriad covenant laws designed to protect the most vulnerable. When these laws are not upheld, it is up to the people to work tirelessly to defend the dignity and rights of the community on God's behalf. (2) *Fidelity.* In the end, the question is not really whether God will vindicate the community (the answer to that question is yes, of course; God's time is different from ours). Rather, the question is whether the community will remain faithful as they await Christ's return.

Ponder

Underlying the Exodus reading and its depiction of the unlikely victory of Israel (the underdog) against Amalek is a metaphor about Moses's persistence, his intimacy with God, and his humility in allowing help from others when he is physically exhausted. The importance of community—and communal help—runs through this passage. It is also a current in the Gospel reading. There the text draws us in to stand aghast at the unjust judge who fails to care for a woman in need and to wonder how her community has also failed to help her. Through her remarkable, God-like persistence, the judge renders her a just verdict. Together, these texts invite us to reflect on how we mirror divine persistence and how we support each other in working toward justice in our communities.

In 2 Timothy, persistence is about proclaiming the truth of Christ even in an environment of corruption and "counterfeit faith." The Gospel then describes persistence in prayer in a way that may contradict our experiences: in real life, persistent prayer does not guarantee that we receive what we (think we) need or want. Yet persistence can bring other, unimagined graces that may surpass our expectations. As you pray with these readings, consider your own prayer life and what these graces have been. Some may be obvious, while others may be more subtle or even unrecognized before today.

Thirtieth Sunday in Ordinary Time

FIRST READING   SIRACH 35:12-14, 16-18

The Lord is a God of justice,
who knows no favorites.
Though not unduly partial toward the weak,
yet he hears the cry of the oppressed.
The Lord is not deaf to the wail of the orphan,
nor to the widow when she pours out her complaint.
The one who serves God willingly is heard;
his petition reaches the heavens.
The prayer of the lowly pierces the clouds;
it does not rest till it reaches its goal,
nor will it withdraw till the Most High responds,
judges justly and affirms the right,
and the Lord will not delay.

We last read from Sirach on the Twenty-Second Sunday in Ordinary Time. The above reading contains at least two main themes: God's justice and the right stance in prayer. God is on the side of both the poor and the oppressed yet does not show favoritism. Instead, God listens to anyone who "serves God willingly" and is "lowly" (or "humble"). Notably, our reading does not suggest that perseverance in prayer is necessary. Instead, a single prayer is so powerful that it "pierces the clouds" and "does not rest" until God responds to "[judge] justly." Like our readings from last week, the promise is that God will respond quickly, without delay, to those who serve God willingly and wholeheartedly.

RESPONSORIAL PSALM   PSALM 34:2-3, 17-18, 19, 23

The Lord hears the cry of the poor.

SECOND READING   2 TIMOTHY 4:6-8, 16-18

Beloved:
I am already being poured out like a libation,
    and the time of my departure is at hand.
I have competed well; I have finished the race;
    I have kept the faith.
From now on the crown of righteousness awaits me,
    which the Lord, the just judge,
    will award to me on that day, and not only to me,
    but to all who have longed for his appearance.

At my first defense no one appeared on my behalf,
    but everyone deserted me.
May it not be held against them!
But the Lord stood by me and gave me strength,
    so that through me the proclamation might be completed
    and all the Gentiles might hear it.
And I was rescued from the lion's mouth.
The Lord will rescue me from every evil threat
    and will bring me safe to his heavenly kingdom.
To him be glory forever and ever. Amen.

This is our last reading from 2 Timothy this season. In it, Paul anticipates his death. He describes himself as a "libation" (a sacrifice or ritual drink offering) and as an athlete who wins a "crown of righteousness" by placing first in a race. We then skip over verses 9-15, in which Paul instructs his disciple Timothy on certain practical matters. In the second part of our reading, the "first defense" refers to the first opportunity of the accused in a court of law to offer an explanation for his "crimes" (which, in this context, means being a follower of Christ). Paul has been freed, it seems, to continue his apostolic mission to the Gentiles. The "lion's mouth" is a biblical image that refers to a physical threat to one's safety (see Dan 6:1-24).

GOSPEL   LUKE 18:9-14

Jesus addressed this parable
   to those who were convinced of their own righteousness
   and despised everyone else.
"Two people went up to the temple area to pray;
   one was a Pharisee and the other was a tax collector.
The Pharisee took up his position and spoke this prayer
      to himself,
   'O God, I thank you that I am not like the rest of humanity—
   greedy, dishonest, adulterous—or even like this tax collector.
I fast twice a week, and I pay tithes on my whole income.'
But the tax collector stood off at a distance
   and would not even raise his eyes to heaven
   but beat his breast and prayed,
   'O God, be merciful to me a sinner.'
I tell you, the latter went home justified, not the former;
   for whoever exalts himself will be humbled,
   and the one who humbles himself will be exalted."

This week we come to our second parable on prayer in Luke 18. The
targeted audience is those "convinced of their own righteousness"
who "[despise] everyone else" (an exaggerated and hilarious statement!). This is a much broader audience than just Pharisees, those
known for being deeply religious, pious individuals (not to be confused with the contemporary, problematic Christian stereotype of
Pharisees as "hypocrites"). Current readers may be prone to dismiss
the Pharisee as legalistic and identify easily with the tax collector,
though ancient readers would have been shocked that a tax collector
could be justified over a religious leader. The reading is a trap, for we
may very well find ourselves repeating the Pharisee's own phrase: "O
God, I thank you that I am not like the *Pharisee*." This interpretation
not only overlooks the Pharisee's positive qualities (e.g., fasting, tithing, marital fidelity, gratitude), but it could erroneously view the tax
collector as a de facto saint. The tax collector stands at a distance,
perhaps because he is employed by Rome, or perhaps because he
separates himself out of contrition. It is here that true repentance
and reconciliation occur between the tax collector and God; the

tax collector beats his breast, a sign of contrition, and goes home "justified" or restored to a right relationship with God. Although the English translation states that the tax collector "went home justified, *not* the former" (emphasis mine), the Greek could also be translated as "went home justified, *alongside* the former" (emphasis mine). In other words, it could be argued that both the Pharisee and the tax collector went home justified. In relation to the first reading from Sirach, only one type of prayer works here: that of a person who is humble, desiring mercy, and who serves God willingly. The parable leaves us to ponder how we embody the qualities of *both* characters in this parable, and it reminds us how easy it is to judge and feel superior to another person.

Ponder

According to Sirach, the prayers of those who "[serve] God willingly" and have a humble stance before God are powerful and are answered speedily. Our responsorial psalm describes the appropriate stance before God as that of one who "bless[es] the LORD at all times" and "glor[ies] in the LORD" (Ps 34:2-3). The Gospel affirms that it is those who understand their appropriate position in relation to God who are justified, not those who glorify themselves for their own righteousness. Our readings prompt us to reflect on our own tendencies in prayer, especially the extent to which we are truly focused on God when we pray, versus being absorbed in ourselves.

In 2 Timothy, Paul states that Christ will reward "all who have longed for his appearance." This is a longing that we also see in our readings about prayer. Sirach states that the prayer of the humble or lowly "pierces the clouds" and calls the Most High to respond. In Luke, the tax collector aches to experience God's mercy. Do we long for the coming of Christ? How does, or how could, this longing manifest in our daily lives, including in our prayers?

Thirty-First Sunday in Ordinary Time

FIRST READING   WISDOM 11:22–12:2

Before the LORD the whole universe is as a grain from a balance
   or a drop of morning dew come down upon the earth.
But you have mercy on all, because you can do all things;
   and you overlook people's sins that they may repent.
For you love all things that are
   and loathe nothing that you have made;
   for what you hated, you would not have fashioned.
And how could a thing remain, unless you willed it;
   or be preserved, had it not been called forth by you?
But you spare all things, because they are yours,
   O LORD and lover of souls,
   for your imperishable spirit is in all things!
Therefore you rebuke offenders little by little,
   warn them and remind them of the sins
   they are committing,
   that they may abandon their wickedness
   and believe in you, O LORD!

For background on the book of Wisdom, see notes for the Nineteenth Sunday in Ordinary Time. The above reading draws from a section that retells the Exodus story and the Israelites' journey through the wilderness. Though some stories in the Hebrew Bible suggest there is a limit to God's mercy, a more important theme (which we see especially in the Israelites' journey through the wilderness in Exodus–Deuteronomy) is God's fidelity toward the people and God's tenacity in loving them, despite the people's constant infidelity toward God. Though some might view mercy as a sign of weakness, a key theme in our reading is the direct correlation between strength and mercy. The verse immediately prior to our text states of God: "[G]reat strength is always present with you; who can resist the might of your arm?" (11:21). Echoing the first creation story in Genesis 1, in which God creates everything and calls it all "good," our reading also affirms that God loves everything in and *into* existence ("all things that are"). It is impossible, according to the writer, that God could loathe or hate anything created by God out of love. The rebuking of "offenders" (literally "those who have fallen away") is how God's mercy is made manifest; when one is touched by this limitless mercy, one cannot help but return to God.

RESPONSORIAL PSALM   PSALM 145:1-2, 8-9, 10-11, 13, 14

I will praise your name forever, my king and my God.

SECOND READING   2 THESSALONIANS 1:11–2:2

Brothers and sisters:
We always pray for you,
   that our God may make you worthy of his calling
   and powerfully bring to fulfillment every good purpose
   and every effort of faith,
   that the name of our Lord Jesus may be glorified in you,
   and you in him,
   in accord with the grace of our God and Lord Jesus Christ.

We ask you, brothers and sisters,
   with regard to the coming of our Lord Jesus Christ
   and our assembling with him,
   not to be shaken out of your minds suddenly, or to be alarmed
   either by a "spirit," or by an oral statement,
   or by a letter allegedly from us
   to the effect that the day of the Lord is at hand.

Until the end of Ordinary Time, we will be reading from Paul's second letter to the Thessalonians. The letter builds upon themes in 1 Thessalonians to encourage those who are facing suffering and hardship and to address two key problems in the early church. The first problem concerns those who erroneously say that "the day of the Lord is at hand." The second (connected) issue concerns those with behavioral problems (3:6-12). Our reading begins with a prayer describing the relationship between human and divine effort. The author then addresses the primary issue, urging the community not to be shaken or agitated by false prophecies that the end times have come.

GOSPEL   LUKE 19:1-10

At that time, Jesus came to Jericho and intended to pass through
   the town.
Now a man there named Zacchaeus,
   who was a chief tax collector and also a wealthy man,
   was seeking to see who Jesus was;
   but he could not see him because of the crowd,
   for he was short in stature.
So he ran ahead and climbed a sycamore tree in order to
      see Jesus,
   who was about to pass that way.
When he reached the place, Jesus looked up and said,
   "Zacchaeus, come down quickly,
   for today I must stay at your house."
And he came down quickly and received him with joy.
When they all saw this, they began to grumble, saying,
   "He has gone to stay at the house of a sinner."
But Zacchaeus stood there and said to the Lord,
   "Behold, half of my possessions, Lord, I shall give to the poor,
   and if I have extorted anything from anyone
   I shall repay it four times over."
And Jesus said to him,
   "Today salvation has come to this house
   because this man too is a descendant of Abraham.
For the Son of Man has come to seek
   and to save what was lost."

Jesus intends to pass through Jericho (a city of the rich and powerful)
on his journey. Seeing Zacchaeus seems to change his mind. The
name Zacchaeus is a Greek rendering of the Hebrew name that
means "pure or innocent one." As chief tax collector, Zacchaeus
contracted with the Romans to collect taxes and extort money from
his people for his own gain. He was therefore rightfully ostracized
by his Jewish community. Zacchaeus was obviously a "sinner" of the
worst sort (v. 7). The story is comical; it is about a very short man
who climbs a sycamore tree to see Jesus (sycamores have short trunks
and wide, lateral branches, which make them easy to climb). Is Zacchaeus simply intrigued, or does he believe that Jesus is a prophet?

The initiative begins with him and continues with Jesus. The text emphasizes the importance of "seeing": Zacchaeus wants to see Jesus, then Jesus sees Zacchaeus. Zacchaeus then shifts from watching Jesus from afar to "receiv[ing]" him in his home and in his heart. His statement of repentance and restitution exceeds the law's requirements (see Exod 21:37; Num 5:5-7) and exemplifies his absolute detachment from his wealth and previous lifestyle. It is a direct comparison to the story of the rich man in Luke 18:18-30. Zacchaeus also exemplifies the tax collector's repentance in last Sunday's Gospel (Luke 18:9-14). In the end, Jesus's final words are directed to Zacchaeus, yet he may also be making a pointed statement to a broader audience. Are the disciples hovering somewhere in the background?

Ponder

Our readings describe a mysterious dynamic between divine and human effort in our relationship with God. In the book of Wisdom, God gently prods, slowly reminding people of their sins so they might "abandon" them or be set free to return to God. Second Thessalonians promises that God will "powerfully bring to fulfillment" our "every good purpose and every effort of faith." And in the Gospel, Zacchaeus's radical act of conversion emerges from his desire to see Jesus and from Jesus seeing him in return. In this dynamic relationship of effort between divine grace and human desire, where do you find yourself today?

_____

"[Y]ou have mercy on all, because you can do all things," states Wisdom. In other words, because God is infinite power (can do all things), God has infinite mercy. Our responsorial psalm affirms the greatness of God's mercy. These readings call us to ponder the connection between power and mercy. Do these traits seem connected or paradoxical to you? Take time to explore this link between power and mercy in your own life, in contemporary examples around you, and especially in your experience of God.

Thirty-Second Sunday in Ordinary Time

FIRST READING   2 MACCABEES 7:1-2, 9-14

It happened that seven brothers with their mother were arrested
and tortured with whips and scourges by the king,
to force them to eat pork in violation of God's law.
One of the brothers, speaking for the others, said:
"What do you expect to achieve by questioning us?
We are ready to die rather than transgress the laws of
    our ancestors."

At the point of death he said:
"You accursed fiend, you are depriving us of this present life,
but the King of the world will raise us up to live again forever.
It is for his laws that we are dying."

After him the third suffered their cruel sport.
He put out his tongue at once when told to do so,
and bravely held out his hands, as he spoke these noble words:
"It was from Heaven that I received these;
for the sake of his laws I disdain them;
from him I hope to receive them again."
Even the king and his attendants marveled at the young
    man's courage,
because he regarded his sufferings as nothing.

After he had died,
they tortured and maltreated the fourth brother in the
    same way.
When he was near death, he said,
"It is my choice to die at the hands of men
with the hope God gives of being raised up by him;
but for you, there will be no resurrection to life."

Belief in the resurrection of the dead was a late development in Judaism. In the Hebrew Bible, we find references to resurrection only in the books of Daniel and Second Maccabees (both of which are later

287

books, dating to the second century BCE). In this story, the Hellenistic Greek king kills seven brothers and their mother for refusing to violate the laws of Judaism. As they die, one by one, the brothers profess their belief in resurrection. In the end, the mother tells her youngest son to be brave as he dies so that she will see all of her sons in the afterlife (2 Macc 7:29). (Note the relationship between the seven brothers here and the seven brothers in our Gospel reading.)

RESPONSORIAL PSALM   PSALM 17:1, 5-6, 8, 15

Lord, when your glory appears, my joy will be full.

SECOND READING   2 THESSALONIANS 2:16–3:5

Brothers and sisters:
May our Lord Jesus Christ himself and God our Father,
    who has loved us and given us everlasting encouragement
    and good hope through his grace,
        encourage your hearts and strengthen them in every good
        deed and word.

Finally, brothers and sisters, pray for us,
    so that the word of the Lord may speed forward and
        be glorified,
    as it did among you,
    and that we may be delivered from perverse and
        wicked people,
    for not all have faith.
But the Lord is faithful;
    he will strengthen you and guard you from the evil one.
We are confident of you in the Lord that what we instruct you,
    you are doing and will continue to do.
May the Lord direct your hearts to the love of God
    and to the endurance of Christ.

Today we near the end of Paul's letter, which closes with thanksgiving, encouragement, and prayers for the community. His focus is Christ's return, a belief that gives "everlasting encouragement and good hope" that will "encourage" and "strengthen" the hearts of Christ's followers. Paul requests prayers from the community for the continued spread of "the word of the Lord" (the gospel), that it might "speed forward and be glorified." Though not all have faith, Paul reminds believers that God is the ground of faith and eternally faithful. Paul ends by praying that the community experience an increase both in the gift of God's love and in the patient endurance of Christ.

GOSPEL   LUKE 20:27-38 [OR 20:27, 34-38]

Some Sadducees, those who deny that there is a resurrection,
   came forward and put this question to Jesus, saying,
   "Teacher, Moses wrote for us,
   If someone's brother dies leaving a wife but no child,
   his brother must take the wife
   and raise up descendants for his brother.
Now there were seven brothers;
   the first married a woman but died childless.
Then the second and the third married her,
   and likewise all the seven died childless.
Finally the woman also died.
Now at the resurrection whose wife will that woman be?
For all seven had been married to her."
Jesus said to them,
   "The children of this age marry and remarry;
   but those who are deemed worthy to attain to the coming age
   and to the resurrection of the dead
   neither marry nor are given in marriage.
They can no longer die,
   for they are like angels;
   and they are the children of God
   because they are the ones who will rise.
That the dead will rise
   even Moses made known in the passage about the bush,
   when he called out 'Lord,'
   the God of Abraham, the God of Isaac, and the God of Jacob;
   and he is not God of the dead, but of the living,
   for to him all are alive."

In the first century CE, three Jewish sects represented three distinct views on resurrection: Sadducees denied it completely, Essenes believed the body died but the soul endured, and Pharisees professed their belief in bodily resurrection. It was this last belief that Jesus followed and that became normative in Judaism and in early Christianity. Meanwhile, Sadducees believed that the Torah alone (the first five books of the Hebrew Bible) was the foundation for Judaism. They therefore denied the resurrection because it was not found in the Torah. In this Gospel passage, the Sadducees try to ensnare Jesus through a story that (they think) demonstrates the absurdity of resurrection. The story recalls levirate marriage in ancient Israel, which protected the economic security of a widow and the continuation of the family lineage should her husband die without giving her children. The widow would marry the husband's brother with the goal of having a child in the name of her dead husband (Deut 25:5; see also Gen 38). In the Sadducees' story, seven brothers marry one woman over the course of time. The Sadducees ask Jesus whose wife she will be at the resurrection (Luke 20:32). Jesus upends the question by stating that marriage is only an institution for this world. In a brilliant maneuver, he professes the reality of resurrection by reinterpreting Exodus 3:6 (remember—the Sadducees believed that the first five books of the Hebrew Bible, including Exodus, did *not* attest to the resurrection of the dead!). To this, some of the scribes praise Jesus, saying, "Teacher, you have answered well" (20:39, the verse immediately following our reading).

Ponder

"[T]he Lord is faithful," writes Paul. What does this mean? It means that God is faithful *to us*. This is an awesome reality and one that can be hard to comprehend. As our readings show, God's faithfulness orients us toward the promise of a world to come that is radically different from this world. Though it is impossible to imagine what this new world is like, the psalmist describes it as one day beholding God's face and being "content" in God's presence (Ps 17:15). This week we are called to ponder God's faithfulness and promise to us, including how we return and extend faithfulness in our lives and in our witness to others.

In the Gospel, Jesus states that for God, "all are alive." Yet our readings also acknowledge the reality of evil that runs counter to life. Second Maccabees even states that for some, "there will be no resurrection to life." Together these readings suggest a paradoxical reality: resurrection is both a promise offered to all and a choice we can accept or reject. This is not a choice we make once and for all but is a daily decision. How do you respond to God's offer of resurrection today?

Thirty-Third Sunday in Ordinary Time

FIRST READING   MALACHI 3:19-20a

Lo, the day is coming, blazing like an oven,
 when all the proud and all evildoers will be stubble,
 and the day that is coming will set them on fire,
  leaving them neither root nor branch,
  says the LORD of hosts.
But for you who fear my name, there will arise
 the sun of justice with its healing rays.

Malachi is the last book of the Hebrew Bible according to the order of books in the Christian canon. Its primary concern is the problem of evil and justice. In this world, the just seem to suffer unfairly, while the unjust flourish. In the above prophecy, Malachi promises that in the coming messianic age, all evil will pass away, while those who "fear" God (i.e., those who revere or live in awe of God's power and holiness) will encounter God as true justice. The phrase "sun of justice" draws upon a common ancient Middle Eastern understanding of the sun as a god because it provides warmth, light, and life. The Hebrew Bible uses the same symbolism but identifies the "sun" as the God of Israel.

RESPONSORIAL PSALM   PSALM 98:5-6, 7-8, 9

The Lord comes to rule the earth with justice.

SECOND READING   2 THESSALONIANS 3:7-12

Brothers and sisters:
You know how one must imitate us.
For we did not act in a disorderly way among you,
 nor did we eat food received free from anyone.
On the contrary, in toil and drudgery, night and day
 we worked, so as not to burden any of you.
Not that we do not have the right.

Rather, we wanted to present ourselves as a model for you,
   so that you might imitate us.
In fact, when we were with you,
   we instructed you that if anyone was unwilling to work,
   neither should that one eat.
We hear that some are conducting themselves among you in a
      disorderly way,
   by not keeping busy but minding the business of others.
Such people we instruct and urge in the Lord Jesus Christ to
      work quietly
   and to eat their own food.

Second Thessalonians ends with warnings and instructions to those who are unruly and idle. An alternative translation of the Greek term *ataktōs*, translated here (twice) as "disorderly," is "idle." In other words, to be a "disorderly" member of the community is to be idle or lazy. Therefore, in this somewhat enigmatic conclusion, Paul confronts those in the community who refuse to work or who live idle lives. This "idle" conduct may have been motivated by the belief that the end times were coming at any moment. Nonetheless, this idleness is not helpful for sustaining and building up a community. Paul urges the community to avoid those who do not follow his teachings and his example of hard work. Yet this avoidance of certain community members is a last resort when all else fails, for the ultimate purpose is to instruct and win people back.

GOSPEL   LUKE 21:5-19

While some people were speaking about
   how the temple was adorned with costly stones and
      votive offerings,
   Jesus said, "All that you see here—
   the days will come when there will not be left
   a stone upon another stone that will not be thrown down."

Then they asked him,
   "Teacher, when will this happen?
And what sign will there be when all these things are about
      to happen?"

He answered,
"See that you not be deceived,
  for many will come in my name, saying,
  'I am he,' and 'The time has come.'
Do not follow them!
When you hear of wars and insurrections,
  do not be terrified; for such things must happen first,
  but it will not immediately be the end."
Then he said to them,
  "Nation will rise against nation, and kingdom against kingdom.
There will be powerful earthquakes, famines, and plagues
  from place to place;
  and awesome sights and mighty signs will come from the sky.

"Before all this happens, however,
  they will seize and persecute you,
  they will hand you over to the synagogues and to prisons,
  and they will have you led before kings and governors
  because of my name.
It will lead to your giving testimony.
Remember, you are not to prepare your defense beforehand,
  for I myself shall give you a wisdom in speaking
  that all your adversaries will be powerless to resist or refute.
You will even be handed over by parents, brothers, relatives,
    and friends,
  and they will put some of you to death.
You will be hated by all because of my name,
  but not a hair on your head will be destroyed.
By your perseverance you will secure your lives."

In today's Gospel, Jesus has made it to Jerusalem, and he foretells the destruction of the temple (ca. 70 CE; see also Matt 24:1-2 and Mark 13:1-2). Luke's Gospel was written *after* the temple's destruction, meaning that Luke's readers have already experienced this deeply traumatic event. Jesus connects this destruction with the end times and teaches his followers how to react and withstand such trauma and suffering. He explains that persecution, political upheaval, and environmental tumult inevitably precede the end times. So do religious accusations of heresy. Jesus instructs his followers on how to withstand such events. First, they are not to "prepare" (literally "premeditate") their response to accusations ahead of time (the Greek term *promeletaō* means to practice or rehearse, as actors might do). Instead, they are to trust that Jesus will give them "wisdom" in that moment. Second and more importantly, they are to practice "perseverance," the necessary endurance or patience to "secure [their] lives," meaning the promise of resurrection.

Ponder

Like the early Christians, we often struggle to internalize Jesus's teachings on the Second Coming. It can seem like a fantasy or far-off reality. But God's kingdom is not so far off. It is both "not yet" and "already come." Malachi describes the "not yet" coming as God's "justice" that will rise or shine like the sun, as does our responsorial psalm: "[God] comes to rule the earth; / he will rule the world with justice and the peoples with equity" (Ps 98:9). Yet as we wait for the "not yet," we are essential to the "already." We are God's hands and feet in this world, called to promote justice and hope where we can. How do we live in ways that are not "idle" (as Paul warns) but that work to perpetuate and incarnate God's justice in our communities?

God's final intervention in this world can be viewed as a threat or a promise. For some of us (perhaps most of us!), passages such as the ones we read this week can be terrifying. If this is the case, we might try reorienting our perspective. For those who persevere in faith, God's intervention is not a threat but a promise, one that is meant to bring comfort and inspire hope in the midst of our present reality. As we prepare for the coming of Advent, our readings invite us to reorient our perspective on Christ's coming and to prepare the way by meaningfully rooting our lives in and toward this promise: in thought, in prayer, and in action.

Our Lord Jesus Christ, King of the Universe

FIRST READING   2 SAMUEL 5:1-3

In those days, all the tribes of Israel came to David in Hebron
    and said:
    "Here we are, your bone and your flesh.
In days past, when Saul was our king,
    it was you who led the Israelites out and brought them back.
And the LORD said to you,
    'You shall shepherd my people Israel
    and shall be commander of Israel.' "
When all the elders of Israel came to David in Hebron,
    King David made an agreement with them there before the
    LORD,
    and they anointed him king of Israel.

The above reading recounts David's anointing as king of Israel. According to the books of Samuel, David's line was key to the continuation of Judah and its Holy City, Jerusalem. After the Babylonians destroyed Jerusalem ca. 586 BCE and forced the people into exile, some exiled Judeans yearned to return to Judah, rebuild the temple, and reinstate the Davidic kingship. Early-exilic messianic ideas were political, rooted in this yearning for the return of the Davidic line and the king as the "messiah" or "anointed one" of the monarchy. Eventually, these political ideas developed into the notion of a religious messiah or "king of the universe." Christians believe this messiah is Jesus Christ, from the line of David (Matt 1:1; Luke 1:32).

RESPONSORIAL PSALM   PSALM 122:1-2, 3-4, 4-5

Let us go rejoicing to the house of the Lord.

SECOND READING   COLOSSIANS 1:12-20

Brothers and sisters:
Let us give thanks to the Father,
   who has made you fit to share
   in the inheritance of the holy ones in light.
He delivered us from the power of darkness
   and transferred us to the kingdom of his beloved Son,
   in whom we have redemption, the forgiveness of sins.

He is the image of the invisible God,
   the firstborn of all creation.
For in him were created all things in heaven and on earth,
   the visible and the invisible,
   whether thrones or dominions or principalities or powers;
   all things were created through him and for him.
He is before all things,
   and in him all things hold together.
He is the head of the body, the church.
He is the beginning, the firstborn from the dead,
   that in all things he himself might be preeminent.
For in him all the fullness was pleased to dwell,
   and through him to reconcile all things for him,
   making peace by the blood of his cross
   through him, whether those on earth or those in heaven.

This hymn-like text depicts Christ's supremacy over the cosmos
and the church. The author draws from the imagery of the early
Jewish figure of Wisdom/Sophia, who is described as dwelling with
God from the beginning of time (see Prov 1–9) to explain Jesus's
relationship to God. We see similar imagery in the beginning of the
Gospel of John, in which Jesus is the "Word" of God who is with God
from the beginning (John 1:1). This passage also incorporates apocalyptic imagery of light and darkness as oppositional forces: light is
God's domain, while "the power of darkness" represents that which
is hostile to God and God's kingdom. Christ represents the ultimate
force of light—the perfect, visible manifestation of God and God's
"firstborn." As God's firstborn and the first to be resurrected ("firstborn from the dead"), Christ is the ultimate ruling authority both on

earth and in heaven. The "fullness" of God's power and presence is manifest in Christ. Those who follow Christ will be delivered from the powers of darkness, redeemed and reconciled through Christ's self-sacrifice and resurrection.

GOSPEL   LUKE 23:35-43

The rulers sneered at Jesus and said,
   "He saved others, let him save himself
   if he is the chosen one, the Christ of God."
Even the soldiers jeered at him.
As they approached to offer him wine they called out,
   "If you are King of the Jews, save yourself."
Above him there was an inscription that read,
   "This is the King of the Jews."

Now one of the criminals hanging there reviled Jesus, saying,
   "Are you not the Christ?
Save yourself and us."
The other, however, rebuking him, said in reply,
   "Have you no fear of God,
   for you are subject to the same condemnation?
And indeed, we have been condemned justly,
   for the sentence we received corresponds to our crimes,
   but this man has done nothing criminal."
Then he said,
   "Jesus, remember me when you come into your kingdom."
He replied to him,
   "Amen, I say to you,
   today you will be with me in Paradise."

According to Luke's account of the Passion, Jesus is crucified between two criminals. With his last breaths, he offers divine mercy to the one who asks for forgiveness. Meanwhile, some of those watching ("rulers" and "soldiers") attempt to humiliate Jesus, jeering at him for being unable to save himself and the people as a true messiah would. They fail to understand that his authority is not of this world. Instead, Jesus becomes the Messiah or Christ, the true king of the universe, through his crucifixion and resurrection (Acts 2:29-36).